THE MEANING OF CONSERVATISM

THE MEANING
OF CONSERVATISM

ROGER SCRUTON

First published in paperback by Penguin Books Ltd 1980
and simultaneously in hardcover by
THE MACMILLAN PRESS LTD
London and Basingstoke
Companies and representatives
throughout the world

First published 1980 in the USA by
BARNES & NOBLE BOOKS
81 Adams Drive
Totowa, New Jersey, 07512

MACMILLAN ISBN 0 333 30478 0

BARNES & NOBLE ISBN 0–389–20082–4

Printed in Great Britain by
BILLING & SONS LTD
Guildford, Surrey

CONTENTS

He that goeth about to persuade a multitude, that they are not so well governed as they ought to be, shall never want attentive and favourable hearers; because they know the manifold defects whereunto every kind of regiment is subject, but the secret lets and difficulties, which in public proceedings are innumerable and inevitable, they have not ordinarily the judgment to consider. And because such as openly reprove supposed disorders of state are taken for principal friends to the common benefit of all, and for men that carry singular freedom of mind; under this fair and plausible colour whatsoever they utter passeth for good and current. That which wanteth in the weight of their speech, is supplied by the aptness of men's minds to accept and believe it. Whereas on the other side, if we maintain things that are established, we have not only to strive with a number of heavy prejudices deeply rooted in the hearts of men, who think that herein we serve the time . . . but also to bear such exceptions as minds so averted beforehand usually take against that which they are loth should be poured into them.
     – Hooker, *Of the Laws of Ecclesiastical Polity*, Book I, Chapter i

There are so many plans, and so many schemes, and so many reasons why there should be neither plans nor schemes.   – Disraeli, to Lady Bradford

PREFACE

I have tried to present clearly and simply the fundamental conceptions which I believe to underlie the conservative view in politics, and in the course of doing so to show the possibility of subscribing to them. This is not a work of philosophy, but of dogmatics: it attempts to describe and defend a system of beliefs, but it is a system which, being directly expressed in action, assumes rather than provides the answers to philosophical questions. Nevertheless, I have drawn on the work of political philosophers, such as Hegel, Marx and Oakeshott, often without directly referring to them, trying always to use a language of my own.

I am grateful to the Rockefeller Foundation for the invitation to the Villa Serbelloni on Lake Como, where the first draft of this essay was begun, and to the friends who encouraged me while writing it. I have benefited from discussions with many people, and in particular from conversations over several years with John Casey and Maurice Cowling. A version of the text was read by William Waldegrave and Ted Honderich, and I was greatly assisted by their criticism.

Many conservatives will find themselves in disagreement with what I say. Nevertheless, it satisfies the first requirement of all conservative thought: it is not original, nor does it try to be.

INTRODUCTION

Philosophy, Policy and Dogma

This is a work of dogmatics: it is an attempt to outline a system of belief, without pausing to argue the abstract questions to which that system provides no answer. The dogmatics of conservatism must be distinguished both from the philosophy upon which it rests, and from the policies which spring from it. The reality of politics is action, but action derives, however covertly, from thought, and consistent action demands consistent thought. Because there is no universal conservative policy, the illusion has arisen that there *is* no conservative thought, no set of beliefs or principles, no general vision of society, which motivates the conservative to act. His action is mere reaction, his policy procrastination, his belief nostalgia.

I shall argue that the conservative attitude, and the dogma which sustains it, are systematic and reasonable. Conservatism may rarely announce itself in maxims, formulae or aims. Its essence is inarticulate, and its expression, when compelled, sceptical. But it is capable of expression, and in times of crisis, forced either by political necessity, or by the clamour for doctrine, conservatism does its best, though not always with any confidence that the words it finds will match the instinct that required them. This lack of confidence stems not from diffidence or dismay, but from an awareness of the complexity of human things, and from an attachment to values which cannot be understood with the abstract clarity of utopian theory.[1] *

It has been common for intellectuals in our time to believe that the conservative position is no longer 'available'. Our century is memorable for nothing so much as its violence, and the attempt to understand this violence has brought with it the rise of political ideology. As the ignorant armies clashed in the night of Europe, the rumour spread that there were 'causes' for which they fought – causes such as 'equality', 'freedom', and 'social justice'. But no report was returned of a conservative banner, and

* Notes are printed on page 193 below.

11

the intellectual drew his conclusion: there is no conservative cause, and therefore no conservative dogma.

We have inherited a world adapted to the needs of conscripts, for whom a creed without a cause suggests no coherent activity. But a new generation, for whom the spirit of war is not the normal one, can again be attracted by the vision of man in his full complexity, unsimplified by theory, or by overmastering ideals. This generation preserves the history of something greater, something for which it has begun to search. But without dogma – in the sense of reasoned belief – it too must lose itself in the transient play of policy. The European mind seeks for a *deep* description of its politics, a description which reflects its real predicament, but which also remains uncontaminated by the day-to-day. Socialists and liberals have contended for this mind, each claiming to provide the system of principles with which to pass from policy to doctrine and from doctrine back to policy. Conservatives, who see value in prejudice and danger in abstract thought, have extemporized, expressing their beliefs in vague and conciliatory language. However, neither the socialist nor the liberal can be appeased. Their bigotry (and there is no greater bigotry, I shall argue, than the bigotry of liberalism) permits no conciliation, while their statements seem clear, definite, founded in system. Until the conservative lays hold again of the principles which motivate him, he will find himself outwitted by those who lay claim to a conviction which they may not always feel but are always ready to express. Without dogma conservatism will lose its intellectual appeal; and (however reluctant conservatives may be to believe it), it is by intellectuals that modern politics is made.

But the alternatives to conservatism, I shall argue, are under-described. The apparent clarity of socialist and liberal thought is illusory, and their obscurity is the deeper for the ease with which it can be concealed within a gospel. By contrast, the conservative attitude is as appropriate and reasonable for the modern mind as it ever was, and, once understood, will be rejected only by those who seek in everything for an overriding purpose or a systematic plan. Such people will be distressed, not only by the conservative viewpoint, but also by the course of modern history, as it overwhelms each successive system in the flood of novelty.

Since my concern is with dogma, I shall not consider the major issues of policy which any government must face. Nevertheless, I shall make extensive use of examples, since dogma is useless if it does not translate immediately into practice. In addition I shall produce abstract arguments, often of a philosophical kind. But it must be remembered that argument is not the favourite pursuit of conservatives. Like any political being, a conservative is 'for' certain things: he is for them, not because he has arguments in their favour, but because he knows them, lives with them, and finds his identity threatened (often he knows not how) by the attempt to interfere with their operation. His characteristic and most dangerous opponent is not the radical, who stands squarely against him, armed with myths and prejudices that match his own, but rather the reformer, who, acting always in a spirit of improvement, finds reason to change whatever he cannot find better reason to retain. It is from this spirit of improvement, the legacy of Victorian liberalism and social Darwinism, that modern socialists and modern liberals continue to derive their moral inspiration.

CHAPTER 1

The Conservative Attitude

Conservatism is a stance that may be defined without identifying it with the policies of any party. Indeed, it may be a stance that appeals to a person for whom the whole idea of party is distasteful. In one of the first political manifestos of the English Conservative Party, appeal was explicitly made to 'that great and intelligent class of society ... which is far less interested in the contentions of party, than in the maintenance of order and the cause of good government' (Peel, *The Tamworth Manifesto*, 1834). Paradoxical though it may seem, it was from this aversion to factional politics that the Conservative Party grew. But it was an aversion rapidly overcome by another: that towards the chronic reform which only an organized party can successfully counter.[2]

In England, therefore, conservatism has sought expression through the activity (or, just as often, through the strategic inactivity) of a particular party, a party dedicated to maintaining the structure and institutions of a society threatened by mercantile enthusiasm and social unrest. In recent years, the Conservative Party has often seemed to be about to break with its tradition; it has joined in the competitive market of reform, endorsing the delegation of power, the code of economic internationalism, the 'free market economy' which it once so strenuously opposed. It has presided over the reorganization of county boundaries, and of national currency, over the entry into Europe and the consequent surrender of legal autonomy. It entertains at present the idea of reforming the House of Lords, and has allowed, while in office, the continued existence of reforming bodies, and the ascendancy in education, economics and penal reform of self-styled experts who may have neither the wisdom nor the responsibility to qualify as the arbiters of political choice. In short, the Conservative Party has often acted in a way with which a conservative may find little sympathy. Most of all, it has begun to see itself as the defender of individual freedom against the encroachments of the state, concerned to return to the people their natural right of choice, and to inject into every corporate body the healing principle

15

of democracy. These are passing fashions, well-meant, not always mis-guided, but by no means the ineluctable expression of the conservative point of view. Rather, they are the outcome of the party's recent at-tempt to provide itself with a set of policies and aims, and with the sketch of a political vision from which to derive them. Some have con-ceived this attempt as politically necessary. Others have wanted it for its own sake. The result has been, either transitory and unmeaning urges to reform, or else the wholesale adoption of the philosophy which I shall characterize in this book as the principal enemy of conservatism, the philosophy of liberalism, with all its attendant trappings of individual autonomy and the 'natural' rights of man. In politics, the conservative attitude seeks above all for government, and regards no citizen as pos-sessed of a natural right that transcends his obligation to be ruled. Even democracy – which corresponds neither to the natural nor to the super-natural yearnings of the normal citizen – can be discarded without detri-ment to the civil well-being as the conservative conceives it.

Freedom and Moderation

Now it is a sign of troubled times – those times when, as I have said, conservatism must feel the need to articulate itself – that advocates of 'moderation', of the sensible 'middle course' between extremes, of the demands of a reasonable (because silent) majority, should be listened to with a respect which they could not normally command. The attraction of 'moderation' to the Conservative Party has been its supposed associ-ation with the 'free' or 'open' society. And it is this free society that socialism is thought to destroy.[3] Hence 'moderation' tries to command the defence against 'Totalitarianism, whether (it is usually added) of the Left or of the Right'. We are encouraged to see national politics, and indeed international politics, in terms of some wholly abstract conflict between 'Freedom' and 'Totalitarianism', between the 'natural' rights to speak and act one's mind, and an enforced, uneasy, slavery.

Properly stated, this distinction need not be naïve, and indeed, has the backing of a whole tradition in political philosophy, reaching from Locke to Robert Nozick.[4] Moreover, it represents an essential part, both of the rhetoric of American government and of the self-image of Ameri-can society, so that political decisions of the highest seriousness are made in its name. This does not show, however, that the distinction can be put forward as though its clarity were immediate, as though it located definite political allegiances which could be defined in advance of the particular occasion for their declaration, or as though the whole of politics could be subsumed under the two disputing factions to which it gives a name. If it is not strange to find so many *soi-distant* conservatives identifying their position with this abstraction called 'Freedom', this is only because it is of the nature of conservatism to avoid abstractions, and to make radical mistakes when tempted by intelligent opposition to make use of them. Thus the concept of freedom – and in particular, such constitutionally derived freedoms as the freedom of speech, the freedom of assembly, the 'freedom of conscience' and the 'right to strike' – this concept has until recently been the only one that has been presented by contemporary Conservatism as a contribution to the ideological battle which it assumes to be raging.

An Example

Later I shall return to this concept of freedom, and to the notion of 'human rights' with which it is associated. But let us consider, in order to make the general issues a little clearer, just one small and topical example: the freedom of speech. It is obvious that there cannot be freedom of speech in any healthy society, if by freedom is meant the absolute untrammelled right to say what one wishes and utter one's views on anything, at any time, and anywhere. And it requires little knowledge of law to see that there is no absolute freedom of speech in the United Kingdom. Liberal thinkers have always recognized this fact. But they have seen the constraints on freedom as arising only negatively and in response to individual rights. Freedom should be qualified only by the possibility that someone might suffer through its exercise. For the conservative constraint should be upheld, until it can be shown that society is not damaged by its removal. Thus the constraints on freedom arise through the law's attempt to embody (as for a conservative it must embody) the fundamental values of the society which it aims to rule. I shall argue that this vision of law is both more coherent and more true to the facts than its individualistic rival.

There is no freedom to abuse, to stir up hatred, to make or publish treasonable, libellous, obscene and blasphemous utterance. In England, as in every civilized country, there is a law which forbids the production and distribution of subversive material – the law of sedition. Now this law also makes it an offence voluntarily to stir up hatred between different sections of the community. Proper application of that law – which makes not only the manipulation of racial hatred but also that of class hatred into a criminal offence – would have made the first Race Relations Act (the Act which still required some element of *mens rea* for its statutory crimes) more or less unnecessary. It was not applied. This was not only because the symbolic gesture of a law specific to racial relations appeared immensely powerful, if not in quelling racial antipathy, at least in appeasing the middle-class conscience over its existence. It was also because the application of the law would lead at once to the curtailing, not only of what was said on the rostrum of the National Front, but also of what is said at every radical demonstration, and at many a Trades Union Congress.

This decline in the very *idea* of sedition has been brought about not by popular agitation, but by the politics of power. The fact is, not that our society believes in freedom of speech and assembly, but rather that it is afraid to announce its disbelief. This disbelief is so entrenched in English law – in the common law just as much as in statutory provisions – that it is impossible to doubt that it could be eradicated without wholly overthrowing the social order which the law enshrines. But it is now principally judges and juries who respond to its demand. Politicians, and especially politicians of the 'moderate' Right, have lost their nerve, for what they seem to represent is not the politics of government, but politics of a professional class, a class which pursues power not for its own sake, but as the by-product of professional advancement. Modern parliaments therefore constantly enact new and selective laws against freedom of speech and assembly, each of which may reflect some serious view as to where evil lies, but none of which is so bold as to recognize that a society really does have enemies, that those enemies seek to undermine it, and that it is the duty of the government, as it is the expectation of the citizen, that they should be prevented by every means to hand.

None of this is to deny the reality of some less absolute ideal of freedom, according to which it would be quite true to say that there is and has been more freedom of speech (and more freedom of every kind) in the United Kingdom than in most other countries of the world. And this Anglo-Saxon freedom is rightly valued by all of us who share its benefits, including the benefit of writing and reading the present essay. But this freedom is not identifiable apart from the institutions which have fostered it. It is a freedom to do precisely what is not forbidden by law, and what is forbidden by law records a long tradition of reflection on the nature and constitution of English society. It is not surprising, therefore, if radicals condemn the 'reactionary' nature of our judges. The English Common Law, which has its roots in Roman law, in canon law, and in the codes of our Saxon ancestors, is the judge's peculiar province, and has become the expression of a deep historical sense, a sense of the continuity and vitality of an existing social order. (It follows that the independence of the judiciary must, for the conservative, be a major political cause.)

Freedom and Institutions

The argument can be generalized. The freedom that Englishmen esteem is not, and cannot be, a special case of that freedom advocated by the

18

American Republican Party, the freedom of pioneering dissenters struggling for community in a place without history, the freedom which is
connected in some mysterious way with free enterprise and the market
economy. It is a specific personal freedom, the result of a long process of
social evolution, the bequest of institutions without whose protection it
could not endure. Freedom in this sense (the only sense which matters)
is not the precondition but the consequence of an accepted social arrangement. Freedom without institutions is blind: it embodies neither
genuine social continuity nor, as I shall argue, genuine individual choice.
It amounts to no more than a gesture in a moral vacuum.

The concept of freedom, therefore, cannot occupy a central place in
conservative thinking, whether about national affairs, international
politics or (what for the conservative is of special significance) the internal guidance of an autonomous institution. Freedom is comprehensible as a social goal only when subordinate to something else, to an
organization or arrangement which defines the individual aim. Hence to
aim at freedom is at the same time to aim at the constraint which is its
precondition. Roughly speaking, it is the individual's responsibility to
win whatever freedom of speech, conscience and assembly he may; it is
the politician's responsibility to define and maintain the arrangement in
which that freedom is to be pursued. One major difference between conservatism and liberalism consists, therefore, in the fact that, for the
conservative, the value of individual liberty is not absolute, but stands
subject to another and higher value, the authority of established government. And history could be taken to suggest that what satisfies people
politically – even if they always used words like 'freedom' to articulate
the first instinctive impulse towards it – is not freedom, but congenial
government. Government is the primary need of every man subject to
the discipline of social intercourse, and freedom the name of at least one
of his anxieties.

The political battles of our time concern, therefore, the conservation
and destruction of institutions and forms of life: nothing more vividly
illustrates this than the issues of education, political unity, the role of
trade unions and the House of Lords, issues with which the abstract concept of 'freedom' fails to make contact. In all such issues the conflict
concerns not freedom but authority, authority vested in a given office,
institution or arrangement. It is through an ideal of authority that the
conservative experiences the political world. His liberal opponent, whose
view is likely to be anhistorical, will usually fail to understand that notion,
and in this he will show how far he is detached from the society upon
which he seeks to impose his rootless prejudices. Now the Marxist (whose
viewpoint I propose to take seriously in this essay, since it derives from
a theory of human nature that one might actually believe) would see the
dispute in quite other terms, seeking to demystify the ideal of 'authority,

and to replace it with the realities of power. 'Authority', for the Marxist, is merely the ideological representation of power – power imbued with a false aura of legitimacy, made absolute and unchangeable, translated from a historical reality into a sempiternal ideal. In preferring to speak of power, the Marxist puts at the centre of politics the only true political commodity, the only thing which can actually change hands. Later I shall try to show how the Marxist's picture in all probability falsifies the realities of politics; nevertheless, it correctly locates the battleground, and for that reason, if for no other, we must take it seriously. But now let us return from our preliminary skirmish to the present task, which is to give some initial description of the conservative outlook, so that its implications as a contemporary political attitude may be explored.

The Search for Dogma

As I have suggested, conservatism – as a motivating force in the political life of the citizen – is characteristically inarticulate, unwilling (and indeed usually unable) to translate itself into formulae or maxims, loath to state its purpose or declare its view. There have been articulate conservatives – Aristotle, for example, Hume, T. S. Eliot. But while they have influenced the course of politics, it has usually been indirectly, and not because of any specific political ideal with which their names have been conjoined. Indeed, if it is true that conservatism becomes conscious only when forced to be so, then it is inevitable that the passage from practice to theory will not be rewarded by any immediate influence from theory back to what is done. Nevertheless, an intellectual will wish to hold his beliefs in conscious suspension before his mind, and will not be content, in a world flustered by faction, to stand without arguments in the midst of the fray.

The task of this essay is to find the concepts with which a conservative might provide himself with a creed, and with which he might define his own position, whether as statesman, or as common political animal. This, let it be repeated, is not an exercise in political philosophy, but in political dogmatics. It is quite possible that the conceptions that I provide will fail to correspond exactly to the intuition which sought expression through them. A political creed, in so far as it is formulated, is partly an exercise in rhetoric, to be revised and restated whenever the times demand that the ruling intuition be given its new dressing of necessity. But we have an important question to settle; how can conservatism be an item of contemporary belief, and how in particular can it recommend itself to that peculiar species to which my readers belong, the self-consciously 'modern' person?

The Desire to Conserve

It is a limp definition of conservatism to describe it as the desire to conserve; for although there is in every man and woman some impulse to conserve that which is safe and familiar, it is the nature of this 'familiarity' that needs to be examined. To put it briefly, conservatism arises directly from the sense that one belongs to some continuing, and pre-existing social order, and that this fact is all important in determining what to do. The 'order' in question may be that of a club, society, class, community, church, regiment or nation – a man may feel towards all these things that institutional stance which it is the task of this book to describe and defend. In feeling it – in feeling thus engaged in the continuity of his social world – a man stands in the current of some common life. The important thing is that the life of a social arrangement may become mingled with the lives of its members. They may feel in themselves the persistence of the will that surrounds them. The conservative instinct is founded in that feeling: it is the enactment of historical vitality, the individual's sense of his society's will to live. Moreover, in so far as people love life they will love what has given them life; in so far as they desire to give life it is in order to perpetuate what they have. In that intricate entanglement of individual and society resides the 'will to live' that constitutes conservatism.

It is sometimes said (and not only by socialists) that the fabric of English society (and I shall assume for the moment that we are discussing English society) is falling apart, that the country is in decline, bereft of everything which constitutes the strength and vitality of an autonomous nation. How, then, can one be a conservative, when there is nothing to conserve but ruins?

This radical scepticism may take many forms, from the apocalyptic vision of Nietzsche and Spengler, to the more homely chatter that accompanies the planning of the 'New Society', whose foundation-stone seems nevertheless always to get mislaid. But, in whatever form, it is surely of little practical interest. A society or a nation is indeed a kind of organism (and also very much more than an organism); it must therefore bear the stigma of mortality. Yet is it not absurd advice to give to a sick man that he should – in the interests of the 'new world' that waits to replace him – promptly set about the task of dying? Even at the point of death the will to live endures and desires its restoration. A society, like a man, may endure through sickness and thrive in death. If a conservative is also a restorationist, this is because he lives close to society, and feels in himself the sickness which infects the common order. How, then, can he fail to direct his eyes towards that state of health from which things have declined? Revolution is now unthinkable: it is like

21

murdering a sick mother out of impatience to snatch some rumoured infant from her womb. Of course there are conservatives who in extremity have adopted the way of revolution. In the ensuing vacuum, however, men are disrupted, aimless, incomplete. The result is bloodshed, and only afterwards the slow work of restoration to some simulacrum of the state that was destroyed. Naturally, therefore, revolution is something that I shall neither advocate nor even consider in what follows.

The desire to conserve is compatible with all manner of change, provided only that change is also continuity. It has recently been argued with some force that the process of change in political life has become 'hyperactive'.[5] Overstimulation of that shallow part of a man's being which constitutes the sum of his articulate views has led to a profusion throughout the public realm of a sense that anything can and should be altered, together with proposals for reform, and political strategies, mounted by those within and by those without the institutions whose life they thereby threaten. This disease is of the kind which any conservative will attend to, first by trying to recognize its nature. The world has become peculiarly 'opinionated', and in every corner of society people with neither the desire nor the ability to reflect on the social good are being urged to choose some favoured recipe for its realization. Even an institution like the Catholic Church has become afflicted with the fashion for reform, and being unable to take Christ's words to Simon Peter in their egoistic Lutheran meaning, has partially forgotten the tradition of custom, ceremony and judicious manoeuvre that enabled it to stand seemingly unshifting in the midst of worldly change, calling to every man with a voice of immutable authority. The Church, an institution with an aim that is not *of* this world, but only *in* this world, sells itself as a 'social cause'! It is hardly surprising if the result is not only empty moralism but also ludicrous theology.

Politics and Purpose

But surely, it will be said, all politics must have an aim, and in the realization of that aim, change and disruption will be inevitable. How then can a conservative both seek to guard his heritage, and not participate in the public pastime of reform? At this point, it will help to step down from the world of national politics, into the microcosm of ordinary human relations.

Some human relations presuppose a common purpose, and fall apart when that purpose is fulfilled or discontinued. (Consider, for example, a business partnership.) But not all relations are of that nature. The pursuit of a certain mechanical analogy has led to the belief (widely held but seldom stated) that an activity without an aim is merely aimless. So that if we are to consider political activity as a form of rational conduct, we should ally it to certain aims – to a social ideal that translates immediately into policy.[6] The rational politician must therefore be able to indicate the form of society at which he is aiming, why he is aiming at it, and what means he proposes for its realization.

Such a view is in fact confused. Most human activities, and most relations that are worthwhile, have no purpose. No purpose, that is, external to themselves. There is no 'end in view', and to attempt to provide one is to do violence to the arrangement. Suppose I were to approach another in the spirit of a given purpose – there is something that I have in mind in, and hope to achieve through, my relations with him. And suppose that the sole interest of my relations with the other lies in this aim. Now there is a sense in which I can still treat him (in Kant's famous terminology) not as a means only, but also as an end. For I may try to accomplish my aim by seeking his concurrence in it. I reason with him, I try to persuade him to do what I want him to do. But, *if* that is my approach, then it is always possible that I shall not persuade him, or that he, in his turn, will dissuade me. A certain reciprocity arises, and the absolute authority of my aim – as the sole determining principle of what it is reasonable for me to do – must be abandoned. And there is nothing irrational in that. If my aim is abandoned in these circumstances it is because it has proved impossible or unjustifiable. In other words it has failed to become part of the fellowship upon which it was first imposed. It follows that, if I am to allow to another the degree of autonomy which his human nature demands of me, I simply cannot approach him with a clearly delimited set of aims for *him*, and expect the fulfilment of those aims to be the inevitable, natural, or even reasonable outcome of our intercourse. I might discover new ends, or even lapse into that state of 'aimlessness' which is the norm of healthy human relations. Indeed, if friendship has a basis it is this: that a man may desire the company of someone for whom he has no specific purpose. The continuity of the friendship will generate its own passing aims and aspirations, but no one of them can ever come to dominate the arrangement without changing it from friendship to something else.

So too in politics. A statesman may have aims and ambitions for the society which he seeks to govern. But a society is more than a speechless organism. It has personality, and will. Its history, institutions and culture are the repositories of human values – in short, it has the character of end as well as means. A politician who seeks to impose upon it a given set of purposes, and seeks no understanding of the reasons and values which the society proposes in return, acts in defiance of friendship. And yet, where else does the right to govern lie, if it is not in a man's fellowship with a social order? The subjection of politics to determining purposes, however 'good in themselves' those purposes seem, is, on the conservative view, irrational. For it destroys the very relationship upon which government depends.

It is the mark of rational intercourse that aims are not all predetermined, that some ends – perhaps the most important ends – remain to be discovered rather than imposed. And in the life of society they are discovered not by the perusal of utopian treatises, but, primarily, through participation. And that means by sharing in the arrangements wherein the ends of political conduct have their life. (Likewise, the 'ends' of friendship are alive in its continuity, and show themselves from day to day, but have no independent existence and die with the friendship.) To participate in a social arrangement is to possess not just a set of beliefs, expectations, and feelings towards one's fellow men; it is also to be availed of a *way of seeing*, through which the value of conduct may be recognized. That value will not be the outcome of some all-embracing principle, applied abstractly, but on the contrary, it will proceed from the immediacies of politics. One might say that, for the conservative, political ends make sense in conduct, but for the most part resist translation into recipes. A politician cannot reasonably propose them until he has understood the social arrangement which he seeks to control, and having understood it, he may find that his ends cannot be 'proposed' in the form of a programme. To propose a recipe in advance of understanding is a sentimental gesture: it involves regarding a society as an *excuse* for political emotion, rather than as a proper object of it. To avoid sentimentality is to attempt to understand the social object, and to measure one's aims and feelings accordingly. It is to recognize, therefore, that a society too has a will, and that a rational man must be open to its persuasion. This will lies, for the conservative, enshrined in history, tradition, culture and prejudice. England, far from being a savage society that would justify the imposition of overarching decrees, is founded in the maturest of national cultures, and contains within itself all the principles of social life. The true conservative has his ear attuned to those principles, and tries to live, as a result, in friendship with the nation to which he owes his being. His own will to live, and the nation's will to live, are simply one and the same.

Immediate Objections

Is it really possible that there should be a political dogma that recognizes no ruling purpose – no purpose beyond that of government? And is it possible that conservatism should derive from a stance of 'political friendship', when for so many people 'conservatism' denotes nothing more than old abuses and unjust decrees?

24

In what follows I shall provide a detailed answer to the first of those objections. I have spoken somewhat loosely of 'nation', 'society', 'government' and 'state'. Beneath those terms lies a host of distinctions which must be brought to the surface and clarified. Eventually, I hope, the metaphor of society as person will be seen to correspond to a clear and literal idea. And then it will be obvious that there can be both dogma and policy without a ruling purpose, and that it can be as reasonable to believe in the one as it is wise to act from the other.

As for the second objection, that too, I hope, will wither away. But a preliminary response is needed, if the reader is to stomach what I have to say. Conservatism presupposes the existence of a social organism. Its politics is concerned with sustaining the life of that organism, through sickness and health, change and decay. (This is not an *external* purpose; it is what government consists in.) There are people who, in their vociferous part, reject the politics of a 'Conservative Party'. But this does not imply that there is not some deeper part of themselves that lies embedded in the social order, motivated and consoled by the forces to which the conservative instinct is attuned. Somewhere beneath the fluster of 'opinion' lies an unspoken unity. It may have evolved, sickened, or moved since it was last identified. But clearly it never *will* be identified unless we forget the opinionated crust which smothers it. Our society is confused by experiences which it has yet to comprehend. A large part of its self-conscious politics is clouded by this confusion. The dogma of conservatism will therefore prove startling and even offensive to many whose feelings it none the less quite accurately describes.

The Pursuit of Power

Nevertheless, even if the conservative is committed, in this way, to the pursuit and upkeep of an underlying social unity, his relation to that unity cannot provide the sum of politics. A society has its diseased and destructive factions, and with these the conservative is at war. And although the modern statesman is inevitably a somewhat 'wounded' surgeon, he must nevertheless continue to practise the healer's art. He must first seek to rule, and must therefore pursue the power that will enable him to do so. Indeed, for the conservative, power will not be able to mask itself as subordinate to some clear justifying aim – it is not the means to 'social justice', or 'equality', or 'freedom'. It is power to command and coerce those who would otherwise reform or destroy, and its justification must be found within itself, in an idea of legitimacy or established right.

The power which the statesman seeks must be, in other words, a power that is accepted. It must be regarded by the people as not just power, but authority. Every society depends upon popular self-respect, respect in the citizen for the order of which he forms a part and for himself as part of that order. This feeling, manifest in patriotism, in custom, in respect for law, in loyalty to a leader or monarch, and in the willing acceptance of the privileges of those to whom privilege is granted, can extend itself indefinitely. And it is from this feeling, which need be neither craven nor endlessly submissive, that the authority of the conservative statesman derives. It will be our first concern, therefore, to describe such a feeling. Thereafter we may derive from it an account of the civil order that renders the conservative attitude both possible and reasonable.

In considering the relation between power and authority, it has to be conceded that the conservative suffers from a singular disadvantage, and this disadvantage makes it necessary for him to be stronger, more cunning, even more Machiavellian, than his usual opponents. For, lacking any obvious aim in politics, he lacks any offering with which to stir up the enthusiasm of the crowd. He is concerned solely with the task of government, and his attitude defies translation into a shopping list of social goals. He looks with scepticism upon the myths of equality and social justice; he regards universal political agitation with distaste, and the clamour for 'progress' seems to him no more than a passing fad, serious only in so far as it constitutes a threat to the political order. What then can persuade the people to acquiesce in his ascent to power? It is well to say, with Burke, that the promises of revolution must be empty (since they can be understood only by presupposing precisely the social arrangement that it is intended to destroy).[7] But what other promises can the conservative provide?

The great intellectual advantage of socialism is obvious. Through its ability to align itself with ideals that every man can recognize, socialism has been able to perpetuate the belief in its moral purity, despite crime upon crime committed in its name. That a socialist revolution may cost millions of lives, that it may involve the wilful murder of an entire class, the destruction of a culture, the elimination of learning and the desecration of art, will leave not the slightest stigma on the doctrines with which it glorifies its action. And yet those lonely restorationists who have committed crimes in the cause of continuity, have – because they fought not for an ideal but for what they took to be a reality – often simply blemished the idea of authority which they hoped to serve. It seems, then, that in these violent times the conservative will find the practice of politics as difficult as he has erstwhile found its theory. But there are places where he can succeed, and England is surely one of them.

CHAPTER 2

Authority and Allegiance

The conservative attitude demands the persistence of a civil order. What is this order? And why should it be conserved?

We must begin by distinguishing state and society – not because they are truly separable but because they should be separately described. Society consists in the civil bond which generates and supports the institutions of government. Historians discuss the origins of the state. Often they write as though the 'state' were a modern invention – arising out of the collapse of ecclesiastical jurisdiction; or out of the palaver of the 'rights of man' (which seemed urgently to require the invention of something against which to claim them); or (yet more parochially), out of the settling of boundaries at the Congress of Vienna. These discussions raise important issues, and I shall return to them. But for clarity's sake we must make the widest possible distinction, and allow any organization in which there is genuine government to possess two aspects, of civil society and state. Neither aspect can exist independently, and the reader must accept therefore that the conservative vision of society – which it is the purpose of this chapter to explore – will already contain strong intimations of the conservative vision of the state.

Nevertheless, conservatism originates in an attitude to civil society, and it is from a conception of civil society that its political doctrine is derived. But a political doctrine must contain a motive to action, and a source of appeal. The conservative, unable as he is to appeal to a utopian future, or to any future that is not, as it were, already contained in the present and past, must avail himself of conceptions which are both directly applicable to things as they are and at the same time indicative of a motivating force in men. And this force must be as great as the desire for the 'freedom' and 'social justice' offered by his rivals. There are three concepts which immediately present themselves, and whose contemporary application we must examine: the concepts of authority, allegiance and tradition.

Authority and Power

It is a remarkable fact that people recognize authority in their fellows, in social arrangements, in institutions, and in the state. It is equally re-markable that this authority can command their allegiance, to such an extent that they might as willingly die for its sake as for the sake of any ideal or any religious creed. In so far as people have shown this disposi-tion to sacrifice their lives for something greater than themselves, then, historically speaking, the nation and the social order must rival religion as the principal beneficiaries of the gesture. A cynic might say that Church and State represent the only powers able to coerce men to sur-render their lives, but such cynicism is baseless. It was no *state* that com-pelled the Achaeans to assemble before the walls of Troy, but a sense of their common social identity, and of their honour and allegiance as Greeks. (The horror and the impersonality of modern warfare naturally make it difficult to sustain this attitude. Honour tends to seek expression in a kind of private grief, in the 'Greater love hath no man than this . . .' of Wilfred Owen, or else in the mere 'solidarity' of those who suffer together.)

'Authority' can mean many things. In particular, it can mean either established or legitimate power. In either sense it can be granted, dele-gated, removed, respected, ignored, opposed. A person who has auth-ority has it from a certain source – although it is well if he has authority in another sense, according to which it means not the legitimate or established principle of rule, but the natural gift to command allegiance. For the Marxist, 'authority', and the concept of 'legitimacy' through which it dignifies itself, are simply parts of the ideology of class rule, concepts belonging to and inculcated by a ruling 'hegemony'. They belong to that immense unconscious conspiracy whereby power has sought to entrench itself in accepted institutions, and whereby the his-torical nature (which is to say, the impermanence) of those institutions is masked. What is historical is presented as natural; power is repre-sented as unchangeable power. But make no mistake, says the Marxist – the only *reality* here is power.

It is important to see that such doctrines, whether true or false, may be irrelevant to the practice of politics. What distinguishes political activity from the biological grouping of the herd is that the structure of the first is determined by the concepts of those who engage in it, whereas that of the second obeys only the inexorable laws of unconscious nature. And you can try as hard as you like to undermine the 'ruling ideology' which first placed legitimacy in the centre of common consci-ousness, but you will not succeed in making people remove from their minds a concept which – in their actual dealings with the world – is indispensable to them. People have the *idea* of legitimacy, and see the world as coloured in its terms; and it is how they *see* the world which determines how they act on it. Now the belief in legitimacy exists and will always exist as part of common political consciousness, and a society is not happy in which men cannot see that legitimacy enacted, in which they see *only* establishment, and only established power. The strength of this belief in legitimacy needs no comment. From the Norman Conquest to the contemporary reactions to trade-union power, the concept of legitimacy has governed political practice, and whether or not there is any reality which corresponds to this concept is a question that may be put aside as of no political (although of great philosophical) significance.

The Social Contract

In order to understand the conservative attitude to authority, we must examine a recent and now seemingly irrepressible political idea, the idea that there can be 'no obligation on any man which ariseth not from some act of his own'[8] as Thomas Hobbes once put it. The most popular version of this idea sees the transition from power to legitimacy as residing in an unspoken, unknown and unknowable 'social contract'. Now no one, least of all a conservative, is likely to believe that government is possible without the propagation of myths. But this particular fiction – which at one time proved convenient in persuading men that the legitimacy of government lay elsewhere than in the divine right of kings – bears about as little relation to the facts as the view that my parents and I once surreptitiously contracted that they would nourish and educate me in return for my later care. Naturally, not every contract has to be explicit: there are implied contracts in law, brought about, for example, by an act of part performance. But even in implied contracts (except for those peculiar cases where a contract is implied by statute) there must be, somewhere, a choice, and a deliberation; a knowledge of consequences and a belief in, if not a mutual recognition of, an exchange of promises. The idea that there *must* be, at the heart of all political, and indeed all social organization, something in the nature of a contract (but a contract which, as it were, arises from social intercourse and does not – because clearly it could not – precede it), that idea stems from a singular pattern of thought which we must analyse, both here and in the chapter which follows, because it bears directly on our theme.

The pattern of thought is this: Human beings, as free, autonomous agents, fall under the rule of Justice. Which is to say, to put it very roughly and once again in the abstract terminology of Kant, that they must be treated as ends and not as means. To treat them as means only

29

is to disrespect their freedom, and hence to sacrifice one's right to any similar respect from them. The fulfilment of a contract is, not the highest point, but the clearest case of just relations. A promise is made, another given, knowingly and in full cognizance of consequences. To promise in such a situation, and to rely on the other's fulfilment, while withholding any intention to return, is to treat the other as a means, to abuse his trust, and hence to act unjustly towards him. Here we can see that one man has assumed a right over another to which he is not entitled; for although the other granted him that right, he did so only conditionally, only on the understanding that he acquired a similar right in return. So now we can distinguish between legitimate and illegitimate claims; the 'rights' so vociferously claimed by Mr Boffin in *Our Mutual Friend* are evidently of the latter kind. The interest of contract is that it consists entirely of rights freely granted, and in that freedom (so both common sense and common law have always suggested) lies their legitimacy. To transfer the language of contract to the social sphere provides us at once, then, with a means to distinguish legitimate from illegitimate power. The criterion may be complex in its application, taking in many subtleties and qualifications as society develops in response to it; but its essence is simple. Does power arise out of and express the contractual basis, or does it claim some right which transcends it? The power of the police might be seen in this light as legitimate, that of the Mafia as not.

It is difficult to be persuaded by such a view. For the very possibility of free and open contract presupposes a sufficient social order, not because it would otherwise be impossible to enforce contracts (although that too is true), but because without social order the very notion of an individual *committing* himself, through a promise, would not arise. Already we have supposed shared institutions and a conception of human freedom, which could hardly have their origin in the very practice of contract which they serve to make possible. This is not to say that one cannot *see* society in this contractual way, in the way of contemporary American liberalism, and so construe all forms of social organization as assemblages of their members, with choice or consent as the ultimate binding principle. But for this vision to capture even the smallest part of what is recognized as the 'authority' of state, the social arrangement must be given plausible historical antecedents (such as those of New England) with which to mystify the inquiring mind. Perhaps the most remarkable thing that has happened in American politics during this century is the recognition that the powers of state in fact transcend their supposed contractual basis, and must therefore look for their authority elsewhere.[9]

Authority and Family

But let us again step down from the political to the private realm. Consider the family. I have already suggested that it would be absurd to think of family ties as contractual, or family obligations as in any way arising from a free relinquishing of autonomy, or even from some unspoken bargain which rises into consciousness, so to speak, at some later stage. Even as a metaphor, the language of contract here fails to make contact with the facts. And it is because of this that extreme individualists – those who can see no virtue in any arrangement which does not in the end derive from conscious choice – have begun to attack the family, to fabricate an idea of its 'dispensability', to declare war on it with the kind of sentimental self-importance that has come to be associated with the language of the 'radical critique'. This critique (which I shall discuss in a later chapter) has found its home in California, and duly taken its place among the anti-authoritarian gestures with which America shakes its fist at the Pacific Ocean.

Were it an accident that human beings grow to love, need and depend upon one another; were it an accident that children feel bound to their parents and parents to their children in inexorable bonds that circumscribe the possibilities of later pleasure and pain; were it an accident that domestic life is even now (except in the case of a minority) roughly as it has been, then the 'radical critique' might have some force. But a conservative will be sceptical. His rare attempts to express the truth about the world are likely to be founded in observation, and to convey a disbelief in the instant changeability of human nature. Hence he will recognize that these facts are not accidental, and that the family bond is dispensable only in the way that pleasure, industry, love, grief, passion and allegiance are dispensable – that is, only in the case of the minority which can persuade itself (for whatever reason) to renounce these things.

The family, then, is a small social unit which shares with civil society the singular quality of being non-contractual, of arising (both for the children and for the parents) not out of choice but out of natural necessity. And (to turn the analogy round) it is obvious that the bond which ties the citizen to society is likewise not a voluntary but a kind of natural bond. Locke, and the other great individualists, who thought otherwise, were also constrained to think that the world contained many 'vacant places' which could be filled by those who chose to withdraw from their inherited arrangement. As we now know, every country sports the sign 'engaged'. And besides, is it not psychological naïvety to think that I, now, at thirty-five, rooted in my language, culture and history, could suddenly do a volte-face and see myself as English only by *accident*, free at every moment to change? If I go elsewhere I take my Englishness with

31

me, as much as I take my attachment to family, language, life and self. I go as a colonial or as an exile, and either sink like the Tibetans or swim like the Jews.

The analogy with the family is useful if we are to understand the role of authority in politics. It is clear from the start that a child must be acted upon by its parents' power: its very love for them will accord to them that power, and parents no more escape from its exercise by being permissive than does an officer cease to command his troops by leaving them constantly at ease. A child is what it is by virtue of its parents' will, and consequently the parent has an indefeasible obligation to form and influence the child's development. In this very process is power, and it is of necessity an established power, since it resides already with the parent at the child's first coming into the world. Now there is a sense in which every child does not only need its parents to exercise that power, but will also demand that they do so, to the extent that it cherishes their protection. There can be no ministering to the love of a child, and no granting of love, that is not also, in the first instance, an exercise of established power. For how is the child to recognize, from all those beings that surround it, the object which is its parent, that is, its principle of protection and its source of love? Surely, it must feel the influence of a will in its life, of a desire *for* its life, besides its own. It must feel the constraint of another's love for it. And it is only in recognizing the existence of an objective power over what it will do that the child is pulled out of its self-immersion into the recognition of its parent as an autonomous being, a being who not only gives love but gives it freely, and towards whom it owes love in return. The kind of personal love that we envisage as the end of family union requires, as its precondition, the sense of established power – the child's unformed recognition that, in respect of at least one other being, he is helpless – combined with the growing awareness that the power of that being is also an exercise of freedom. And it is a similar recognition of constraint, helplessness, and subjection to external will that heralds the citizen's realization of his membership of society; in this recognition love of one's country is born.

Consider the other side of family loyalties. We are apt to think of children as having a responsibility towards their parents, a responsibility that in no way reflects any merely contractual right, but which is simply *due* to the parents as a recognition of the filial tie. This sense of obligation is not founded in justice – which is the sphere of free actions between beings who *create* their moral ties – but rather in respect, honour, or (as the Romans called it) piety.[10] To neglect my parents in old age is not an act of injustice but an act of impiety. Impiety is the refusal to recognize as legitimate a demand that does not arise from consent or choice. And we see that the behaviour of children towards their parents cannot be understood unless we admit this ability to recognize a bond that is 'transcendent', that exists, as it were 'objectively', outside the sphere of individual choice. It is this ability that is transferred by the citizen from hearth and home to place, people and country. The bond of society – as the conservative sees it – is just such a 'transcendent' bond, and it is inevitable that the citizen will be disposed to recognize its legitimacy, will be disposed, in other words, to bestow authority upon the existing order. He will be deterred from doing so largely by acts of arbitrary power, or by a general 'unfriendliness' in the public order, of the kind experienced by the deprived and unfostered child.

Authority, in the sense that we have considered, is an enormous artifact. By which I mean, not that authority is intentionally constructed, but rather that it exists only in so far as men exercise, understand and submit to it. The condition of society presupposes this general connivance, and a conservative will seek to uphold all those practices and institutions – among which, of course, the family is pre-eminent – through which the habits of allegiance are acquired. As we shall see, this necessary corollary of conservative thinking is incompatible with any suggestions that the conservative is an advocate either of liberal ideals, or of the so-called 'minimal state'.[11] It is as possible for a conservative as it is for a socialist to be, should the need arise, 'totalitarian' – although, naturally, it is not the height of wisdom so to declare oneself. In fact, what is objected to as 'totalitarianism' is not the power of state, but power arbitrarily constituted and arbitrarily exercised. No serious person *can* believe that there ought to be a power greater than that of the state, a power that can, if it chooses, put itself beyond the reach of law. The conservative believes in the power of state as necessary to the state's authority, and will seek to establish and enforce that power in the face of every influence that opposes it. However, his desire is to see power standing not naked in the forum of politics, but clothed in constitution, operating always through an adequate system of law, so that its movement seems never barbarous or oppressive, but always controlled and inevitable, an expression of the civilized vitality through which allegiance is inspired. The constitution, therefore, and the institutions which sustain it, will always lie at the heart of conservative thinking. The conservative places his faith in arrangements that are known and tried, and wishes to imbue them with all the authority necessary to constitute an accepted and objective public realm. It is from this that his respect for tradition and custom arises, and not from any end – such as freedom – towards which these practices are seen as a means. This point is of the essence, and I shall elaborate it further.

Allegiance

Consider, then, the concept of allegiance. It is allegiance which defines the condition of society, and which constitutes society as something greater than the 'aggregate of individuals' that the liberal mind perceives. It is proper for a conservative to be sceptical of claims made on behalf of the value of the individual, if these claims should conflict with the allegiance necessary to society, even though he may wish the *state* (in the sense of the apparatus of government) to stand in a fairly loose relation to the activities of individual citizens. Individuality too is an artifact, an achievement which depends upon the social life of man. And indeed, as many historians have pointed out, it is a recent venture of the human spirit for men and women to define themselves as individuals, as creatures whose nature and value is summed up in their unique individual being.[12] The condition of man requires that the individual, while he exists and acts as an autonomous being, does so only because he can first identify himself as something greater – as a member of a society, group, class, state or nation, of some arrangement to which he may not attach a name, but which he recognizes instinctively as home. Politically speaking, this bond of allegiance – which, seen from the heights of intellectual speculation as 'my station and its duties', is experienced as a peculiar certainty in the activity of day to day [13] – is of a value which transcends the value of individuality. For the majority of men, the bond of allegiance has immediate authority, while the call to individuality is unheard. It is therefore wrong to consider that a statesman has some kind of duty to minister to the second of these, and ignore the first. If the two impulses are not in conflict, as they perhaps were not, for example, in the society described by Fielding (and defended by Burke), then well and good. But if the second threatens the first – as it must do in a society where individuality seeks to realize itself independently of the institutions and traditions that have nurtured it – then the civil order is threatened too. And the business of politics is to maintain the civil order, and to prevent the 'dust and powder of individuality' that was once described as its ruin.[14]

I have sketched the formation of allegiance in the family bond, and the residue of respect or piety which grows from that, ripe for transference to whatever might present itself as a fitting social object. The primary object of allegiance is, as I argued, authority, which is to say power conceived as legitimate, and so bound by responsibility. In the family this authority and responsibility have their foundation and end in love, but from the beginning they transcend the personal love of individuals. (There is, surely, a great mystification involved in the Freudian idea of the 'family romance'. Freud was getting at something of immense importance, which is the connection – perceived also by Hegel and Wagner – between the prohibition of incest and the existence of the family as 'home'. But this surely need not persuade us that the natural bond is always and inevitably erotic. In this area the distinctions, and not the similarities, have the greatest meaning.) Authority and responsibility arise from and sustain the sense of the family as something greater than the aggregate of its members, an entity in which the members participate, so that its being and their being are intermingled. Man is increased and not diminished through his participation in such arrangements.[15] Mere individuality, relinquished first to the family, and then to the whole social organism, is finally replaced by the mature allegiance which is the only politically desirable form of 'freedom'. It is obvious that such allegiance is a matter of degree, being fervent at some times, passive or failing at others. The possibility of conservatism supposes only that it exists to some degree, and in most active people.

It would seem, then, that the healthy state or nation must command the allegiance of its subjects. Patriotism of some kind – the individual's sense of his identity with a social order – is politically indispensable. Patriotism has had many detractors, not all of them as sentimental as the ageing Tolstoy. But it is hard to deny its power to instil a measure of generosity even into the meanest spirit, or to quieten the instinct to profit from another's helplessness or loss. If it be objected that patriotism (or 'nationalism') has been a major cause of war and suffering, then the answer is, first, that it has been the single greatest obstacle to civil war, widely recognized to be the worst of human misfortunes, and secondly that, since the cause of war is the struggle for power, war can be carried on as easily in the name of an 'international' ideal as in the cause of national grandeur. And in the former case, as we know from the religious wars of Europe, and from the constantly fomented struggles of the 'people's armies' of Africa and the East, the result is war practised without honour, law or mercy.

There is a long-standing tradition of political thought (of which Machiavelli is by no means the first representative) that considers aggression abroad to be a condition of peace at home. If that is so, then of course patriotism becomes a necessary bond of civil society. But it is the hope of every modern citizen that the Machiavellian intuition contains no necessary truth, and that a habit of bargaining under international law will come to replace the previous pattern of belligerence. Nevertheless, it has to be recognized that patriotism is not simply a stance towards the international world. It is in the first instance a condition of private life, and occupies a unique place in the deliberations of the citizen. To understand it we must refer again to two axioms of conservative thought. I call them axioms, although, naturally, they are implicit and unspoken in the instincts of *homo conservans.*

35

The National Focus

The first axiom is the simple principle that, lacking an overmastering ideal (in the sense explained in Chapter 1), conservatism must necessarily take many forms. Solon, asked what is the best form of government, replied 'For whom? And at what time?' It is a *particular* country, a *particular* history, a *particular* form of life that commands the conservative's respect and energy, and while he may have an imaginative grasp of other real or ideal arrangements, he is not immersed in them as he is immersed in the society that is his own. No utopian vision will have force for him compared to the force of present practice, for while the former is abstract and incomplete, the latter is concrete, qualified by familiar complexities that may be understood without describing them. To the extent that there are arrangements that have been proved in social life, and which have power to command the loyalty of their participants, to that extent is there variety among the forms of conservative politics. Moral scruples may turn the conservative from condoning the practices of others of his kind; but his preferred form of political life will not be a deduction from abstract principles sufficient in themselves to forbid what he finds distasteful. Englishmen may loathe the Chinese practice of trial by ordeal (or 'struggle' as it is quaintly called). But this is not a reason to press the Chinese to revise this particularly conservative aspect of their 'revolutionary state', when the constitution of that state is in any case hardly intelligible to anyone who observes it from outside. This is not to espouse the view (associated with such sociologists as Talcott Parsons) that alien 'cultures' are in some deep way inaccessible to judgement. It is rather to emphasize that political understanding, as a form of practical judgement, does not readily translate itself into universal principles, and that conservatism, which takes its main inspiration from what *is*, has little competence to meddle in what is merely possible.

The Priority of Appearance

The second axiom is more difficult, although equally fundamental to the conservative creed. This is that the political activity of the citizen is determined by his own conception of his social nature. The *reality* of politics is not to be found outside the motives of those who engage in it, and whatever Marxists may say about the relation between base and superstructure, or about the economic causation of social behaviour, its truth does not bear on the *political* understanding of humanity. (This is a point to which I shall return in Chapter 5.)

The argument may be illustrated by an analogy from the science of linguistics. Suppose that a linguist presented a law of English speech, which told us when a man will say 'The house is white', and when he will say 'Something is white'. Given sufficient theory, this law would provide a complete account of the relation between those sentences, since it would tell us all the facts about their utterance: when, where and why. But in another sense it would be incomplete. For there is a connection between those sentences that may have nothing to do with causality, and yet which is of the first importance, a connection of meaning. It is this connection which is grasped by the man who understands them, and he may have a *complete* understanding of them while being ignorant of the linguist's laws. And conversely, the linguist may have a full knowledge of causal laws, and yet lack the native speaker's understanding of what is said. For his laws may not issue in a dictionary.

Similarly, whatever the economic, social and biological determinants of a man's behaviour, that behaviour is *understood* by him and his fellows in another way: in terms of its *meaning*. To describe this meaning one would have to use the concepts available to the agent, and not the specialized classifications of a predictive science. Moreover, a man's intentions and acts derive from his own conception of the world; there can be no 'impartial observer' of human behaviour, if that means an observer who has no imaginative understanding of the concepts which determine agency. To engage in political activity is to understand, and in varying degrees to share, the common way of seeing things. This may require an act of imaginative identification; but it does not involve (and indeed is largely incompatible with) the application of any neutral 'science of man'.

What is this 'surface' of social affairs, this thing that is understood in participation but which may resist translation into words? In the first instance, to put the matter very simply, one may refer to the 'culture' of a society, race or nation. By 'culture' I mean all those activities which endow the world with meaning, so that it bears the mark of appropriate action and appropriate response. It is this which constitutes the individual's understanding of his social nature. Such understanding is given not through choice, but rather through concepts and perceptions embodied in the social organism, practices (such as that of marriage) which it does not make sense to think of as the products of individual will, or the outcome of some 'social contract' the terms of which no one can state or remember. A practice belongs to culture whenever it leads its participants to perceive the *value* of what they do. This perception may not be fully available to an outsider, but it may be essential to the intention which underlies a social act.

There is, to put it bluntly, something deeply self-deceived in the idea of a fulfilled human being whose style of life is entirely of his own devising. The cult of 'authenticity' – emphasizing the truth that the individual self is in some sense an artifact – espouses the self-contradictory position that it is by himself that he is made. This myth of self as *causa sui* is one to which few people now subscribe. Clearly the artifact of self is not of *my* making; it was cast first in the mould of a social arrangement and lives with that shape stamped permanently upon it, more or less distorted or embellished by later acts of choice.

I shall argue that, once we have rejected the cult of 'authenticity', we shall be forced to reject along with it the entire apparatus of dissent. In particular, we shall have to abandon the attempt to erode whatever is 'established', whatever has a vested power to overcome opposition, which is the first principle of liberal as of socialist thought. Which is not to say that we must *accept* all that is established; but we will be forced to acknowledge that, whatever we postulate by way of an ideal, the ideal itself may have little life outside the social arrangement which provided the concepts and the perceptions of those who pursue it. And once it is clear that a major and perhaps central part of those concepts and perceptions is inherited, then custom, tradition and common culture become ruling conceptions in politics. If these provide the common man with a sense of the value of his acts, then his self-identity and his allegiance to public forms are ultimately one and the same.

Patriotism

We now begin to see the relevance of our second conservative axiom – the axiom that politics deals with the surface of social consciousness. A full understanding of the idea of allegiance will require in its turn an understanding of tradition, custom and ceremony – of the totality of practices through which the citizen is able to perceive his allegiance as an *end*. For the liberal, allegiance to society is a means: 'stick to this arrangement and on the whole you'll be left to yourself'. But the conservative cannot see it as a means to an end, since there is no description of the end in question that does not refer back to the values – and hence to the customs, institutions and allegiances – of those who pursue it. It follows that while the forms of patriotism will be many and varied, they will seek always to translate themselves into *symbolic* acts, acts which resist translation as 'means to an end'.

Consider the Englishman's allegiance to the Crown, as he envisages and enacts it. Monarchy is an institution, with a complex constitutional background, that elevates the person of the monarch above the realm of individual character and endows him or her with the dignity and, so to speak, the objectivity of office. It is not the personal qualities of the Queen that draw the Englishman to her nor is it any considered knowledge of the function and history of the Crown. It is rather a sense of the monarch as a symbol of nationhood, as an incarnation of the historical entity of which he is a part. His loyalty to the monarch requires ceremonial enactment, customary usage, an established code of deference: for this is the style of all symbolic gestures in which society and individual are merged.

Now a conservative is likely to value the institution of monarchy, and the kind of patriotism that it engenders. For the legitimacy of monarchical rule arises 'transcendentally', in the manner of the duties and obligations of family life. The monarch is not chosen for his personal attributes, nor does he have obligations and expectations which are the subject-matter of any 'social contract'. He is simply the representation of sovereignty, and its ceremonial presence. His will as monarch is not his individual will, but the will of state. The monarch forms part of that surface of concepts and symbols whereby the citizen can perceive his social identity, and perceive society not as a means to an end, but as an end in itself. Attachment to the monarch is therefore patriotism in a pure form, a form that could not be translated into attachment to a policy, or to a choice of means.

As a matter of fact, even when the titular head of state is 'chosen' – where there is an elected president, say, who offers 'promises' to the people – the choice is not in fact a choice of policy. The aims of politics, as they arise from day to day, are beyond the voter's competence, the ideals of social policy largely beyond his care. Usually, therefore, the president is chosen not as a means to an end, but as a peculiar kind of end in himself – as a 'figure of state'. Once again, he is a symbol. In a world of mass communication this means that a president will be chosen for his 'style', where style carries an implication of inward identity between president and nation, an identity that derives from no common end to which they might both be moving. This attachment to style represents an attempt to escape from the burden of democratic election, to escape from the 'contractual' element of the choice, to escape most of all from the sense of the state as constantly remade at each election, like a machine that has become outclassed. It is an expression of the conservative instinct, the instinct to make a future in the image of the past.

But just as the past constrains the future, so does the future commandeer the past. The past enacted by the citizen is the past *directed* to the future. Continuity is a selective aim; it looks both backwards and forwards with a measure of distrust. But we must remember the distinctive place of the past in our practical understanding: unlike the future, the past is *known*. How then should it enter our political calculations?

Tradition

That question brings us to the final concept that will be necessary in giving articulate voice to the conservative instinct towards society, the concept of tradition. Under this concept I include all manner of custom, ceremony, and participation in institutional life, where what is done is done, not mechanically, but for a reason, and where the reason lies, not in what will be, but in what *has* been. It does not matter if the reason cannot be voiced by the man who obeys it: traditions are enacted and not designed, and none the less conscious for the lack of speech.

The power of tradition is twofold. First, it makes history into reason, and therefore the past into a present aim (as the whole history of the nation is enacted in the ceremony of coronation). Secondly, tradition arises from every organization in society, and is no mere trapping of the exercise of power. Traditions arise and command respect wherever the individual seeks to relate himself to something transcendent. They arise in clubs and societies, in local life, in religion and family custom, in education, and in every institution where man is brought into contact with his kind. Later, in considering questions of politics, we must show how the state can bring authority, allegiance, and tradition together, in order to define the citizen as *subject*.

I am aware that any reference to tradition will cause scepticism among those who believe themselves free from its charm. And there is no doubt that, while the concept may be essential to conservative dogma, it will also (like the 'equality', 'freedom' and 'social justice' which rival it) have to bear more weight of political argument than any single conception can sustain. But we must do our best for it. Whatever difficulties may attend the enterprise of defending tradition, the fight concerns no fiction but a genuine reality. Now it is salutary at this juncture to compare the realms of politics and art. Both activities are imbued with significance and purposefulness, and yet neither (on the conservative view) has any real external purpose. Art shows in microcosm the great architectural problem of politics as we are beginning to envisage it. And the comparison enables us to see why we should consider again the complaint that conservatism holds no prospect for the 'modern man': that it is far from being the impulse of life in death, but rather the will for death in life. For in art too we have felt the cravings, the disorientation, the overwhelming estrangement of 'modern' man, and in art too it has seemed necessary to present as self-conscious what was previously felt as nature, instinct and life.

But in the very sphere where the embattled consciousness of 'modern man' has most displayed itself, so too has the conservative principle been repeatedly affirmed. By this I do not mean that the artists who brought

40

about the major aesthetic achievements of our century were, politically, of a conservative cast. If this is true, then it is only an instance of a more general truth – swallowed with some difficulty by critics of the New Left – that significant artists can be, and very often are, that way. (It is interesting to note the frequency with which it has been assumed, since the Romantic movement, that art must necessarily be a revolutionary force, simply because it has revolutionized *itself*. The assumption looks very odd when set beside the varieties of social conservatism expressed and advocated by James, Conrad, Yeats, Pound, Eliot, Joyce, Waugh and Lawrence – to name only the greatest of those who created our modern literature.)

What does it mean, then, to say that the conservative principle has been repeatedly reaffirmed in contemporary art? Partly this: that for most significant artists – for Eliot, Pound and Joyce, for Schoenberg and Stravinsky, for Braque and Moore – the problem of giving articulate voice to the modern consciousness was conceived as the problem of making that consciousness part of a *tradition* of artistic expression, and so bringing it back, by whatever complicated route, to the point where it might be understood. For Schoenberg the tradition of German music was what principally mattered: the problem was to re-create it, through self-conscious understanding of its inner life. The 'live tradition' that Pound hoped to 'gather from the air' was conceived in equally self-conscious terms. Eliot went so far as to represent tradition as an individual artifact: to belong to a tradition is also to make that tradition; to be part of history is to have created history.[16] However, this process, which begins in loss and in conscious exploration, ends too in genuine discovery, the discovery that 'History is now and England'. In that discovery is a restoration of the whole of things.

It would be interesting to digress further into the transformation of the idea of tradition in the mind of alienated man. But let us simply draw the obvious conclusion from our parallel. Just as tradition circumscribes the possibilities of artistic expression, and so must be constantly re-created in artistic change, so too does it lay down the forms of political life, and must be re-created in every conscious political act. Now it is both difficult and yet (it seems) at the same time necessary for the modern consciousness to create tradition, setting itself in the centre of tradition as it sets tradition in the centre of itself. It may require an act of imagination, insight and will for a politician, in the midst of confusion, to reassert the identity of the society that he seeks to govern, even when, in their most secret innervations, it is just such an adventure that the people require from him. His route back to that place he started from will not find the place unchanged, and the way will be hard and uncertain. He will need exceptional qualities – the qualities of a De Gaulle or a Disraeli – if he is to reaffirm as a statesman the reality which he knows as a man. Yet, if he has the will to live, and the will to govern, nothing short of that can satisfy him.

As one writer has suggested,[17] there is no general explanation of *how* men re-create and accept traditions. Nor is it easy to draw the line between genuine re-creation and the establishment of new and divergent social forms. But in all attempts to restore, re-create and assimilate tradition, the feature of continuity remains. When a man acts from tradition he sees what he *now* does as belonging to a pattern that transcends the focus of his present interest, binding it to what has previously been done, and done successfully. (This is obvious from the case of artistic creation.) Naturally there are rival traditions, and it would be vain to pretend that there is reason to belong to *all* of them. There are traditions of torture, crime and revolution. The traditions which the conservative fosters and upholds must therefore satisfy independent criteria. First, they must have the weight of a *successful* history – which is to say that they must be the palpable remainder of something that has flourished, and not the latest in a series of abortive starts. Secondly, they must engage the loyalty of their participants, in the deep sense of moulding their idea of what they are and should be. (Contrast the traditions of family life with those of torture.) Finally, they must point to something durable, something which survives and gives meaning to the acts that emerge from it.

But what does this tradition concretely amount to? No simple answer to this question can prove satisfactory: the task of dogma is to bridge the gap between philosophy and practice, and it is only in practice that the sum of our traditions can be understood. Nevertheless, it still belongs to dogma to delineate the *kind* of thing that is intended, and to present some partial exposition of its instances. Tradition, then, must include all those practices which serve to define the individual's 'being in society'. It constitutes his image of himself as a fragment of the greater social organism, and at the same time as the whole of that organism implicit in this individual part. The institution of the family, as it has variously developed, provides a clear example. No man who participates in that institution can remain unaffected in his conception of himself. He can no longer regard the fact of fatherhood, for example, as a biological accident. In seeing himself as father he finds himself entangled in a social bond, a bond of responsibility. And the reason for this bond and for the actions which express it, lies in the fact that this is how things are. Moreover, they are like this because they have been like this. The idea of 'family', through which his responsibilities, aims and preoccupations are from day to day defined, is one inherited without thought from his own participation in the arrangement which it designates. This is what is 'given'. Had he not conceived his activities as exemplifying the historical pattern contained in that concept, then he would nevertheless have needed some adequate replacement, some rival conception in terms of which to define his ends. And if this conception does not belong to tradition it will make way for the dangerous thought: 'Perhaps I do this, not for its own sake, not for what it *is*, but as a means to an end. Where then is the end? Where is the profit?' This thought signifies the emergence of the individual from social life, and the first glimpse of the empty solipsism that waits outside. Tradition restores the individual to the present act: it shows the reason *in* the act, and stills the desire for a justifying aim.

The family is of course an obvious example. But there are others, such as the customs which surround the momentous occasions of birth, coupling and death, the customs of hospitality, rivalry and class allegiance, of manners, dress and common courtesy. There are also the institutions of religion, in which man's desire for an identity greater than his nature provides reaches out of history altogether, to what is outside time and change. Only some of these institutions, it might be thought, are truly political. But to take such a view is to take too narrow a view of politics. Every tradition of any importance in the life of the citizen will tend to become part of the establishment of a state. This principle – which we might call the law of establishment and which I shall illustrate in Chapter 8 – is part of the natural history of politics, and shows the continuing necessity for political action to extend beyond the bounds of economic management. It is illustrated not only by the explicit establishment of the Church and, through the operation of law, of the family and private property, but by the implicit establishment of class rule in parliamentary institutions, by the more recent establishment of the traditions of organized labour in the trade-union movement, and by the extension of law (less automatic in America than in England, but manifest even there) to protect every aspect of social life, just so soon as it seems to be of more than individual concern.

A Note of Scepticism

What of the conservative attitude to social transformation? What 'tradition' has force, in comparison with the violence of industrial expansion and of over-population, with the spread of irreligion, and the growth of the urban working-class? Is there not an element of make-believe in the view that allegiance, authority and custom might have survived these historical convulsions, so as still to provide the bond from which politics derives its inspiration and appeal?

If this scepticism is the prelude to a rival politics, then it calls for only one reply: what other bond are you imagining? And how will you bring it about? But usually it takes a more unsettling form, the form, as one might put it, of the 'broad historical perspective'. It makes no recommendations, espouses no policies, and stands above the particular beliefs of the communities which it seeks to observe. The historical perspective looks down on the world of men from a height where their activity is seen only as the movement of impersonal forces, which propel the politician precisely when he most believes that he is guiding them. Withdrawing to this height, it may for the moment seem as though the task of discovering and asserting continuity is a hopeless one, that all things have changed utterly, and that in nothing is there a lasting principle of government.

I shall try to answer certain common forms of this historian's doubt. But two things should be said at once in reply to it. First, some of the items of dogma that I have considered have a philosophical basis which places them beyond the reach of historical criticism. The view of society as requiring forms of allegiance, and a recognition of authority, both of which transcend the operation of any contractual bond, is a view not of this or that community, but of the essence of civil life. It is this transcendent bond that constitutes society, and which is misrepresented by the liberal theories of contract and consent. Moreover, one particular tradition, which both embodies a transcendent bond, and also reinforces social allegiance, has survived all the upheavals of recent history. This is the tradition of family life. Even a 'revolutionary state' will find itself dependent upon it, and placed under the necessity to create (usually through the old expedient of belligerent foreign policy) the corresponding bond of social unity.

Secondly, it may be true that particular bonds of allegiance have decayed or fallen apart. But if some people *think* (in their vociferous part) that the bond of English citizenship has been loosened or undone, this does not show that their thought corresponds either to reality or to the true political sentiments which guide them. Much is disturbed; old allegiances have gone under and new ones risen in their place. But through all this, I shall argue, the conservative can find and uphold a genuine continuity. And his reason for doing so will be apparent in the attempt.

Concluding Remarks

I have surveyed the great 'datum' of civil society. What, then, are the dogmas to which that survey gives support? There are two principles so basic as to constitute axioms of conservative thinking. First, the principle that there is no general politics of conservatism. The forms of conservatism will be as varied as the forms of social order. Second, the principle that conservatism engages with the surface of things, with the motives, reasons, traditions and values of the society from which it draws its life. There are further dogmas, abstract in their origin, but specific in their implications. Society exists through authority, and the recognition of this authority requires the allegiance to a bond that is not contractual but transcendent, in the manner of the family tie. Such allegiance requires tradition and custom through which to find enactment. But tradition is no static thing. It is the active achievement of continuity; it can be restored, rescued and amended as grace and opportunity allow.

Having discovered the allegiance of society, the conservative seeks to lend to it the support of a constituted state. It is therefore to the political implications of social life, and the constitution of the order in which it is lived, that we now must turn.

CHAPTER 3
_____

Constitution and the State

Burckhardt wrote of the 'great modern fallacy that a constitution can be *made*'.[18] It would be equally true to speak of the greater modern fallacy that a constitution can be endlessly and in every particular *reformed*. The customs, allegiances and traditions to which I have referred form the life of a civil society: they do not yet amount to the constitution of a state. And yet clearly they owe their continuance to presiding power, and that power (which is the power of state) must contain in itself the authority of something 'given' if it is to protect and enshrine allegiances that arise from no individual choice.

The Making of a Constitution

Liberalism, which sees the state as means to the end of individual freedom, is bound to consider the civil society as absolutely separate from the state, and to require of the latter only that minimum of interference in the life of society which the aim of freedom requires. It therefore must naturally tend to the view that a constitution *can* be made (for if it is no more than a means to an end, it suffices to understand the end in order to calculate the most effective means to it). The liberal will perhaps point to the example of the American constitution as proof of his contention. But the example is a bad one. It ignores the American inheritance, and the peculiar circumstances that led to drawing up a document designed both to secure the unity and to safeguard the eccentricities of the original participant states. It ignores all that language and custom had already established – in particular the tradition of English common law which both preceded and survived the break with the Crown. It ignores the unique social position of the Founding Fathers, educated gentlemen who could propagate the myth of a 'new constitution' while enjoying the privileges of an established order which already defined their social goal. (Madison was able to say in Federal Convention in 1787: 'our government ought to secure the permanent interests

46

of the country against innovation'; it is part of the genius of such men as Madison and Jefferson that they were able to fulfil that aim.) It ignores the conflicts which were suppressed in the final ratification, and which still persist. It ignores the already constituted rights and liberties which made the conscious adoption of a 'constitution' into a coherent gesture. In short, it ignores the fact that the written constitution of the United States – like any written constitution – is an abstract formula, of no more concrete significance than the *Déclaration des Droits de l'Homme et du Citoyen*. It is true even now that the very meaning of this slender document is something that can be decided only by judicial process.[19] And judicial interpretation takes account – whether consciously or unconsciously – of issues that determine the fabric of civil life. It is history and not the written word which reveals the constitution of America, and that part of it which is usually identified as the whole is no more than a delicate superstructure, resting on a deep and unfathomed base.

State and Civil Society

Now it is clear that, while the conservative may require a loose connection between the state and civil society (looser, say, than that which exists in China), he will wish to see the state as end and not as means, just as he sees civil society. The state as means (as administrative machine, or business enterprise, or welfare officer, or whatever) – such a state is not one to which the citizen can *belong*. Nor are the ends to which the state is supposed to be subordinate really capable of description outside the order which embodies them. This is certainly true of the liberal end of freedom. Naturally, one's neighbours may interfere with one, to a greater or lesser extent, but until we are given some concrete description of the social and political arrangement, it is impossible to say whether more or less of this interference is desirable. The 'interference' proper to a rural community in Zululand is greater than anything experienced in a Soviet city. Yet it would be sadly misguided to call it a loss of freedom, when subjection to this kind of interference is precisely what it is to *be* a Zulu. And as soon as there is interference, there is a form of rule, and therefore a state, however loosely constituted. Without some move in this direction, towards constituted power, a person is neither free nor unfree, but lives like the nomads of the anarchistic commune, in a perpetual hallucination of freedom that can be translated only into solipsistic acts.

To treat the state as end and not as means is to see the aims of state as arising internally, out of its own life and self-interaction. It is wholly natural to see institutions in some such way. Consider a football team,

47

an institution to which men belong and to which others swear undying loyalty. It commands this loyalty not as a means but as an end: it is *this* group, acting in *this* way that matters. It is not a means to the end of scoring goals (an activity which, outside the institution of football, would make no sense). Nor is it a means to the pleasure of those observing it. It is, rather, something to which one may belong, in a variety of ways, and the benefit of which resides precisely in the bond of membership.

The conservative is recognizable as a political animal partly by his respect for constitution (for the state as 'given'), and by his reluctance to effect any complete separation – either in theory or in practice – between state and civil society. It is (as I remarked) a fundamental tenet of liberal thought that this separation exists in theory, and ought also to exist in fact. One modern writer has compared fascism and communism in our times by saying that, whereas the former elevates the functions of civil society to the level of state, the latter allows the state to swallow the functions of society.[20] But such rhetorical juggling misrepresents the nature of the relation. There are not two entities here, but rather one entity seen under separate aspects. Similarly a man is not two entities – soul and body – but one entity which can be seen in both a material and a spiritual way. Liberalism is like a political survival of the Cartesian theory of mind, an attempt to represent the mind of society as functioning in accidental relation to its body. And in order to verify this image to itself, the massive conscience of liberalism has laboured to sunder the life of society from its spiritual 'form', and contemplated with increasing amazement the result, which is, of course, not the life but the death of the 'body politic'. The conservative will see the constitution as the inherited principle of the life of the state, and see the state in its turn not just as the guardian but also as the expression of a social entity. He will not be occupied with 'alternatives' – for to speak of alternatives suggests that we are considering rival means to some universal end. For the conservative end and means are the same: the life of the body politic. Moreover it is as deep an instinct in a conservative as it is in a socialist to resist the champions of 'minimal' government, and to recognize the essence of politics in established power. Where they differ is in their idea of legitimacy, which, for a conservative, stems not from results but from origins. The reasons that he acknowledges refer not to any hypothetical or abstract future, but to a real and concrete past. It is in the past, and the past as it makes itself present, that he will find his reasons for the pursuit of power. And that pursuit will again be seen not as means but as end, as an *expression* of his political identity. The pursuit of power by political men is simply a part, and a necessary part, of the life of the state, and the true statesman is the one whose personal ambition and personal success coincide with the existing forces of civil order.

Human Rights

How is this attitude to the state to be translated into dogma? I shall approach this difficult question negatively. First, the conservative will be loath to found his political enterprise upon any doctrine of 'universal' or 'natural rights'. In the international dispute which is wrongly identified as the conflict between 'left' (or 'right') and 'centre' (the safe place where, believing nothing, you can never be wrong), the conception of 'human rights' has played a major part, with the implication that the moral force of western democracy is great enough to endow it with the imperial and ecclesiastical supremacy enshrined in the doctrine of natural law. Of course there are good states and bad states, tyrannies and peaceful communities; and the conservative will be ready to judge between them. And as we shall see, he will not deny himself the use of such epithets as 'just' and 'unjust' in the process. But to think that the whole difference can be summed up in terms of a simple body of abstract rights, which can be specified for all men, independently of their origin and station, is neither feasible politics nor plausible doctrine. There are only rights where there are obligations; and whose is the obligation to provide? No doubt the United Nations Charter of Human Rights contains many moral truths; but what social arrangement, what community of common interests, what mutual understanding between man and man, gives rise to the *political* obligation to comply with it?

There is no political reason why the 'rights' of the Soviet citizen should coincide with those of an Englishman, or be made to do so. The latter is the fortunate inheritor of a long tradition of social life and established power; his rights have been granted and won through a process in which the nature and identity of the nation was seldom at risk (and which was never more at risk than when the doctrine of the rights of man gained sudden ascendancy). Naturally his rights, constituted in the state, grant to him a measure of freedom, and an expectation of just treatment, that his Soviet brother does not enjoy. But does this give the Soviet citizen – heir to a confused empire, emerging from a state of revolution, and searching once again for its lost autocratic past – some equivalent 'right' to 'dissent' because he is not provided for? We may wish to pass judgement on the Soviet state, but this is surely not the best language in which to do so. There can be no international charter for dissidents, and only one respectable reason for one state to lend support to seditious utterance in another, which is the pursuit of power. In the absence of that pursuit, all this shadow-boxing is meaningless. Certainly it brings us no nearer to conservative dogma.

Rights and Privileges

It is worth considering the notion of 'rights' a little further. There is no doubt that it has achieved an unnatural predominance in the language of politics. The conservative would conceive the power of state as an embodiment of privilege, rather than as a source of gifts. A privilege is part of the apparatus of state, and not separate from the exercise of political authority. (Thus the title 'Duke' is a privilege only if it represents some form of social or political precedence, otherwise, as Huckleberry Finn discovered, a Duke is a very ornery kind of thing.) A gift, on the other hand, is a benefit that is separate from the apparatus of state. It requires neither service to, nor position in, nor even membership of the state. A council house, for example, is a gift, which consequently confers on the recipient no political status; while it is often claimed as a 'right', it cannot possibly be so conceived by someone who takes the conservative view of politics. Moreover, such gifts involve a transference of power without any transference of authority (in this they differ markedly from political privilege). Indeed, this illustrates one of the channels through which authority flows away from the heart of politics, and transforms itself into the mere power of the underdog, who has nothing political but his 'rights', and no reciprocal obligations which would establish a genuine title to them.

Now the conservative is not opposed to charity, and, as I shall later argue, he will be constrained to accept some version of the welfare state. Nevertheless he may be reluctant to subscribe to the universal transfer of charity to the offices of state, and for reasons which the example demonstrates. In fostering the illusion of a 'natural' right to home, health, wealth and comfort, the state erodes both the individual's will and its own authority. The state becomes a kind of machine, a centre of distribution, an alien object which sometimes grants, and sometimes withholds, what is thought of as an independent right. For the conservative the state is not a machine, but an organism – more, a person. Its laws are those of life and death, sickness and regeneration. It contains reason, will and friendship. Not all its citizens lie at an equal remove from it; some enjoy privileges that others may not have. For its substance is power, and its form authority. There is no equal distribution of the first of these, that does not dissipate the second. In Chapter 8 I shall ask the question how, and for what reason, might power become authority, and what are the privileges that emerge, or ought to emerge, when it does so.

The State as Person

The last two sections have given covert content to the metaphor which lies at the heart of conservative thinking. People are organisms: they are born, they flourish, they sicken and die. Our attitudes are conditioned by mortality: it constitutes our impetus and limitation. But we are not mere animals, we are also rational beings. It is not that we are *two* beings, joined by some Cartesian knot, but that our organic forces are subject to a peculiar living principle, and the proper functioning of this principle constitutes our happiness. We have the capacity to argue, to persuade and to be persuaded. We can form ties and obligations, recognize rights and duties. We have consciousness of self and other, and a system of values which stems from that. Our world is imbued with will, directed from past to future. Reason *informs* our organic life, lifting it from the immersion in present appetite, and casting it in the dramatic roles of self-conscious reflection. Hence, just as reason depends upon organic life, so does life's continuity come to depend upon the exercise of reason.

Likewise the organism of society takes the form of reasoned intellect. This intellect is the 'constitution' through which the self-image of society is formed. Such a constitution, like the rational principle in men, will recognize ties, obligations, privileges and duties. It has arguments; it persuades or is persuaded. (Hence there is a distinctly political *process*, which is not the process of revolution, nor the mere pursuit of power.) Constitution endows the life of society with continuity and will. It creates history in the place of succession. But the state depends upon its organic base: its will and self-image require the continuity of the social organism, just as the organism comes to depend upon the forms of constituted power. State and civil society permeate each other; in their sundering lies the death of both. It is hardly surprising therefore that, in a healthy nation, the constitution remains tacit, general, and inexplicit. To suppose otherwise is like supposing a rational being to control himself from outside, in accordance with a programme of instructions that remain unchanged by the appetites and passions of his body. Just as reason permeates the life of man, so does constitution permeate the movement of society. If we speak of a 'bond' that joins society and state, this is only because their peculiar mutuality exists in varying degrees. In the primitive tribe society barely translates itself into governmental forms: all is instinct, organism, outside history and change. In the Stalinist state, society marches rigidly, bound in the fetters of a constitution that hampers its movements and deadens its life. It is the body of a puritan marching in the chains of his conscience. The ideal of relaxed personhood, in which reason and passion flourish together, is reached differently at different times. In the political sphere, it is reached when social life and constitutional forms exist in harmony. But of course it never *is* reached; only approached, in manners which exhibit no universal pattern and no external aim. We must therefore look to the ways in which *our* society has come near to its ideal, and the ways in which it falls from it.

I hope that enough has been made of our metaphor to give it cogency. The arguments for its truth are deep and difficult. I shall hint at them, and sometimes bring them forward. My purpose in doing so will be not to prove the underlying philosophy, but to articulate and give support to crucial items of conservative dogma.[21] But here we see why we must reject the language of the 'rights of man'. No more than a person can a country represent the privileges which it confers as 'natural'. A country's relations with its citizens reflect the same principle that is embodied in the citizens' relations among themselves: the principle that to claim a right is also to confer one. The doctrine of the 'natural' right is an attempt to avoid the penalty which all true rights impose. Hence its immediate appeal. And hence its political vacuity.

Essence and Identity

To reject the language of the 'natural' right is to take a step towards the Burkean idea of a national 'essence': the idea that there is a core of political life which generates the activities of state. This essence will be the true 'constitution' of the state. It cannot be sufficiently emphasized that a constitution, whether written or unwritten, is not a body of rules. What rules there are can be interpreted only in terms of a background of custom, habit, convention and a certain 'style' which shows how things are done. This is evident in the conduct of the British Parliament, where it is impossible to separate rule from custom without doing violence to both. (It is customary for the sovereign to ask the leader of the party which commands a majority in the Commons to be his minister. This is not a rule, nor is it a habit: but it is presupposed in the entire practice of government. The flexibility of the sovereign power in this respect can be immediately verified in the exercise of George V's prerogative in the matter of the National Government of 1931.)

If the constitution is not just a body of rules, how are we to identify it, and how are we to separate it, if at all, from the customs which constitute civil society? The answer, to put it briefly, is that the constitution consists in those rules and customs through which men engage in the exercise of power: it is what guides, limits and authorizes power, and thus manifests itself primarily through law, through the 'style' of law, and through the position of the citizen as defined by law. It may change and develop in accordance with its own inner logic – the logic of precedent, practice, and judicial abstraction.[22] The conservative instinct is not to prevent that change – since it is the vital motion of the state – but to guard the essence which survives it, and which enables us to say that its various stages are stages in the life of *one* state or nation. And the constitutional essence guards in its turn the social essence. Here then, is the conservative cause in politics. Civil society, once destroyed, can seldom be revived. Yet this living thing is vulnerable. It demands protection and fulfilment in the constituted state. And the business of the conservative politician is to fight the contagions which oppress the state, and uphold the institutions which nourish it. I shall describe some of the contagions, and then later attempt to show the constitutional essence which has so far survived them. This is not the place for either optimism or pessimism; to borrow the image which was once used to such effect by an Indian chieftain: men drink the water of life from many cups, and ours is not broken.[23]

Democracy

Let us begin with the contagion of democracy, now raging so wildly that it is possible to mistake its high flush of fever for the light of health. De Tocqueville wrote of this disease that it 'not only makes each man forget his forefathers, but it conceals from him his descendants and separates him from his contemporaries; it ceaselessly throws him back on himself alone and threatens finally to confine him entirely in the solitude of his own heart'.[24] That is a strong way of putting it, and one that reflects the bitterness spread by the French Revolution in the hearts of all its descendants. But it contains a truth. The constitution that we have inherited has been slowly, and comparatively recently, subject to the democratic principle, not on account of popular pressure so much as of political faction. It is hard to know whether unenfranchised citizens are happier or unhappier than their fellows; hard to know whether they lament their state, or rather borrow their lamentations from others whose interest is not franchise but power, hard to know whether the right to vote would be missed by the populace were it now to be removed from them. Naturally people have rioted in the cause of franchise, as in every other cause that has seemed to spell the instant remedy for present evils. But outbreaks of agitation, whether in Bristol or Barcelona, Moscow or Tehran, show nothing about the value of what is called for, and nothing about its lasting popularity. (In all such matters one must remember the quip of Defoe, that the streets of London are full of 'stout fellows that would spend the last drop of their blood against Popery, that do not know whether it be a man or a horse', a remark amply illustrated, not only in such minor madnesses as the Priestley Riots of 1791, but in the whole tradition of the free-born English trouble-maker.)

The defects of democracy are easy to catalogue, but hard to weigh against the defects of every other arrangement. The social fragmentation presaged by de Tocqueville is as elusive as it is virulent, while the supposed legitimacy of the democratic process is a conception of permanent and vivid appeal. Should a politician wish to dispel for a moment this collective hallucination he must represent himself as opposed, not to democracy, but to some local or specialized form of it – proportional representation, say, or the single-chamber parliament, or the plebiscite. But these specialized forms exemplify the same principle that he must also claim to be defending, the principle that, in matters of government, it is the opinion of the governed that confers legitimacy upon what is done. It might be possible to argue against the use of a referendum, on the grounds that twenty million people ought not to be asked to make a momentous decision concerning a matter about which all of them know nothing (for example, whether to join or not to join the European Economic Community). It might be possible to argue against proportional representation, on the grounds that it will generate a parliament that is weak, irresolute and peppered with crackpots. But all such arguments rely on a principle that denies the basis of democracy. For they assert that popular opinion is a legitimate guide only in so far as it is authorized by government. Hence the legitimacy of government cannot be conferred merely by democratic choice.

It is for some such reason that, when Burke first tried, in his great essay on the French Revolution, to locate the principle of constitution, he could not see total franchise as a necessary part of it, or as having anything to do with the legitimacy of rule. And it is quite possible that even now the constitutional essence of our country would remain unaffected were the franchise to be confined to people of position, education, wealth or power – to those, in other words, with a self-conscious interest in the fortunes of the nation. When Disraeli suddenly snatched from the Liberals the banner of electoral reform, it was certainly not because he had regarded universal suffrage as a Tory principle. The gesture was strategic and opportune. It also satisfied his sense that conservatives reside as much at the bottom as at the top of the social scale, and that it is in the middle class, with its contempt for the prejudice of others, that liberalism finds its natural home.

The extent of the ensuing commitment to democracy should not, however, be underrated. It survives in the doctrine (given increasing rhetorical impetus at every general election) of the 'mandate', the doctrine that a party programme is a kind of promise to the people, and that election success is tantamount to a contractual bond to honour it. (If the programme contains more than one such 'promise', then a party may obtain a majority from an electorate all of whom had voted in a minority on the issue which most concerned them. To whom, then, is it fulfilling its obligation? This is no curious exception, but in all probability wholly normal. The view of electoral success as creating a quasi-contractual obligation is therefore nonsense.)

The commitment to democracy can be seen too in the recent Conservative Party report on the future of the House of Lords, in which it is taken for granted that the Upper House stands in need of reform simply *because* of the undemocratic process whereby it is filled. This argument, taken seriously, would lead to the subversion of any institution (such as school, hospital, college, monastery) which depended for its health on a privilege to govern arising independently of the 'mandate' of its members. (Indeed, the recent Bullock report on industrial democracy has prepared the ground for the subversion of private business in just such a way.) The underlying idea is again the profoundly anti-conservative one, that legitimacy can reside only in contractual or quasi-contractual agreement, and not in established usage. Hence, it is thought, the only legitimate government, or procedure, is one that has been 'chosen' or consented to by its subjects. Yet as soon as one considers the highly artificial circumstances of democratic choice, one must see that this 'choice' presupposes in its turn that the citizen should recognize some prior legitimacy in establishment. When a citizen votes, his choice lies between a small number of parties, none of which would be in a position to attract his vote had they not already been incorporated into the political order. Their right to form into parties, and to regiment their members, is a right of establishment, determined independently of the will of the electorate, and necessary if the citizen is to have any clear idea of what he is *doing* when he casts his vote. Once in parliament, a member, rightly subject to the discipline of party, ceases to represent his constituents in any matter of state. He is part of the apparatus of state. What he does is determined by the established interests that seek expression through his party, and not by any 'promises' that he once made at the hustings. Democracy is simply one means of gaining power, and so of freeing oneself from the immediate demands of the multitude. Moreover, it may be no more obviously satisfactory than any other means, and certainly not possessed of some *a priori* legitimacy which its rivals lack. What are called election 'promises' are no such thing; they can be revoked at will, and were given in exchange for nothing more than a favour born from constraint. It is impossible for a politician to think that he is bound by them or that his presence in parliament is made legitimate just because a sufficient vote was cast in support of him (for reasons which will have nothing in common other than the citizen's sense of the established style and authority of his chosen party). If we were to think that this process – of constraining people to choose between two independently constituted powers – were sufficient in itself to confer legitimacy, then any form of banditry could be legitimate tomorrow.

Legitimacy, however, must be more *concretely* constituted. Consider those many institutions (school, church, university) where there *must* be a principle of authority (as legitimate power) and where there *cannot* be democratic procedure without the immediate collapse of the institution.

No conservative, then, is likely to think that democracy is an essential axiom of his politics, even though he is likely to value an independent thing which is often confused with it, which is the individual's ability to participate in government, and at the same time to avoid the encroachments of arbitrary, unconstituted power. This ability, exemplified in the entire course of English history, pre-existed democracy, and lay, indeed, from the beginning, implicit in the common law of our Saxon ancestors.

The House of Lords

Now the United Kingdom is fortunate in that its constitutional essence is not entrusted to one institution, and that the House of Commons finds its power limited at every point by bodies which are relatively free from organized reformist enthusiasm. The most obvious of these – the House of Lords – is a body that explicitly represents the established interests of the country as these have evolved through history; and its authority must inevitably prove irksome to a reformer, even though, as is now clear, it is an authority that can be exercised only in response to constitutional threat. The most evident disadvantage of democracy is that it gives power to demagogues, and to men of merely individual will. Government is a matter of individual will only in the adopted leader, the being whose will is (or ought to be) identical with the will of state. For the common politician, will should be, not his own invention, but merely his own discovery, arising from the political education afforded by his station. It is no bad arrangement in which men should sometimes be granted power without having to debase themselves in the pursuit of it. If there is an institution which confers offices and responsibility, and which requires only some gift of inheritance in order to qualify for it, how can this be condemned outright as inimical to the well-being of the nation? To say that the hereditary principle (even when refined as it is by the constant creation of peers) is 'antiquated' is to say nothing; it needs but a glance at the state of international politics to see that the same is true of democracy. And to argue that the hereditary principle confers office and responsibility at random, and without consideration to the fitness of the person who receives them, is to repeat an objection to every mode of preferment. Is it to be supposed that the ability to fascinate an electorate (as Hitler did) has some connection with the fitness for public office? It is odd, indeed, listening to the present debates in the House of Commons, to reflect on the fact that the author of *Troilus and Criseyde* once belonged to it. But the fact ceases to surprise, when one remembers the activities which are now needed to arrive there.

Why, then, should a Conservative Party seek to reform the House of Lords? The question is not one of policy: for if ever there were an issue ʿ ɔrinciple it is this. The House of Lords is a feature of English political life as complex and deep-rooted as the constitution itself. It is not a feature which could be subject to a 'commission of inquiry'. No such body would have the 'inward' knowledge that a great institution demands, nor could its conclusions have an authority that does not derive from the constitution which it seeks to arbitrate. The matter is, therefore, one of dogma, to be approached in a spirit of conviction.

But there are reasons, even for the conviction that nothing should be done. The movement to reform the House of Lords has arisen in the face of a threat to abolish it. Politically speaking, such a threat means two things: first, that the present power of the Upper House is sufficient to thwart those whom the conservative wishes to thwart; secondly (and consequently), that a conservative reform must *strengthen* that power. Would a system of election produce such a result? Or would it create yet another branch of our vast and burdensome civil service, with neither the will to oppose, nor the authority seriously to endorse, the decisions to which it adds its rubber stamp? The arguments here are difficult, and not all on one side.

An upper house that derives its membership from those whose social and political dignity is inviolable has one remarkable quality which will always be absent from an assemblage of elected members – the quality of leisure. Leisure transforms argument into conversation. In our Upper House views and interests may be consulted which, being useless to the demagogue, must be passed over in the scramble for power. Moreover, peers such as the Law Lords, whose office is consequent upon their learning, will have the great benefit which conversation confers and argument removes: they will carry the day on all issues which they alone are competent to decide. It is the Law Lords, indeed, speaking not to a body of agitators, but to a gathering of listeners, who have stood in the way of much radical legislation. Their presence in the Upper House increases their authority in the affairs of state, and, as I shall argue, it is essential to conservative dogma that their authority should prevail.

In recent years the Conservative Party has responded to the aggressive tactics of its opponents with gestures of reform and amendment which have seemed more like appeasement than a preparation for war. There are reasons for this, the chief among them being that conservative politics does, in the end, require a consensus of feeling that transcends party allegiance. Nevertheless, policy apart (and policy here is vast and delicate), it is important to see that the issue is of the essence, and that the conservative cannot allow himself to give ground. Any move to alter the constitution of the Lords must be calculated both to strengthen its powers and to conserve its detachment. Bagehot, in his spirited defence of the Upper House, regarded two reforms as imperative, not in order to reduce its power, privilege or dignity, but in order to restore them.[25] (These two reforms – abolition of the proxy vote, and the creation of life peers – have since been calmly effected.) Our constitution vests power in institutions that are partially immune to democratic pressure, and requires that those institutions remain autonomous. It is their autonomy which has lent to British political life its admirable mixture of continuity and flux, so conserving national unity through decades of European unrest.

The Contagion of Democracy

It is, then, the conservative hope that our hierarchical institutions will accommodate the principle of democratic election, without according to Party the power that belongs to State. Some politicians have been moved by an ideal of parliament, and by the delightful notion of 'representational government'. They have seen the House of Commons as the debating chamber of the nation, the guarantee of liberties, the defender of the common man. This pearl, grown around the sand of popular opinion, has often, it is true, rendered that opinion harmless to the social organism. But it is a cultivated pearl. It is there because the constitution placed it there, and it has no rights which the constitution has not bestowed on it. In a series of cancerous growths it has begun to swamp the shell which harbours it, and so transform the institution of government into a lifeless bauble, on offer to whomsoever should play the highest card.

The problem consists in a loss of organic balance. Our parliamentary institutions, admired alike by those subject to them and by those who observe them from afar, have evolved from the need to reconcile competing powers, to resolve, in a manner compatible with social continuity, the complex vectors of establishment. It has therefore proved necessary, since the massive upsurge of power among classes previously unused to it, to contain that power within parliamentary forms. Democracy has been seen as the most effective means to this. Unfortunately democracy is the name of an ideal which power itself does not recognize: power seeks to coerce and rule. Too much of the democratic principle unsettles the balance of parliament, giving rise to the 'professional' politician, the opportunist who wishes to advance as far and as quickly as possible in an institution which maintains sufficient outward dignity and glory to make the pursuit worth while. But the real powers in the nation remain indifferent to this display of glamour and pursue their purposes relentlessly, often outside the reach of government control. So long as politics is regarded as a profession, where men scramble for office with the assiduity and insolence of salesmen, then the House of Commons must remain a battleground, whose best quality lies in its power to exhaust its members. It is possible even now to envisage a kind of politics which is not one of 'career', a politics nearer to the pursuit of learning or office than to the bargaining of the market-place. But to aim at such a politics is to subdue the presentation of politics. It is to remove from the public mind the delusion that the decisions made in parliament are, or ought to be, a reflection of its own transient appetites, and to replace that delusion with a political truth, that the best decisions of government are those of a constant and self-conscious will, which remains indifferent to fashion, and contemptuous of fleeting urges to reform.

The contagion of democracy is great. For a while, there has been no course but to let it rage. It has seized hold of many smaller institutions – of universities, of professions, of the church – and wrought its havoc there. If conservatives tremble now at the power of the unions, then let them at least recognize that power is only relative, and that one can dominate as easily through the weakness of others as through a strength of one's own. The call for a more 'democratic' structure in the management of union affairs is to some extent an admission of defeat, an attempt to spread to one's imagined opponent the disease that has weakened oneself. The true nature of the relation between state and trade union will be understood only when the democratic principle has been put aside.

There are other contagions, which have been too frequently described to bear much comment at this juncture. Perhaps the most important among them, egalitarianism, is also the one from which public life will most rapidly recover. There are signs that a brief acquaintance with its reality has served to inoculate many who thought they might benefit from its spoils. The doctrine of the 'equality' of all rational beings – unless read in the spirit of some philosophical abstraction – is so manifestly false that it seldom attempts to translate itself from the language of slogans into a description of reality. But one particular slogan will later occupy our attention – 'equality of opportunity'. For it has been thought that, so qualified, 'equality' can be both coherently described and politically provided. And, in the subsequent rush to make it available, many autonomous institutions are pushed towards the brink of destruction.

Judicial Independence

Let us now consider the positive aspect of conservative dogma. How does the conservative envisage the constitution, and how, and for what reason, will he set about its defence? Since it is not possible to describe the entire constitution of the Kingdom, I propose instead to consider one small part of it, in order to show how the conservative attitude might display itself in the intricacies of power. I shall consider the issue of judicial independence. Parliamentary battles are often fought over this issue, but always fruitlessly, since no politician has yet thought of a way of undoing this constitutional knot. Nevertheless judicial independence has proved an obstacle to the policies of the Left. Indeed, there is a fashionable argument, of the kind that is associated in England with no coherent remedy, that since judicial decision is founded in the ideology of a 'middle class' it must automatically stand in the way of legislation which seeks to damage the self-interest of that class. In China, where such arguments *do* lead to recommendations, almost nothing of the judicial process remains – simply peremptory trials conducted by local dignitaries. *The Compendium of the Laws and Regulations of the People's Republic of China* originally consisted of one medium-sized volume published every year. By the later fifties it had become very slim; publication ceased in 1964. By then law had become entirely a matter of party directive and local custom. For, as every good Leninist knows, the withering away of the state involves the withering away of law.

Now it is an inevitable consequence of serious socialism that the existing apparatus of state be held subordinate to something which lies beyond it. The state is what it is for the liberal – a means; the end being 'social justice', a word which, in so far as it stands for anything, stands for a society that we do not have, and may equally not desire. Naturally the Labour Party has hesitated to identify itself with that view, since it is far from representing an exclusively socialist, or even anti-conservative, attitude. There is a residual respect for the British constitution which reflects both the citizen's own native respect for law, and also the urgent desire of the trade unions to become part of the political establishment.

For the conservative, the matter is simple. He will regard the axioms of egalitarianism as conveying no concrete idea of future reality; by contrast, the constitution of the Kingdom displays an order which we enact from day to day. The maintenance of that order is an intelligible goal; 'social justice' is not.

Judicial independence is an intricate phenomenon, rooted in an ambiguous area of politics where fact and fiction conspire. It has the history and the myth proper to every rooted constitutional device. In reality it can be neither absolute, nor self-sustaining. It is customary, following Montesquieu,[26] to divide the powers of state into three: the executive, the legislature, and the judiciary. Although the instinct is a sound one, there is no clear theory to sustain it. It is of course neither necessary nor desirable that the process of administration, the making of law and the execution of justice should all lie in the hands of a single body. But the three functions cannot be disentangled, and, in some sense, the *will* behind each of them is one and the same. The British Cabinet, for example, could not govern if it attempted to separate its legislative and its executive powers.[27] Moreover, a law-making body is powerless unless it can compel the judges to apply its laws. The titular head of the judiciary must therefore be answerable to the legislative power. Thus our Lord Chancellor is answerable to the Crown, and to the will of the Crown as this is enacted through Parliament. Here we see one of the advantages which spring from the myths of monarchy: that a power may be both one (as for government's sake it must be) and at the same time many (as civil obedience demands). But how, then, do we describe the constitutional *fact* of judicial independence?

What we call judicial independence is a relative thing. In the United Kingdom it has three main causes, the first being that legal reasoning and procedure remain autonomous. Indeed, the ascendancy of Equity in Scottish and English law (brought about, paradoxically enough, by James I, in his attempt to bring the judiciary to heel) entails that no parliamentary edict could in fact control the mode of judicial argument. This element of judicial independence exists in every country where legal decisions are arrived at through the application of abstract principles of evidence and natural justice, principles which all men (even politicians) must accept in their daily undertakings.

In the second place, judicial decisions cannot be reversed by Parliament, but only by due process of law. There is (in normal circumstances) no retroactive legislation. However, we must remind ourselves that the highest court of appeal in the land – the House of Lords – is also a parliamentary body, and it is only a constitutional convention of the utmost delicacy that prevents peers who do not hold judicial office from casting judgement there.

Finally our law is not (or not yet) codified. It is based in a system of precedent, or common law, expanded, restricted and amended by statute. The law has therefore evolved often through judicial, and not political reflection, and when suddenly it may seem as though Parliament has advanced, simplified or clarified matters – as in the formulation of the Property Acts, the Theft Act, or the exemplary Occupier's Liability Act of 1957 – this may be because an order has been seen in, and extracted from, the judicial reasoning that already existed. The judicial mind has been applied directly to the facts of our native society, and in that process it has incorporated into the law of the land a lasting image of the nation, an image often provokingly invoked by Lord Denning in his snubs to Parliament.

A barbaric state is one in which it is impossible to distinguish the 'due process of law' (the will of state) from the will of party or individual. In such a state the law has no independent authority, only delegated power. The constitution of the United Kingdom defends us from such barbarism partly because of the three principles of judicial independence. There are qualifications. In times of war judicial procedures may be peremptory, and legislation may be retroactive (again as a result of war). But these are abnormalities.

The Ascendancy of Statute

There is, however, a perfectly normal method through which the activity of the judiciary may be controlled; and while it is a method which *appears* constitutional, the appearance is misleading. There is no constitutional rule which governs the matter; but in so far as the motive of the practice arises independently of the governing principle of the Kingdom, it is, to that extent, not unconstitutional, but against constitution, expressive of the ethos of the state as means. I refer to the attempt to remake the nation through statute, and to substitute statute wherever possible for common law, even in defiance of natural justice. When this happens, it is to statute that the judge must bow.

But in a constitution adapted to the world of men, obedience becomes a complex and creative thing, by no means to be understood as a punctilious servitude to rule. It has often been noticed that the judicial mind has been given to seek, not the letter, but the spirit of the law, and (for all its necessary protestations of obedience) it will not regard the spirit of the law as vested in Parliament alone. Parliament is therefore part of the apparatus of state, but not the state itself; the consequences of this for the English nation are enormous. Thus it has been one of the strengths of our constitution that judges have been able to reinterpret harsh, absolute or confused legislation in the light of their own existing principles. It is natural for a judge to look for some means to hold a man to his freely chosen bargain, or to infer an obligation when someone has been deliberately encouraged to act to his detriment. Legislation designed to overcome such judicial foibles has to be draconian, and drafted with an exactness which, in times of hyperactivity, is naturally somewhat rare. Manifestly unjust laws – laws such as the 1968 Rent Act, which have the intention of rewriting contracts to the consistent detriment of one of the parties, bills of expropriation and nationalization, statutes which attempt to eliminate *mens rea* from offences which may nevertheless be severely punished – all such laws have to be most carefully set out, in order not to die the death of judicial qualification.

Now this procedure depends upon a balance between judicial and parliamentary power, and the conservative is likely to add his weight to the first. For judicial reflection is governed by no ruling purpose other than the pursuit of justice within the framework of a given social order, while parliamentary reflection, being purposeful, is inherently dangerous to the state. The balance can be turned by an exaggerated quantity of statute law, and the associated attempt to restrict the law-making capacity of the judges. Naturally it is not possible to dispense with statute; all administration depends upon it. But in England statute has normally been a deliberative affair, constrained as much by judicial precedent as by 'reasons of state'.

Now a politician given to the pursuit of 'social justice' is apt to be impatient with those who prefer the more 'natural' kind. He therefore seeks statutes that are immune from judicial qualification. And they must come in fast succession, forbidding time to the community in which to take stock of change. (Consider the recent attempts to enforce comprehensive education, in the face of which judges continued to dispense remedies wherever they were able.) Inevitably, in the fever of fomented change, the judiciary must act as a conservative force. For judges seek to align the decrees of parliament with an established legal system, and hence (indirectly) with institutions that find protection under the existing body of law. A politician who sought to destroy those institutions would therefore desire to remove law-making capacity from the judges and vest it entirely in Parliament, specifically, in the House of Commons, where the judiciary is neither directly represented, nor overtly influential.

Those who suspect the judiciary, under existing arrangements, of being a conservative force, are surely right. A judge acting under the disciplines of British law can do no other than respect the social arrangement that is *expressed* in law. In doing justice he removes resentment and so indirectly restores some part of the *status quo*. The ethic of 'social justice' might demand that whole classes of society be punished on account of their privileges, success, talent, intellectual or material superiority. Neither the constitution, nor the ethic of natural justice, can be made to recognize such a law. Hence, indirectly, the law-making capacity of the judges impedes the formation of the egalitarian state.

The Law of Charity

I propose to consider a neglected but from the conservative point of view significant example: the law of Charity, which is one of the most deeply 'embedded' of our constitutional artifacts. 'Charity' is loosely defined in the preamble to an Elizabethan statute. But to understand what charity means at law one must look to four hundred years of subsequent judicial reasoning. This reasoning has been influenced at every turn both by an unspoken conception of the common good, and by an awareness of the fiscal privileges accorded to charity. It is to the judges, therefore, that we owe the continuity of our greatest schools, the endowments of the university colleges, the strength of private and public medicine, the maintenance of churches, and countless other aspects of the moral and political life of the nation that have been of concern to charitable men, from the relief of poverty to the upkeep of the National Trust (which are both, in turn, ways of perpetuating the aura of class rule). Through charity a man is able to look back over his life from the point of maturity, and reassert the will with which it began; it is thus that an individual realizes his loyalty to the social arrangement that surrounds him, and to its continuity through time. (It is out of some such spirit that American individualism has been able – almost against its nature – to foster institutional life, to create brilliant simulacra of European institutions, offshoots of private property and public nostalgia.)

It is also to the judges that we owe the inability of political activism to wear a charitable mask. Politics has enjoyed no fiscal privileges in English law; had it done so, the spread of socialist propaganda might have been as rapid and contagious as the spread of the non-conformist church.

Now private charity, as an offshoot of private property, has profound political implications, and represents the determination of wealth to relinquish individuality and turn itself into a social force. And this force, as we have seen, is almost always turned towards continuity. Politicians might therefore seek to wrest the law of charity from the judge's hands.[28] It has come to embody part of the self-consciousness of English society. It hampers at every point the imperatives of fashion, and exerts a cool authority over testamentary whim, making sure that no man can perpetuate himself as a mere individual, but only through institutional forms. (See the Scottish case of *McCaig* v. *University of Glasgow*.)[29] It exemplifies the continuity of the nation's life, the enduring basis of its politics, and the vitality of those autonomous institutions which the conservative (as we shall see) finds himself committed to uphold. Without judicial independence in this matter, a whole section of public and private life might already have been merged into the apparatus of a socialist state.

Government and Party

There is a further danger to judicial independence, as to all matters which lie balanced within the constitution by deep historical forces. This lies in the constitutional irreverence that must naturally accompany political activism. A politician whose aim is to change the established order cannot regard his aim as open to qualification from the existing constitution. He will respect the constitution only in so far as it serves his aim; otherwise he will seek to ignore it or cast it aside. It is for this reason that sections of the Labour Party have recently made light of the distinction between government and party. Now the judiciary is answerable to Parliament, and, through Parliament, to the Crown. Certain parliamentary officers – such as the Attorney-General, and the Lord Chancellor – have the function of mediating the relations between those who make, and those who administer, the law. But such officers are officers of the Crown, answerable through the Crown to the interests of state. Democratic politics requires (although this is no more than a constitutional convention) that those officers be appointed through the dominant party; but they are not directly answerable to that party. It is important to see, therefore, that a constitutional threat is already present when these officers are compelled to act in response to party pressure – for example, when disciplining a judge (the case of Judge Mackinnon). It is necessary for the conservative to force every assailant of judicial independence into speaking not with the authority of state, but only with the influence of party. He will then find himself far more confused as to his meaning.

This brings us to an aspect of the constitution which is, and must be, of the greatest concern to the conservative, which is the nature of Parliament, and the role of party politics in determining its affairs. Now it was Burke, a conservative whose factional association was with the Rockingham Whigs, who first urged his parliamentary friends, in the face of the threat of constitutional reform, to organize themselves into a party. Some might suppose that this division into parties is both alien to conservatism and destructive of the constitutional balance. But I doubt that this is so. Burke was surely right in his intuition that party politics is a bastion against the fragmentation of political life which might otherwise ensue under the process of democracy. Through the influence of party, votes are cast not as an expression of individual wish (for this or that feature of national life), but largely as a gesture of allegiance to a style of government; and the continuity of the party is felt as the nearest substitute for the continuity of the nation, as the conservative and the common citizen desire it. But the corollary of this is that party politics must be taken seriously: a conservative party constantly faced by drastic measures of reform, must, when in office, wield as much power as its opponents in order to undo those measures; not because such toing and froing of domestic policy is a healthy thing, but because this is the only way to bring it to an end. It is a means of forcing the parties to recognize a common cause, so that they become once again not 'movements' but factions, equally committed to the national interest and to the constitutional authority, conflicting in this or that attitude over matters of state, but over nothing so much as their common desire for power. The composite image which they will come to form must contain large conservative fragments. In order to achieve this it is important to keep government and party separate, to vest as much power in the former as is assumed by the latter, and in particular to vest power in those aspects of government that do not lie within parliamentary jurisdiction. (It is uncharacteristic of conservatism to make a fetish of 'parliamentary privilege', for example, or to try to represent this fragile convention as some kind of unspoken rule of state.)

Civil Society and the State

In order to understand what is at stake in the constitutional issues I have raised, we must return again to our earlier reflections and discuss the nature of civil society, and its proximity to the state. It is basic to a conservative view of things (I suggested) that the individual should seek and find his completion in society, and that he should find himself as part of an order that is greater than himself, in the sense of transcending anything that could have been brought about through his own enactment. He must see himself as the inheritor, not the creator, of the order in which he participates, so that he may derive from it (from the picture of its 'objectivity') the conceptions and values which determine self-identity. He will see his extension in time from birth to death as taking on significance from civil stability: his world was not born with him, nor does it die when he departs from it.

It is natural to conclude that a constitution adapted to the realization of a conservative outlook will make room for, and certainly find nothing wrong with, principles of hereditary government. The existence of hereditary establishment itself depends upon and expresses the strength of family life. Moreover, it reinforces the connection between family and property which, being part of human nature, is also part of the 'natural' politics that the conservative proposes. Here we see an aspect of constitution (hereditary privilege) reflected, first, in a feature of civil society, and, second, in a demand of fiscal policy. It is impossible here to separate 'matters of state' from all the sustaining features of civil life with which they are associated. To see the precise way in which a conservative might formulate belief in the hereditary principle (or in any other aspect of the constitution) we shall always have to discuss matters far more serious and more elusive than immediate policy. We live in a nation so constituted that state and society move together, pointing always to the common end of national sovereignty. To envisage a political future for our nation is to aim at both its outer continuity in politics, and its inner cohesion in social life. As the example of hereditary government indicates, and as I earlier argued, it will be impossible to separate the two. However, in certain matters of state, it has been liberal policy to enforce a separation between government and society, in order to achieve, through the former, ends which are at variance with the latter.

Consider, for example, the issue of devolution. For a variety of reasons politicians have advocated this constitutional change, partly in answer to local sentiment, partly by way of reducing the centralization of power. Neither of those motives can arise from a conservative outlook, despite the view, held by some, that the conservative aim in politics should always be to remove power from central government and return it to the people. A nation must necessarily have a centre and a periphery, and unless the periphery is governed with the same strength and resolution as the centre, the nation falls apart. In our new 'English' kingdom, founded on the hegemony of Hampstead, what is to prevent the dissatisfied Northumbrian from asserting his native right to independence? What will deter the oil-rich town of Yarmouth from self-government? Who will rule over the republic of Brixton when its customs, manners and language seem to provide so little application to the laws of distant Westminster?

Moreover, a Kingdom that is sure of its boundaries, requires government *within* those boundaries, and autonomous decisions that can be identified by the people as in some way stemming from the bond which already unites them. From the constitutional point of view this means legislative autonomy. It is certainly hard for a conservative to accept the strange and voluntary renunciation of sovereignty which has argued that British law is better made in Brussels than at home. Now the law of the Common Market, being of commercial intention, has largely benefited companies engaged in international trade. Indeed it has grown out of the kind of thinking which imagines that economic well-being is the whole of politics and the true aim of law. This thinking is dangerous, not only because it tramples on the fact of constitution, but also because it enables the easy transfer of power to any party that is prepared to put the accumulation of power before the accumulation of wealth. As the decisions of the European Assembly begin to reflect more nearly the ideology of its members, many things will be imposed on Britons of a kind that they do not like, but which they will be powerless to reject except through the total rupture of a treaty under which the economic life of the nation might by then have been totally subsumed. It is necessary to take note of the rise of 'Euro-communism', and of the scale of European socialism. For these are political positions with *international* aims, and aims which are not primarily concerned with 'trade': they therefore have a strength and will which no conservatism could ever match. While conservatism is founded in a universal philosophy of human nature, and hence a generalized view of social well-being, it recognizes no single 'international' politics, no unique constitution or body of laws which can be imposed irrespective of the traditions of the society which is to be subsumed under them. As a political position 'Euro-conservatism' is nonsense – unless, of course, it means the maintenance of close alliances and commercial ties, or perhaps something more wild, like the restoration of the Holy Roman Empire, and the sovereignty of the Church.

The issues just discussed are constitutional, but they reflect a view of the civil order. Conversely there are issues which arise out of popular sentiment and yet which seek expression in decisions of a constitutional kind. This is true of all those sentiments which compose the inarticulate idea of nationhood, and which impose upon the government the necessity to lay down, as constitutional fiat, a legal determination of citizenship. The law has been formulated comparatively recently, under the pressure of universal migrancy. But it is unclear to the common man either what it means or why he should accept it. Many Britons, who have never heard of the Nationality Acts and the laws on immigration, feel strongly about something which was once called 'the alien wedge'. And surely it cannot be doubted, even by those who profess allegiance to the 'pluralistic society', that our society, unlike America, is not of that kind, and therefore that immigration cannot be an object of merely passive contemplation on the part of the present citizenship. There is perhaps no greater sign of the strength of liberalism (a strength which issues, not from popular consensus, but from the political power of the semi-educated) than that it has made it impossible for any but the circumlocutory to utter an illiberal sentiment on this subject, and on the subject of race which forms such a substantial part of it.[30] But while it is a long-standing principle of British law that the fomentation of hatred (and hence of racial hatred) is a serious criminal offence, it is not clear that illiberal sentiments have to be forms of hatred, nor that they should be treated in the high-handed way that is calculated to make them become so. On the contrary, they are sentiments which seem to arise inevitably from social consciousness: they involve natural prejudice, and a desire for the company of one's kind. That is hardly sufficient ground to condemn them as 'racist', or to invoke against them those frivolous fulminations which have been aptly described as 'death camp chic'. The politician is not concerned with the justification of illiberal feeling; it suffices that it should be a natural offshoot of an allegiance upon which even the liberal élite must depend, in depending for its privilege upon the peaceful continuance of the nation.

In all the issues which I have mentioned it has been the business of liberalism to prise state and society apart. The conservative ideal of the constitution as something generalized and tacit can be enacted only by holding the two together. The reason why such matters as devolution, legislative autonomy, immigration and so on are of the first concern to conservatives is that they indicate battles which could be immediately won. The magnetic pull of civil society is here at its strongest; it is only necessary to place the constitution within its field. What holds it back is no more than a collection of statutes, orders, and books of inapplicable, perhaps even illegitimate, law.

Pessimae republicae plurimae leges. The words of Tacitus are beginning to apply even to England, of which Joseph de Maistre wrote that 'the true *English Constitution* is that admirable public spirit ... which leads and saves everything, whereas that which is written down is nothing'.[31] But, as I have tried to show, de Maistre's ideal, modified as it inevitably has been by the passage of time, and by the complexity of modern administration, is still exemplified by the United Kingdom. It suffices to know the points at which the 'deep' unspoken constitution still reveals itself. For they are the places where the conservative must fight.

Concluding Remarks

Of necessity this chapter has been discursive. The topic of constitution is vast, and at every stage debatable. A constitution is not a book of rules, nor can it be cast as one. It permeates the body of society, just as man's self-image permeates his organic nature. It is not founded in a 'natural' right, for it grants rights as it grants privileges, so as to demand obeisance in return.

The unity between state and society demands no democratic process; indeed, at present, democracy is nothing better than a menacing disease. But there is a greater menace in the liberal desire to remake the constitution, so that it matches no *particular* social order, and answers to no *particular* historical identity. In resisting that attempt, I have argued, the conservative must seek to vest the power of state outside the forum of speculative change, in particular, outside the opinion-ridden turmoil of the Commons. Hence he must uphold the judiciary, the House of Lords, and every autonomous institution through which the processes of state find tacit and faction-free enactment. For a conservative the movement of the constitution must express the movement of social

69

feeling, and not the opportunistic aims of that small professional class – the class of politicians. But if a conservative belongs to that class, then he must fight boldly and warily, taking a stand at every point where the bond of society lends support to him, and allowing no party to usurp the loyalty which, because it stems from the social order, belongs not to Party but to State.

It is time to leave the topic of constitution, and to progress towards the more detailed considerations of conservative dogma. We must now consider, not the state as such, but the will of state; and the will of state is law.

CHAPTER 4

Law and Liberty

If we were to remain on the level of 'party politics', we should begin by discussing the process whereby the Conservative Party has come to be regarded as a symbol of 'law and order', opposed to all those factions which defy them. But, whatever the present truth of the matter, 'law and order' is simply the business of government, and there can be no political party which spoke or acted as though it were not concerned to uphold them. The truth was given by Machiavelli, in one sharp sentence which everybody recognizes to be true the moment he feels the reluctance to believe it: 'The Prince must use first law, which is natural to man, but must be prepared to use violence, which is bestial, in order that the rule of law be maintained.' The issues that will concern us are those of the nature of law, its scope, and its 'image' in conservative thinking. The rest is a matter of tactics, and irrelevant to our purpose. Theoretically speaking 'law and order' can be left to look after itself.

The Sphere of Law

The conservative needs some conception of the legitimate *sphere* of law. What can, and what cannot, be subject to law? And to what extent may he law define and limit the activities of the citizen? Again he is unlikely to be content with a single and absolute answer, framed for the use of every nation and every institution, regardless of its history and character. Nevertheless, he has still to contend with his liberal opponent and, in the sphere of law, liberalism is all-powerful, being, so to speak, the first thought that comes to mind. Since the Enlightenment, it has seemed quite natural to suppose that the cause of 'individual liberty' is what is at issue in every question of law, and while this is not how the law *is*, it is how it has been theorized. Should we remove *this* man's liberty, to protect *that* man's? Such a philosophy sees the law as legitimate only to the extent that it protects individuals from harm; and it must allow the maximum of individual freedom that is compatible with that aim.

Clearly, it would be impossible to dismiss the liberal view out of hand: it has a respectable intellectual history, and a perennial intellectual appeal. But it is important to see that the conservative is in no way forced to accept it.

As I have already suggested, the liberal view is individualistic. It sees the individual as potentially complete in himself, and possessed of reason, which he can use either well or ill. To use it well is to use it freely – to live one's life according to the precepts of 'autonomous' (or even 'authentic') choice. It is from the exercise of this autonomous choice, argued Kant,[32] that all the good of human nature derives, and the single most important degradation of that nature lies in the 'heteronomy of the will' – action according to precepts that are not self-commanded. It is easy to see in this philosophy – ancestor of Sartrean existentialism, and the quintessence of the Enlightenment concept of man – a ground for the view that the well-being of man is freedom, and that all government is valid only as a means to that end. One does not have to go so far as Dostoevsky's Grand Inquisitor in pointing to its defects. Kant thought that he could derive from the overriding principle of autonomy certain subsidiary laws of action, the moral laws, which each man would be constrained by reason to accept. But these laws remained, as Kant recognized, purely 'formal', and his own attempt to derive from them specific rules of conduct was not only somewhat strained, but also remarkably apolitical in conception, giving no indication of the kind of social organization that would best serve the moral ends of man. Indeed, the operation of the moral law seemed to require that man conceive himself as belonging, not to this, but to some other world, an ideal member of the 'kingdom of ends'.

It seems to me that the liberal conception of politics is no more nor less plausible than the Kantian idea of the free, autonomous being. The conservative view begins from a conflicting premise, which is that the abstract ideal of autonomy, however admirable, is radically incomplete Men have free will; they make choices, act on reasons, are guided in everything by a conception of what they are, and what they wish to be But the 'form' of freedom requires a content. Freedom is of no use to a being who lacks the concepts with which to value things, who lives in a solipsistic vacuum, idly willing now this and now that, but with no conception of an objective order that would be affected by his choice. We cannot derive the ends of conduct from the idea of choice alone. We must show how the agent values what he intends to do. Through what concepts, and through what perceptions, does he represent his end as desirable? To recognize something as desirable, is to view it as an achievement. This means seeing it as conferring merit, dignity, respect ability – in short, as conferring social recognition. (I speak of the norma

72

case, not of the hyper-sophisticated examples, such as you and me, who must be defined by extrapolation.) This sense of the merit of something is not as a rule to be translated into words: it suffices that it be real and vivid. Without this kind of ready perception of the value of things, there can be no autonomy, and the perception cannot be acquired through an act of choice. It is brought about, not by freedom, but by the struggle for freedom, not through self-obsession but through knowledge of others. In short, value is the perception of the self as other, and only from that perception can freedom begin. There is no autonomy that does not presuppose the sense of a social order, and if the order may be ideal, this is only because it was once experienced as real. The autonomous individual is the product of practices which designate him as social. The individual man is the man who recognizes that he is no mere individual. Anarchy (which is freedom from the sense of a public realm) is not the *gain* of individuality, but its loss. Individual freedom is the great social artifact which, in trying to represent itself as nature alone, generates the myth of liberalism.

'The Consenting Adult'

The meaning of the last paragraph will be clearer in the application. What I have said stands opposed not only to liberalism, but to the more pragmatic conception of law, which sees it simply as the power of government to constrain the wicked and uphold the good. It is the exercise of that power without which the life of man is, in the famous words of Hobbes, 'solitary, poor, nasty, brutish and short'. But such a view might still have its liberal expression. It could be said that the legitimate function of law had been fulfilled as soon as it possessed the power and the machinery whereby to restrain individuals from interfering with one another's 'rights' – for example, the right to life, health, peace, privacy and property. (And no doubt, the view would find some natural, universal, basis, in an implied contract, or in some Kantian version of the 'natural law'.) It follows that the function of law is largely protective, and, having given its protection, it cannot legitimately infringe the 'natural' right of the citizen to do as he please, provided he also pleases those 'consenting adults' who do it along with him.

Everyone feels the attraction of such a view, for everyone, in some small portion of his psyche, is a 'consenting adult in private', anxious to retire from the surveillance of state into the sphere of the merely personal. Like the great Athenians, we seek to be, 'Free and tolerant in our private lives; in public affairs obedient to the law'.[33] And no modern state can flourish without a careful attitude towards this hyper-civilized yearning for privacy, even when its principal manifestation lies in the freedom of the Sunday newspapers to provide vignettes of privacy to those who have never achieved it. Nevertheless, the view cannot stand alone as definitive of the 'new' social order, or indeed of any social order at all.

The Right of Property

To take one small example: the right of property. On one extreme liberal view, there can be no legitimate interference with a man's right to dispose as he thinks fit with that which is legally and morally recognized as his. (Let us assume, for a moment, that there are no complications introduced by the division of legal from beneficial ownership.) But it is absurd to think that a merchant has some indefeasible right to throw his grain into the sea, or even to withhold it from the market in time of famine (whether or not the motive of this act be profit). Naturally, no one doubts that his behaviour is immoral – as indeed is some of the dealing in short-term commodities at present permitted in England – but surely a state that refused to make it also illegal would be refraining from exercising the very power vested in its constitution, the power to ensure the continuity of a human society. Perhaps, it will be said, the example is an extreme one, and that there should be something like a 'rebuttable presumption' that a man may deal freely with his own. But that too is questionable. What, for the common man, *is* his own? Let us consider his house, since that is closest to him psychologically, and the locus of all that is 'private'. Whether he holds it as tenant or as freeholder is irrelevant, since these are both property rights in English law, representable as exchange values. For a long time it has been recognized that a man may not deal freely with his house, and not merely because some ways of dealing with it directly 'harm' his neighbours. He may not demolish it, alter it, even (on occasion) redecorate it, without the consent of legally authorized bodies. And the reasons for this might be entirely aesthetic, matters of 'local character', 'traditional appearance' – in short a public expectation as to how a man's property should *look*. Nor should it be imagined that this legal respect for aesthetic principles is a modern thing, a protection against the suddenly mobile market in 'real estate'. In sixteenth-century Venice the very pattern on the prow of a gondola was determined by law. The ascendancy of the aesthetic in matters of planning is of immense significance. For it shows the law enacting a will for visual continuity that can have no other legitimate origin than in the vested power of state, conceived not as means to individual freedom, but as the expression of social consciousness. Such a law becomes legitimate only if we abandon the individualistic picture of human nature.

Morality and Law

What, then, is the legitimate sphere of law? The law is the will of state, and the domestic expression of its power. And since state and civil society are interdependent, the legitimate sphere of law will be all that matters to social continuity, all that can be taken as standing in need of state protection. The law must cover all activity through which the bonds of trust and allegiance are cemented or broken. Obvious instances – the upholding of contract, the outlawing of gratuitous violence, the common essence of civil and criminal law – follow from this view as from any view. But so too do more controversial instances, concerning matters in which the dominance of liberal ideology is likely to be the cause, not of freedom, but of licence.

Consider the case of public decency, and the massive propaganda issued (partly through the medium of 'sex education') on behalf of an experimental approach to sexual relations. These are difficult matters to write about: for one thing, people will dispute that there is any connection (or at least that there ought to be any connection) between the issues of public decency and private morality. For another thing, this is an area which, because it concerns the quality and not the quantity of something (the quality, namely, of the bond of love) does not yield itself to statistical investigation. As a result, the bureaucratic mind, which can imagine that it has some grasp of issues like 'television violence', and 'romanticized crime', is apt to think that there is here no decidable issue, and therefore no issue at all. In fact, as everyone feels instinctively, there *is* an issue. Moreover, in *none* of these matters do statistics have any serious relevance. Suppose statistics were to show that, in societies which periodically arrange spectacles involving the martyrdom of consenting Christians in public, before wild beasts or knife artists, incidents of public violence are fewer than in other arrangements, where these healthy, cathartic practices do not occur. Does that prove anything? Naturally not; for the evil lay, not in the results of the thing, but in the thing itself. And not, primarily, in the suffering of the victims (who may well have desired and gloried in what was given to them), but in the mental degradation of the crowd. That is clearly what matters also in questions of public decency. It is irrelevant that more or less people do or do not go away after pornographic films and engage in this or that practice. That is not the primary, the social fact.

Now in all these issues it seems that the opinions of a minority have commanded more attention than the inarticulate feelings of the common citizen. Those feelings, which grow from the constraints of the family, and the abstinence attendant on a working life, deserve not contempt but civil protection. It is only an exaggeratedly liberal view of

75

politics that can refuse to see that matters of private morality and public decency *are* connected, and that both are of urgent political concern. It was a source of surprise to some that a jury was recently able to return a verdict not only of obscenity but also of blasphemy at a public trial. But it would cause no surprise to anyone who has observed, either in himself or in another, the strength of the feelings which find their fulfilment in family life, and the fear with which the common man – the man whose life as citizen begins with the family – must contemplate their dissipation. This may seem a small matter, but surely it is far from small. For it is through the channelling of libidinal impulse that the bond of society is formed. (And whether or not that channelling spells its eventual doom or merely its daily 'discontents', is neither here nor there.) A conservative is unlikely to be persuaded by that particular brand of German-American sentimentalism which imagines the free expression of sexual impulse and the true harmony of social intercourse to be deeply compatible, and which sees the ills of society as stemming from some single experience of 'repression'. That is surely just wishful thinking, as false to human nature as it is self-deceived.

Let us put to one side for a moment the vexed problem of sexual conduct, and concentrate on that of public decency. It is surely difficult to contemplate with ease the free marketing of sex as a spectacle, and the consequent transference of erotic passion from personal commitment to abstract desire. To borrow a Marxist concept: this fetishism of the sexual commodity is also a source of sexual alienation. It places a barrier between man and his fulfilment, turning the meaning of the sexual act into a caricature of itself: not the consummation of moral choice, but the gratification of a fleeting appetite. This kind of 'fetishism' is the enemy of the human spirit: it is the hallucination of freedom, meted out by the vacillation of the sexual market. It marks the obsession of man with his animal nature, and the theft of his social essence. It has been objected repeatedly since the trial of *Madame Bovary* that censorship threatens art and culture. But one must distinguish the individual work from the culture which engenders it. And having done so, why not be sceptical? There was no civilized period previous to ours that lacked effective censorship, and few periods so seemingly devoid of artistic inspiration, so driven – in the pursuit of a cut-price originality – to fanatical desecration in the name of art.

Consider now the question of sexual mores. Surely, it will be said, *these* at least are not within the sphere of law? But we know that they are, and that law moves in a slow and complicated way in obedience to what one can only call the convulsions of civil society over these matters, matters where the animal and the rational natures of man are sometimes in direct and irreconcilable conflict. Consider the legal fiction of 'consent'. It is a crime to make love to a willing, or importunate, schoolgirl, a crime which grows in seriousness as a man discovers the ease of committing it. And yet, says the law, the girl has not consented. Behind that legal fiction lies a moral fiction, and one which is vital to the self-image of society. It is the fiction, the myth, or (from the political point of view these are all the same) the value, of 'innocence'. It is through a conception of innocence that sexual relations are experienced and understood – understood, that is, as something other than a merely animal performance. It is this conception (and the corresponding idea of personal maturity) that makes possible the representation of sexual love as the *consummation* of something; as the *end* of courtship. The existence of this law, can therefore be seen as legitimated by an indispensable moral conception. The conception may in fact correspond only very approximately to the way people behave, but most normal citizens wish to *see* their behaviour in this way, and to see their values enshrined in law. This is the kind of law which liberals find difficult to accept. The proponents of 'sex education' might even consider the whole concept of 'innocence' to be profoundly unhygienic. (But I suppose the proven capacity of the human race to survive without their advice enables us to discount them.)

The example is a minor one. But it is important. For it shows how a conservative stance towards civil society might begin to translate itself, without violence to its sense of the legitimate activity of state, into laws which seriously restrict what some would call the 'freedom' of the citizen. And these laws make no reference to 'harmful' consequences; or if they do it is only because 'harm' is being redefined in the process. You cannot say that the doctrine of an 'age of consent' corresponds to a prior conception of what is 'harmful' to the young. Men extend their idea of 'harm' to cover such difficult conceptions as those of innocence and maturity only by imbuing the idea with all the moral force of those conceptions, so justifying the translation of a moral intuition into a legal rule.

Freedom and Harm

That last remark brings us into direct confrontation with the liberal view of law, as stated and defended by Mill and his successors. The issue has been discussed many times, not only in the great controversies of the Victorian era,[34] but even now, many years after Utilitarianism has fallen into disrepute. Its most recent outbreak – precipitated by Lord Devlin's *The Enforcement of Morals* – led not only to fervent protestations of liberal faith throughout the intellectual world, but also to the Wolfenden Report, and to the subsequent measures designed to remove from our legal system every imprint of sexual intolerance. Since

77

the Sexual Offences Act 1967 many of the issues must appear parochial. But this testimony to the vitality of liberal thinking cannot be ignored. A perusal of the issue reveals two fundamental principles at work in the liberal mind. The first constitutes its premise: that the criminal law should be concerned solely with the protection of the citizen from harm. The second constitutes its method, which is that in all questions of law and morality there is room for debate, and that the onus of proof lies upon the man who would retain some precept rather than upon the man who would have it abolished. The liberal is the one to ask 'why?' of every institution, never the one to doubt the premise from which the possibility of such a question springs, the premise of unbelief. The ground of morality, as of the law which embodies it, remains obscure and inaccessible. The liberal, who knows no more than anyone just why it is wrong to rape, to steal, to make public display of obscene or gory spectacles, delights in tricking his opponent into inconsistencies over matters which – because they lie at the limit of human understanding – must breed either inconsistency or naïvety whenever they are the subject not of prejudice but of speculation. What is meant, when it is said that a given practice does no 'harm' to its participants, is that it can be viewed (from some position of secure and emancipated detachment) with no more than the vestiges of moral sentiment. What else is the invocation of harm capable of signifying? The idea is clear enough in its physical application: we know what it is to damage or destroy a human body. But physical injury is not the normal accompaniment of rape, a crime which must therefore be condemned largely on account of the 'psychological', 'spiritual' or 'moral' harm which stems from it. But am I harmed by something purely because I do not *consent* to it? If that is the criterion, then we must change the fiscal, educational, and environmental laws of the country. Am I harmed by the spectacle of a public execution? How do we find a serious answer that does not stretch the concept of 'harm' to embody the finest shade of moral disapprobation? Again, am I harmed by the destruction of a beautiful building or a work of art? The only answer that will generate the law which most liberals would wish to see (since they belong to the class which shudders at such things) is that I *am* harmed, and in a way that quite transcends the minor grievance of the property developer made bankrupt by the enforcement of the law. Finally, am I harmed by the opportunity to engage (in private) in practices against which (unknown to myself) my whole moral nature may at some later stage revolt? Clearly no sensible answer to any of these questions is forthcoming, until we begin to embody in the concept of 'harm' precisely the moral and social sentiment which the liberal wished to remove from it. The whole dispute, represented as that between dark intolerance and enlightened reason, is nothing more than a clash of prejudices. And while one side frankly admits that the feelings he brings to this dispute are moral, the other hides his bigotry behind a mask of reason, serenely expecting to carry the day.

This is not to deny that there could be such a thing as a genuine liberal consensus. The invocation of that consensus would give grounds for a corresponding shift in the law. And it may be true (though I doubt it) that the liberal morality is not, after all, the property of an élite, and that it corresponds to the developing instincts of the nation. How could one know? The answer is not to be found by argument, but by the test that has always been used – by the response of magistrates and juries. As moral feeling recedes so too does the desire to convict or to subject to punishment. Thus it became necessary to invent the offence of Causing Death by Dangerous Driving; for what juryman, seeing another accused of an act which he himself barely avoids each day, will find for a verdict of manslaughter, and a possible ten years' imprisonment? Likewise, it could be that popular feeling about the age of consent is changing, and beginning to show itself in court.

To advocate this traditional test is not to preach the doctrine of *vox populi vox Dei*. It is simply to keep the law within the sight and understanding of those who are governed by it, to refuse to assume a consensus before it is proven in the only forum where men are forced to be truly serious. To suffer the opinion of the majority is the natural penalty of an education which condemns majority values; and the sense of a common moral order is the greatest force which reconciles that majority to eccentricities that it can neither understand nor emulate. Pursued for its own sake, and in defiance of civil feeling, liberalization must breed resentment, whether in Christian Europe or (to take a topical example) in Islamic Iran.

Constitutional Rights

It is worth pausing to mention another liberal manoeuvre in the face of the grave problem of popular morality. This is to argue that the law is a distributor of constitutional rights, these rights being formulated in accordance with the axioms of state. And if the constitution involves a commitment to 'moral pluralism', then the citizen will have no legitimate expectation that the law may enforce *his* moral code against another's, even when the rival code is postulated merely for the sake of argument. On this view, however strong the consensus, law is public, morality private. Moreover, the purpose of law relates to one thing alone – the constitution which confers the rights which are contended for in open court. It is in this way that American jurists tend to see their law; and while one may naturally concur in the view that the rights conferred by law are constitutional, one may doubt that the commitment to 'moral plural-ism', even when set against the accepted mythology of the American judicial process, is a coherent one. The myth here is the old one of the social contract – how could any American bind himself to a morality that is not his own?[35] From which it follows that those incapable of joining the social contract cannot benefit from the protection of the law. A foetus, for example, is in just that position, as was definitively proven in the American case of *Roe* v. *Wade*. Not being a 'person', said Mr Justice Blackmun, the foetus can naturally claim no benefit from a law which, while conceding nothing to morality, concedes everything to the contractual bond of state. For liberalism to have advanced to such a position from its initial premise is astonishing. But a conservative will not wish to pursue the argument. He would prefer to go back to the premise itself, and so see 'moral pluralism' for what it is: a devious but peculiarly bigoted form of the Kantian Moral Law. 'So natural to man-kind', after all, 'is intolerance in whatever they really care about' (Mill, *On Liberty*).

Law and Society

The truth is, then, that there could not be a conservative outlook that did not require that the law be so closely connected with the civil bond as to exercise all the authority contained in it. The authority of law, however filtered through the apparatus of state, depends upon the sense of social cohesion. And no law which tries to transcend that sense will ever have the firm allegiance of the citizen. Likewise any area of social life which is vital either to the strength of the social bond, or to the social image of its participants, will be one into which the law may in-trude with the full authority of a constituted order. Thus, it is inescap-able that there should be family law, planning laws, laws which regulate the days and times when men may work, drink or seek recreation, even laws which control the nature of permitted intoxicants. (Just as Islamic law recognizes the conflict between the outlook which it expresses and the consumption of wine, so does our law recognize a conflict between the foetid banter of the public house and the menacing gentleness of 'grass'.) It is a great merit in the conservative view of law that it can explain these things and make them intelligible. On the liberal view, it seems to me, almost the entire legal system of our country, outside a small central core of criminal and civil law, becomes indefensible.

One could go further: *how* far is a matter of the actual politics of the day, the full details of which must lie outside the scope of conservative dogmatics. It is a very difficult matter to adjust the workings of the law to the movement of society, and to attempt to follow only that movement which proceeds from its life rather than that which foreshadows its demise. On the whole, it seems to me that judges have been better equipped to make this adjustment than Parliament; consider the fine shades of obligation that have been introduced recently into the relations between man and mistress, using purely judicial concepts (such as that of the constructive trust) in order to accommodate difficult cases without distrubing the fundamentals of family law.[36] And should the enthusiasm of the Master of the Rolls here sometimes overstep itself, judicial adjustment is still possible, without the need to unravel the complex knot of law, and weave some other conception of the established family.

Liberalism, which is the creed of an élite, and an impossible substitute for the pieties of ordinary existence, has been the guiding force in the many bodies devoted to the 'reform of law'. Their overriding aim has been to loosen the relation between law and civil life – extending the myth of 'liberation' into every area where men seek not permission but constraint. Liberalism seeks to remove from the law the image of a *particular* social arrangement. For the conservative this is simply not possible. Just as the private individual needs to find himself reflected in the social order, so as to recognize externally the value of what he does, so must that order find its image in the state. Civil society cannot provide its own self-image, any more than an individual can rise to self-consciousness by staring in a glass. The civil society is confirmed in the institutions of state; law, as the will of state, is therefore the concrete reality of civil life. To the extent that, one by one, customs, manners, morals, education, labour and rest are 'liberated' from the jurisdiction of law, so too does the sense of their social validity suffer a decline, as the citizen finds the gulf widening between his own allegiance to social forms, and the constituted authority of his country.

Punishment

Having adopted the conception of law that I have outlined, one will find little difficulty in accepting punishment as an essential part of its enactment. Intellectual confusion over the problem of free will has conspired with a certain sentimental love of the underprivileged to provide a philosophy of universal forgiveness, and a conception of the law as an instrument, not of enforcement, but of cure and reform. I do not propose to debate these issues, which are of great complexity. I shall simply make a suggestion, which is that any philosophy which purports to eliminate from the understanding of human affairs either punishment or blame must also dispense with reward and praise, with anger, resentment, diffidence, respect and admiration – in short, with all those attitudes which constitute the realm of rational will. Such a philosophy must finish by clearing from the world the elaborate superstructure of human values, leaving in its place a behaviouristic desertland, where soulless computers may thrive, but men never. To take that philosophy as a basis for moral life and for political activity is to remove the significance from both.

What then of punishment? The question to consider is not that of law and order, but that of how the law and its infringement are *conceived*. And we must recognize a fundamental opposition between those who see the conflict between crime and law as a conflict of will, and those who see it in terms of the 'adjustment' or 'maladjustment' of the individual (or of society). The first view is common to both conservatives and subversives, who each conceive the criminal as acting deliberately, and for his own ends, in defiance of the social will. It may not be his purpose to oppose the 'General Will' (in Rousseau's phrase) – unless, like Genet, he attempts to find his self-image in just that way, turning the garment of society inside out so as to dress up in its seamy side. Nevertheless his purpose is antagonistic to the will of society, and to the extent that he is subject to its authority in the state, so too does he bestow on the state the need to punish him. The reason for his punishment lies in what he does. The effects of it are irrelevant. It is unimportant that he be reformed, cured, or subdued into acquiescence : it suffices that he acted as he did. It follows that the motive of punishment – being essentially backward-looking – is founded in some respect for the established order, and for the system of authority of which the crime constituted a violation. Punishment does not seek to redress a wrong (for that is the province of civil and not of criminal law), but to express and propitiate outrage. Thus while there may be forgiveness of a civil wrong, for a crime there can be only mercy. The healthiest form of punishment will be immediate, intelligible, even violent, conceived by the citizen as a natural retaliation, which takes away the sting of resentment and removes the necessity for private revenge. The institution of punishment simply transfers to the law the authority that is invoked in every act of retaliation.

Now such a motive is perfectly intelligible, not only to the political observer, but also to the citizen, since it is nothing but his own motive rewritten in the larger characters of state. To conceive punishment in such a way is to uphold the ideal of the state as person, as will and as end in itself : that is the ideal of conservatism. Its intelligibility and coherence are the mark of its political common sense; and the fact that it can generate a clear and humane *canon* of punishment is a mark of its reasonableness – for clearly, the way is now open to the suggestion that the mode and severity of punishment should be directly determined by the nature and seriousness of the crime.

Let us now consider the view – which it would be not unfair to regard as one of the premises of modern 'penal reform' – that the true reason for punishment is to be found, not in its antecedents, but in its effects. On this view, it is legitimate to punish just so long as the criminal, or the public, in some tangible way benefit from the act, so that the true nature of punishment must lie in the protection of society, or the reform of the individual. It becomes at once extremely difficult to explain why we should not reserve the death penalty for minor motoring offences (a move that would eliminate them for ever), and punish murder by a course in sociology at the University of Essex (a punishment which, for such private, domestic crimes, must prove at least as reformatory as prison). Nor is this kind of absurdity the only defect in the 'forward-looking' approach to the institution of punishment. There is the more serious defect that it makes the institution unintelligible. For it removes from the description of punishment any reference to the evil of what has been done, presenting the crime in neutral terms as a kind of biological accident, generated by a disorderly organism which it is now our sole concern to 'cure'. That attitude (clearly described in *A Clockwork Orange*) represents the crime and its penalty as not inhuman but unhuman acts, removed from the sphere of common understanding, motiveless, aimless, valueless. It constitutes a surrender of the indispensable concept of freedom to a vulgar misconception, dressed up as the 'objective', 'scientific' view of man.

As the established power of government has become adulterated by the expert and the careerist, this woolly minded humanitarianism has begun to replace the natural sanctions which are the intelligible opposite to crime. Humanitarianism is in fact a sign of an unwillingness to take full responsibility for the offices of state, while nevertheless enjoying the advantages which stem from them. It may represent itself as 'conscience', with all the associated trappings of 'sincerity', although in considerations of such importance, one cannot but feel tempted by the opinion of Oscar Wilde, that it is style and not sincerity that matters. For the common man punishment is conceived simply as a moral necessity, which has nothing to do with any humanitarian aim. It is sought as retribution, and as institutionalized revenge, the desert of the criminal as much as the right of his victim. To replace punishment by 'reform' is to separate the law from its unspoken moral base; it is also to assume a right of forgiveness which lies with the victim of crime alone. This reinforces the sense, either that crime is 'subjective', so that acts are criminal only by convention, or else that the objectivity of crime goes unnoticed by the powers of state. The first of those thoughts spells the decline in the standards of common conduct, while the second fosters the desire for personal, rather than institutional revenge.

83

What form, it might be asked, should this 'illiberal' system of punishment take? Are we to take our example from the cruel and emphatic law of Islam, and institute flogging and maiming as the expression of civic virtue? The answer cannot be abstractly determined. But there is no doubt that one vital feature of punishment – which is the vivid sense that there is human agency and not unhuman mechanism at its source – must be restored if the institution is to have the place in social arrangements that the conservative would accord to it. Modern writers, from Kafka to Genet, have sufficiently described the plight and the degradation of man in a world without agency: such a world is a world beyond morality, and beyond politics, a world which it would be irremediable folly to bring into being. Now consider the institution of prison. Is it obvious that this is the best way of conveying either to the criminal or to the public an adequate sense of punishment as a *response* to crime; in the way that a human action may constitute a response? The answer is by no means certain. The demoralizing effect of long sentences, the natural tendency of prison (persuasively described by Genet) to create a criminal society with values and traditions of its own, the corrupting and disturbing effect of a social life without the benefit of home, all conspire to render prison both cruel and dangerous. Moreover, its nature as deterrent and retribution is rendered nugatory by its inscrutable exterior, and to retain prison as the only form of punishment is to give rise to an absurd mathematics of crime, according to which it seems that the robbery of a mail train is roughly four times as bad as premeditated murder – a result which is deeply repugnant to the normal conscience. Now the natural conclusion from those reflections is not always drawn, for fear of the barbarous and the primitive in men. But unfortunately, the barbarous and the primitive are there, and have expressed themselves no more terribly than in our pampered times. They have to be answered, and their expression must be channelled towards a reaffirmation of what they will otherwise most certainly destroy.

The Natural Law

A criticism of some significance is always made against conservatism, which is that, to direct one's political aspirations towards an established order removes the means of social criticism, and requires one to uphold whatever arbitrary despotism might have achieved or usurped the power of state. The idea of the *good* state simply slips away as irrelevant. The challenge of such a question can be met, but the conservative's answer, unlike the reformist's, is not easy to formulate. The conservative cannot criticize the existing order because it is an inefficient means to some end that he designates as the sole aim of politics. He must find,

84

within the operation of law itself, the saving criterion of its validity.

A state is not despotic just so long as the law represents a power that bears authority. The unwritten constitution of the United Kingdom, which vests the making of law in institutions many of which are only indirectly answerable to the sources of power, makes despotism unlikely. For the important part of English criminal law stems not from parliamentary enactment but from what I shall call (to use an old and much misused label) 'natural' justice. By natural justice I mean a process of reflection recognized (but not always obeyed) by all men in their mutual dealings, a process without which no human intercourse could be conceived in the spirit of friendship. I previously criticized the cant of 'human rights' with which politicians wage their current war of words, not because there is no intelligible notion which attaches to that label, but because it is thought to sum up the entire legitimacy of government, and to generate, as a principle of universal politics, the parochial preconceptions of western democracy. The notion merely obscures the major issues of foreign policy in connection with which it is used.

Nevertheless, there are natural rights, to the extent that there are natural obligations – to the extent, that is, that a concept of 'just dealing' arises naturally among men. In using the word 'natural' I do not mean that the authority of these rights can be exercised independently of the protection afforded by a constituted state. But they can be independently understood, and they are in some sense 'nearer' to the citizen than those rights and obligations which define his membership of a specific social order.

In administrative law, certain formal or procedural principles are given the name 'principles of natural justice' – the right of representation, the obligation not to be judge in one's own cause, and so on. But apart from this residue of principles derived from canon law, the distinction between the 'natural' and the artificial is made only indirectly, through the distinction between equity and law. Nevertheless, the distinction is intuitively obvious. It is undeniable that the very process of development from child to adult, from animal to rational being, involves a man in relations with his fellows which, were they not mediated by an instinctive conception of what is just, would be without the benefit of friendship, benevolence and love. It is unjust to strike a man who has given you no cause, unjust to appropriate another man's property without his consent, unjust to force another to submit to sexual desire ... and so on. The list is long, and even in the application of laws which derive only from the political constitution, an independent judiciary will follow principles of reasoning which have their intellectual basis, as those elementary principles have their basis, in a conception of justice that is presupposed in every social arrangement, and which cannot be conceived as the mere creation of the sovereign power. The question of the origin and justification of this sense of justice is philosophical: is it a reflection of that fundamental principle of practical reasoning which Kant derived from the idea of autonomy (the principle that one must treat all rational beings as ends and not as means)? Or is it, perhaps, simply part of the natural history of friendship? The answer is of no concern to us; for what is important, politically speaking, is that the sense of justice is immediate, part of the surface of social intercourse. It cannot be eradicated from human feeling by any political power, nor by any process of 're-education'. The best a despot can do is to prevent its expression. And just as natural justice is an essential ingredient in friendship between men, so must the laws of a state embody it if that state is to command the friendship of its citizens and be honoured as end and not as means.

Social Justice

It is here that we must recognize, however, that 'natural' justice has an unnatural enemy: the 'social' justice of the egalitarian reformer. To illustrate their conflict it is best to consider a specific example. I shall consider the law of property.

'Natural justice' finds its principal application to human action, and, by extension, to the characters from which those actions spring. It has no application to a state of affairs as such, judged independently of the agency which served to create it. The sense of justice, being founded in and expressive of our reciprocal dealings with our kind, arises only because we can see the justice of individual actions, and feel drawn towards the will from which they spring. If, at some later stage, we come to extend the idea, and speak of the justice or injustice of social and political realities, we mean to refer, not to their nature, but to their cause. It is not unjust that one man is born better looking, or more intelligent than another. Indeed, the conservative would say that our understanding of this idea of a 'just state of affairs' is so uncertain that we could not say that it is unjust that one man is born richer than another, or that such and such a proportion of citizens hold such and such a proportion of the national wealth. These things happen, but they are unjust only if they are brought about through injustice. If they are to be criticized then it must be in other terms, and terms which, unless they make reference to human agency, will be more aesthetic than moral.

In order to employ this concept of 'justice' in political debate, therefore, the advocate of 'social justice' creates a peculiar unconscious fiction: the fiction that really all wealth, and perhaps all advantage, belongs to a single owner (the state), who (in some way inexplicable to man) has

86

the duty to ensure its 'distribution'. And, given a sufficiently bare, and unhistorical, description of the facts, it might seem that it would be unjust to distribute wealth unequally among people who are all equal in their right to claim a portion of it (equal, simply in the fact of being citizens); just as it is 'unfair' to divide the sweets unequally at a children's party. But this fiction of 'distribution' is so often in conflict with the immediate perception of what is just that one can come to believe it only through repeatedly and ritualistically rehearsing its desirable implications: namely, that it succours the poor and casts down the rich. It can nurture itself then, not on feelings of natural justice, but rather on the kind of cavilling egalitarianism which has not reason but resentment as its source.

To illustrate the conflict between social and natural justice, I shall consider an example that is likely to be of great political importance in our times: the 1968 Rent Act, which provides statutory protection to most classes of private tenant. I choose this example, not because it is an easy one to discuss, but because it illustrates the *depth* at which the fight between natural and social justice occurs. (There are easier examples, such as that of the Bakke case in America, or the parallel proposals in East Germany to grant university education only to those whose parents had been (as the fiction goes) 'deprived' of it.)

The Rent Acts confer powers to interfere in contractual bargaining, and so grant rights in law which transcend the rights contracted for. Now, it is not alien to the spirit of natural justice to refuse to uphold a contract, or to impose conditions that were not contained in it. It has always been recognized that the freedom with which a promise is made is a relative thing, and that a man may contract away his life, like Antonio, if the necessity lies upon him. Part of the exercise of natural justice might involve undoing, or rewriting, contracts, in order to remove whatever element of oppressive usage might otherwise be sanctioned by them. And it is clear that, since it is necessary to a man to have a home, it is unlikely that the law will stand aside from contracts concerning residential (or, for that matter, industrial) property. From the earliest feudal times the law has offered 'rights' – even to squatters – without which relations between landlord and tenant could have become despotic, as they were (and are) in Russia. It follows that, since contracts for the use of land are and have been subject to close judicial and statutory control, it will be very difficult to provide a formula which defines the uniquely just arrangement. Nevertheless, it can hardly be considered just that a certain kind of contract must *always* and *inevitably* be rewritten in the interest of one of the parties, and in such a way as to effect a transfer of ownership to someone who was contracting only for a right of use. Suppose that a statute existed which declared that anyone

who freely contracted to hire a car could at once rewrite the contract so as to claim the use of the car for life (and for the life of some
chosen dependant), at a reduced rent, and with all obligation of repair
still resting with the hirer. Natural justice would be outraged, and
common sense would bring such contracts to an end.

Now the sense of justice is bewildered by the more complex case of
land, for the reasons I have mentioned. Clearly, a man's attachment to
his home and to the place which surrounds it; the difficulties of moving
house, of finding another place to live compatible with retaining his job,
and so on – all these put a tenant at the mercy of a landlord who chooses
to raise his rent, or terminate the tenancy. Nevertheless, the difficulty
of steering the sense of justice through this complex web of free and
unfree bargaining should not give grounds for a complete adoption of
the ethic of 'social justice', and the consequent attempt (manifest in the
Rent Acts) simply to redistribute property, so that tenants acquire the
property rights that were previously vested in their landlords. (Just as,
in my example, ownership of a car is effectively transferred under the
name of an 'agreement to hire'.) The example will be very important;
for having caused the demise of private letting agreements, except under
very special circumstances, it has reduced the number of ways in which
property might be held. It follows that if, like most young professional
people, one is both too rich and too mobile to qualify as a council tenant,
and at the same time too poor and too unsettled to purchase a home of
one's own, one has a strong motive to emigrate. (It is precisely such
things which make the *beginnings* of middle-class existence so difficult
in England, and which have led to the kind of emigration on the part of
talented people that democratic governments deplore, while tyrannies
prevent.)

It is clear that the statute in question *can* be understood as an exercise
of 'social justice', since, other things being equal, it will effect a transfer
of wealth from rich to poor. But it is also clear that its provisions are so
strict in the favouring of the 'weaker' party that they constitute a direct
violation of natural justice. They effect a transfer of ownership, even
where there is a contract to rent an apartment for no more than a week.
Consider the following case, which is not uncommon. (Those used to the
practice of law will recognize it as more frequent than socialists may
wish to believe.) A widow, being left with nothing more than the matri-
monial home, and a little money, buys for herself a small apartment,
hoping to live from the rents provided by her house. This house was pur-
chased over many years, at considerable sacrifice, and is the principal
fruit of her and her husband's labour. Having installed tenants, the
widow finds that she cannot move them, and has little control over them.
The house can no longer be sold. Moreover, the widow cannot raise the

rents to keep pace with inflation, and her statutory obligation to repair the house encumbers her with expenses that she is unable to meet. The result is not merely hardship, but destitution. It is of course not the hardship that is in question: to appeal to that is simply to invoke the very concept of 'social justice' that led to this iniquity. What is wrong is the natural injustice of the law.

The example, as I said, is a complex one, because it deals with that area of law where historical and contractual rights intermingle, and where each is constrained by necessities that cannot be subject to the vagaries of individual choice. As I shall argue in the next chapter, 'freedom of contract' is at best an ideal, and subject to determinations of state that make it impossible for the conservative to rest his case in this concept alone. Social complexities will always force us away from the paradigm of just relations. But it is precisely in examples of the kind I have discussed, where these complexities modify and inform the oper- ation of 'natural' justice, that the conflict between 'natural' and 'social' justice can be seen to be both genuine and deep. If this is so, then the adoption of the ethic of 'social justice' in the practice of government will already cause an unnatural strain in the social bond (the bond which is founded in friendly relations between citizen and citizen, and between citizen and state). Moreover, its effects are never more than temporary; consisting in the transfer of wealth to the ineffective. Social justice can- not, in the nature of things, root out those deep inequalities of skill, in- dustry and talent which will once again cause some to rise and others to fall. The recent history of Russia perfectly illustrates this point.

It is in the concept of natural justice, therefore, that the conservative will find one answer to the sceptic, and a partial criterion of the social good. And natural justice, far from being an external aim of state, will be inextricable from legal procedure, qualifying and varying the very laws and customs that constitute the state.

The Broad Historical Perspective

A familiar ghost now comes to trouble us. I have avoided philosophical argument, and presented the conception of 'natural' justice through a single vivid instance. Dogma requires concreteness. But to talk of what is concrete is to enter the purview of history. What, it will be asked, does this 'natural justice' amount to, when surveyed from the uncommitted standpoint of the historian? The answer may seem disconcerting. Natural justice has its antecedents in the *jus gentium* of Roman law. This remnant of law applied, not to citizens, but to the mass of con- quered peoples from whose customary procedures it provided a con- venient appeal – convenient because, in representing Rome as the final arbiter of justice, it also confirmed Rome as the final ruling power. The *jus gentium* passed into canon law, to be upheld as the 'natural law' of the medieval jurists and theologians. But what did that transmission amount to, historically, if not the attempt of the Church to constitute a court of appeal from the local laws of European sovereigns, and so cling to the ascendancy of Rome? And why again did the *Code Napoléon* lean so heavily on the rhetoric of natural law, if not to bolster the political hegemony which sought expression through its counsels? Let us take a more recent example. The Northern Rhodesian Order in Council of 1924, providing for the administration of that protectorate, enacted that in civil cases courts must be guided (where possible) by native law, provided that law should not be 'repugnant to natural justice'. Again, the constraint of natural justice is the constraint of a ruling power. The singular failure of Grotius to extract a coherent 'international law' from the remnants of ecclesiastical jurisdiction at the Reformation only serves to confirm the 'historical' view. 'Natural justice' is the slave of a ruling class. Where there is no such class (as in the matters arising between nation states), then there is no natural justice to enact.

It is impossible to consider the issues of fact, diplomacy and legal theory that our historian raises. Let us rather stand him on his head. Why, let us ask, was anyone (not already a member of some ruling class) taken in by the doctrine of a 'natural' law? Not (as honest historians will admit) because of an attachment to the 'rights of man'. It is plausible to suggest, therefore, that the doctrine arises, as it claims to arise, quite 'naturally' – which is to say, from the exigencies of human nature. And that is *why* it is in the interest of a ruling class to uphold it, as it is in the interest of a ruling class to confirm and consolidate every natural sentiment of its subject people. The feeling of injustice which attaches to gratuitous violence, to rape, theft and fraud, to imprisonment without trial – this feeling is an inescapable outcome of the experience of society. Why that should be so is a question not for the historian but for the philosopher; that it *is* so is given. And that is how we could begin to *explain* the power and durability of Rome, of the Church, and of the *Code Napoléon*. Far from being besmirched by its proximity to political power, natural justice constitutes one of the justifications of power, since power has been necessary to make justice possible.

But there is also power without justice. In modern history, one might say, it is 'social justice', and not 'natural justice', that has done most to sustain that possibility. The first represents a political aim (the aim of social equality); the second merely translates into law a vital principle of society. And, as my example was designed to show, at some point the conflict between the two will be inevitable and open.

The Rule of Law

Natural justice exists not absolutely, however, but in varying degrees. One cannot suppose that the rapacity of men's nature could be so overcome that justice alone would serve to govern them. So we must return, after all, to the remark of Machiavelli's with which this chapter began. While the authority of the state prevails, then the allegiance of the citizen is assured, and he may struggle for whatever liberties and benefits may seem desirable without threatening either the social order or his own fulfilment within it. In such a state, natural justice may be at the heart of every constitutional device and inhabit every judicial decision. But it is too much to hope of human nature that the authority of state will go unchallenged, or that civil society will not contain elements which regard established institutions not as expressions of authority but as mere instruments of power. In every legal system, therefore, there must be provision against sedition, laws which enable the power of state to reassert itself against antagonists, and these laws may stand wholly outside the rule of natural justice, being determined by the principle of necessity alone. This truth is so evident that no political dogma can dispense with some soothing rhetoric that will serve to make it palatable. It is unquestionable that, if the power of state is threatened, so too is its authority, and with it the structure of civil society. To sacrifice power for the sake of justice, is to make the exercise of justice impossible. It cannot, therefore, be an insuperable defect in a law of sedition that it provides for imprisonment without trial, a reduced judicial process, or summary execution. What matters is the extent to which such laws must be invoked. If this invocation constitutes – as in Russia – a major portion of the judicial process, then clearly the power of state transcends the allegiance of the citizen. The whole arrangement stands on the brink of illegitimacy.

Here we see what might be called the dialectic of justice and allegiance in the state. The exercise of justice is only possible within the framework of established institutions which command respect. To command respect it is not sufficient to make just pronouncements: it is necessary also to have the power to enact them. And that power must be seen to be *embodied* in judicial decisions, so that a single power translates itself into the commands of state, the enforcement of law, and the resolution of private quarrels. A general piety towards the established order is required for the exercise of this power, and hence for the just dealings which the citizen expects from it. In return for this expectation of justice, the state expects the allegiance of its citizens; they are constrained in conscience to sanction the most violent and even 'unnatural' methods in the suppression of rebellion.

91

The conservative view of law will therefore pay special attention to the constitutional artifact known as 'the rule of law'. The rule of law is the sign of a successful constitution – for it is a sign that all exercise of power can be described and criticized in legal terms. Hence it enables the citizen to make a prompt distinction between the authority of state and the power of some dissentious or rebellious body. It is an essential feature of the conservative state that this 'rule of law' should prevail, not because law has an authority greater than the power of state, but because the power of state and the authority of law should be ultimately one and the same. The power of state achieves its full dressing of authority only when it is constituted in law. In upholding the rule of law the conservative does no more than to vest the power of government outside the principal purveyors of social change, transferring it to the complex institutions of state, among which the House of Commons is, and should be, only one. In such a way the impatient desire to change the law, meeting with frustration, can be turned at once into an attempt to defy it. And so long as the constitution is strong, that attempt will fail, not the least because it will divide the loyalties of the citizen. Trade unions, half realizing this, saw at one point that they stood in danger of isolating themselves from the popular support which they had always supposed themselves to command. Within very little time they changed from instruments of reform to an unsettled mixture of revolution and reaction. The conservative hope is that the constitution is strong and flexible enough to confront and survive these forms of dissentious sentiment. There is nothing irrational in such hope, nor in the political activity that it engenders. But it is a hope that requires strong and definite laws, and which resists the attempt of factions to place themselves outside the law. As we shall see, political dispute is always represented by conservatives in legal terms. In industrial relations, in habits of assembly, in the control of monopoly and the curtailing of individual power, even in the sphere of international relations where 'the state of nature' still prevails, it is through law that the conservative seeks his solution rather than through the confrontation of subject powers.

Concluding Remarks

The conservative view of law is, I have suggested, clear, consistent, and, through being in harmony with normal feelings, at variance with received ideas. As the will of state, the law must enact the will of society. The idea of 'individual freedom' cannot suffice to generate laws that will be either acceptable to the normal conscience or compatible with normal administrative needs. Nor is it cogent to claim that law derives its legitimacy solely through preserving the individual from 'harm'. Legitimacy arises from the civil bond alone. Such an attitude to law necessitates a corresponding attitude to punishment. This attitude, which may seem harsh when initially stated, is in reality as humane as its liberal competitors.

I considered the possibility that there might be *general* principles of justice, which carry an authority greater than the authority of a particular constitution. I claimed that there are such principles, that they are in deep and inevitable conflict with the ethic of 'social justice', and that they cannot be viewed as the instrument of power. Their generality stems from the general condition of the social order. Hence, even the conservative view of law, which gives special weight to existing social arrangements, can generate a criterion of validity that applies beyond the *status quo*. In virtue of that, it is possible for a conservative to deny that each and every arrangement deserves to be conserved. But when an arrangement deserves that favour, it demands along with it the institution of a rule of law.

CHAPTER 5

Property

It may seem surprising that I have advanced so far in describing the conservative attitude without mentioning what some take to be its principal fetish. But the reader will begin to see that there is a world of difference between the political outlook that I have described, and the view which sees all politics as a question of ownership, and of the creation and distribution of wealth. Nevertheless, a political dogma that said nothing about these things would be hard enough to believe, and even if it be fashionable to over-emphasize matters of wealth and ownership, that only constitutes a yet stronger reason for taking them seriously. We must, in particular, examine the nature of private property, and determine how and to what extent a conservative is committed to its safeguard.

Wealth and Management

Economics is the major preoccupation of practising politicians. Moreover, in so far as there is a consistent popular image of the machinery of state, it is that of a corporation, with a 'management' directed towards the overriding urgencies of profit and loss.[37] This image is fostered by the media of mass communication, which, being necessarily the expression of a popularizing intelligence, can hardly be expected to convey more than a rudimentary impression of the affairs of state. However, it is also fostered by politicians themselves. Our concern will be with its actual and potential truth.

If the question of ownership is central to conservatism, then this is not because that is how conservatism is *defined*. There is no logical identity between conservatism and capitalism, for example. The connection arises because the need for private property stems automatically from the basic attitude of conservatism as we have already described it. It may still be no part of conservatism to be associated with any particular economic policy, or even to align itself with the pursuit of wealth.

94

Perhaps the most simple-minded case for something called 'conservatism' consists in the argument that a 'free market' economy is a guarantee of national wealth, and the best way to maintain or raise the 'standard of living', by ensuring that each man, through pursuing his own material well-being, has the incentive to pursue the well-being of the whole. And if that is so, then the true enemy of 'conservatism' – now identified as 'socialism' or 'public ownership' – must necessarily deprive the citizen of that material incentive upon which the nation depends for its prosperity.

Such arguments – while they may once have provided the content of electioneering slogans – present us with a vision of politics that is desultory indeed, as though the sole aim of social existence were the accumulation of wealth and the sole concern of politics the discovery of the most effective means to it. No doubt there is truth in the contention that public ownership destroys incentive; and no doubt the attempt to erode the institutions of private property *is* incompatible with the highest economic objectives. But it is not clear that these objectives are the sum of politics. The socialist, for example, is more interested in the distribution of wealth than in its accumulation. And he commands popular support on that basis alone. There was a time, indeed, when the English Tory party stood against the 'market' economy, not in the interests of national wealth, but in the interests of a social order which it felt quite rightly to be threatened by it.

One cannot ignore the question of national wealth, which must inevitably bear on every issue of domestic and foreign policy. But there exists no persuasive theory of politics or of human nature which shows wealth to be an unmitigated good, or poverty an unmitigated evil, and it is perhaps only the desire to reduce all human goods to something measurable that would represent things in such a way. Nobody is likely to consider that the wealth enjoyed by the Eskimo through his labour in the fish-canning factory means anything when set beside the impoverished existence that he once enjoyed in fellowship with his kind. Naturally, material wealth is important in international politics and in national security. But the vast wealth of America counted for little in the Vietnam war, no more than the amassed resources of England, Holland and the Empire did against the resolution of the French who followed Louis XIV. It has been argued, too, that wealth is the great precondition of domestic order and of national culture: do not Venice, Holland and Florence give proof of it? But then one must forget Greece, and Japan, forget the destitute world of Piers Plowman, forget most of all that every nation in the West possesses wealth far in excess of what was conceivable in Renaissance Italy, while not one of them can produce an artist to match the least among the hundred who briefly flourished in the tiny town of Florence. The fact is that the relation of wealth to social and political well-being is a mystery, and to cast all politics in economic terms is to surrender the known facts of human life to the flimsiest speculation.

This is not to say that the production of wealth has no part to play in political deliberations. It is, rather, to insist on the ascendancy of policy over production, where policy means the directing of activity towards the maintenance of social life. So conceived, the creation of wealth is not a sufficient policy. If it is thought to be so, this is partly because the creation of wealth is believed to be a necessary guarantee of economic stability. The emphasis on the 'standard of living' in politics – while it is a natural effect of the democratic process – has its most important explanation in the experience of uncontrolled inflation, economic depression, rapidly fluctuating and changing material circumstances, as these have afflicted western society in the present century. And these sudden reversals have been accompanied by 'social, political, and moral disasters which the general framework – the patterns of behaviour, habits, outlook, language, that is, the "ideological superstructure" of the victims – could not sustain'.[38] It is the truth encapsulated in that remark of Berlin's that has led politicians to seek for some understanding of these things, and to attempt at all costs to avert the drastic fluctuations experienced in the inter-war years. A citizen's allegiance requires fixed expectations, a settled idea of his own and others' material status, and a sense that he is not the victim of uncontrollable forces that might at any moment plunge him into destitution or raise him to incomprehensible wealth. In so far as that sense is integral to the authority of state, then it becomes part of the responsibility of state to settle and uphold the common currency and all the material expectations that are associated with it. But, as conservatives have until recently always realized, this argues not for a free market but for something like its opposite. Indeed, it has led to the acceptance by the Conservative Party of economic theories – such as that of Keynes – which regard the interference of the state in the market process as a social and economic necessity.

The Ascendancy of Economics

Before considering the institution of private property, however, it is important to reflect on the ascendancy of economics in matters of policy. Some might consider this to be a sign of the wholesale adoption of the Marxist view, the view that 'the mode of production of material life determines the social, political and intellectual process . . .', and that one should always distinguish 'the material transformation of the economic conditions of production, which can be determined with the precision of

a natural science', from the 'legal, political, religious, aesthetic or philo-
sophic – in short, ideological – forms in which men become conscious of
this conflict and fight it out'.[39] In other words it might seem to be tantamount to the theory that the true understanding of the facts of social
life is to be found in the 'science' of economics. Politics is nothing more
than the unruly attempt of consciousness to express and control a reality
which in fact proceeds in obedience to laws which no merely political
conception can grasp.

In fact, matters are worse than that. For Marx's high-spirited attempt
to subvert the deliverances of political common sense was redeemed by
a theory which restored, at the so-called 'economic' level, all those features of human self-consciousness which it seemed to invalidate at the
level of surface politics. The 'labour theory of value' is less a theory of
economics than a theory of political exploitation. 'Labour' is a concept
integral to the self-consciousness of man, and in describing it as the
economic reality Marx was at the same time describing the thoughts and
feelings through which citizenship is enacted.[40] Until recently the
'economic advisers' who surround our statesmen were possessed, as a
rule, of theories which both claimed to be more scientific than Marx's,
and also remained wholly divested of any reference to the moral life of
man. Citizenship was reduced to consumption, and the triumph of
economics coexisted quite happily with the downfall of political understanding. Other less managerially minded politicians fell victim to those
economists who – while preserving the appearance of scientific expertise – disguised as economic theorems the political prejudices which could
not be deduced from them. It came to seem as though a Galbraith, a
Hayek or a Friedman could speak about political matters with the authority of a scientist, when in fact his political dogma remained detachable
from his economic theory, the theory itself being as scientifically un-
adventurous and as empirically arbitrary as any of its competitors. As a
result of all this, one response to the ascendancy of economics has been
scepticism, scepticism most of all about its scientific pretensions, about
its predictions, concepts and results, many of which, in the hands of
established 'advisers', seem to derive directly from the antecedent policies
of party, and not from the axioms of an impartial science. (The point is
evident in the 'neo-classical' theories of the market; it is only slight-
ly less evident in the recent American attacks on 'oligarchical business'.[41])

Nevertheless, scepticism is premature. The recent acceptance by our
major parties of similar economic policies (partly under pressure from
the International Monetary Fund) suggests a minimum of received wisdom in economic matters. Wisdom which triumphs over party ideology
might well encapsulate the basic truths of some budding science. But

now, suppose that there is this science, and that it has all the power to predict and explain which Marx and others have claimed for it. Should not a politician avail himself of its results, and will he not thereby enhance his political understanding?

In answer to that question it is necessary to remind ourselves that no natural science of man *could* replace or subvert the mode of understanding that we call political. We can of course imagine a neutral, predictive, science of social behaviour; but the result may make human action not more intelligible, but less, since it may have to eliminate from its account of things all reference to how action is conceived. Economics stands to politics in much the same relation as neurology stands to personal affection. While I *could*, in principle, regard my friend as an organism activated by a complex system of nerves, and base all my knowledge of him and all my anticipations of his behaviour in that description, I certainly would not thereby understand him as I understand him instinctively through friendship. He would have become, for me, a mechanized corpse, towards which love and hatred, liking and anger, admiration and contempt, indeed all emotion that is distinctively human, would be more or less impossible. I would be forced to turn away from him as something alien and unintelligible.[42]

In just such a way the purely scientific economist might have to see civil society as a corpse, moving in obedience to scientific laws which can be formulated without reference to the conceptions, values and feelings through which men understand themselves as political beings. The only result of that scientific enterprise would be to render politics incomprehensible, to retreat from direct involvement in it, and to cease to want either to belong or not to belong to the social arrangement by which one is surrounded. Some such objection, I shall later argue, applies to all 'deterministic' economic models, and in particular to the Marxist theory of history, which seeks to replace political understanding with a 'value-free' predictive science.

The Right of Property

None of this is to dismiss the importance of economics, or to suggest that there is no room for a genuine 'political economy', tempered by the priorities of politics in much the way that domestic economy is tempered by the needs of family life. But, before laying emphasis on this unborn 'science', we must study the principles from which the politics of property will spring. The conservative's concern is not merely with the *creation* of wealth. Will he then turn his attention, as the socialist does, to its distribution? The answer is that he will, but only indirectly, and only because of a certain view about private property. This view is difficult to state, for the simple reason that the intuition from which it derives lies in the very centre of the social sense of man. It is only by ignoring this intuition that it has been possible for the opponents of conservatism to regard political issues as concerned with 'control of the means of production', and to set up a simple-minded dichotomy between socialism and capitalism as containing the whole of contemporary politics. For a conservative that dichotomy is naïve, for it simplifies beyond recognition the principle of his outlook, which is man's absolute and ineradicable need of private property.

This dogma represents the common intuition of every labouring person. The problem is to translate it into an articulate view. The first thing to be said is that ownership is the primary relation through which man and nature come together. It is therefore the first stage in the socializing of objects, and the condition of all higher institutions. It is not necessarily a product of greed or exploitation, but it *is* necessarily a part of the process whereby man frees himself from the power of things, transforming resistant nature into compliant image. Through property man imbues his world with will, and begins therein to discover himself as a social being.

Those high-flown sentiments belong to Hegel;[43] they demand translation into the plain talk of government, and the task is not easy. But a first step is made when we see how near is the idea of private property to the notions that I put forward in Chapter 2. For consider what man is without the institution of property. He cannot identify in the world any object as his own; hence he cannot freely avail himself of objects and expect others to accord him the use of them. Everything he desires he sees as the object only of desire, and not of right. Nor can he see any part of the world as connected (except by some accident of strength or interest) with anyone else. A man who wields power over woods and fields has no more authority to dispose of them than does his neighbour. The concepts of 'right', and 'possession' fail to inform their common understanding of a world which, in consequence, remains alien to each of them, and a battleground for both. Nor can the battle be terminated by a gift, since gift supposes property. Objects can therefore play no part in establishing or reinforcing social bonds. Instead they stand wholly apart from the world of men, an inanimate, inhuman scenario to their unformed transactions.

If a man is to awaken from this state into true self-consciousness – consciousness of himself as one of a kind – then he must see the world in different terms, terms of right, responsibility and freedom. The institution of property enables him to do this. Through property an object ceases to be a mere inanimate thing, and becomes instead the focus of rights and obligations. These rights and obligations need not be (in the first place) contractual. Indeed the question how they arise is of little immediate importance. The point is rather that, until they arise, until property passes from 'effective control' (to use the Marxist expression) to institutional right, it contains no contribution to human society. Through property, and the rights associated with it, the object is lifted out of mere 'thinghood' and rendered up to man. It bears now the imprint of human social relations, and reflects back to its owner a picture of himself as a social being. By instilling the world with the rights of ownership man remakes the world as an image of his true – his social – self. He is now at home where before he was merely let loose.

It is for this reason that a man's principal proprietary attitude is towards his immediate surroundings – house, room, furniture – towards those things with which he is, so to speak, deeply mingled. It is the home, therefore, that is the principal sphere of property, and the principal locus of the gift. (Hospitality is the only form of gift that imposes itself as an obligation: for it arises when another has been invited into the sphere which defines one's own.)

There is, then, a deep connection between private property and self-realization. If this has been doubted it is partly on account of a common confusion between possession and consumption. The activity of consumption does not presuppose ownership, and takes place even in that 'state of nature' where philosophers locate their primeval men. In the civilized state, however, consumption is also an exercise of right, and implies ownership of the things consumed. Nevertheless consumption is only a part of property, and not the part which reveals its social essence. The important aspect of property is its stable aspect, in which ownership is conceived as permanent or semi-permanent. For the full fruition of the sense of property there must be permanent objects of possession. It is this which explains the enduring place of land in the psychology of ownership. The true gift is not the thing which is consumed (and which does honour only in the process of hospitality), but the thing which is kept beyond foreseeable consumption. This thing is the embodiment of a right of use. The right may be exclusive or qualified, permanent or semi-permanent, absolute or defeasible: there are many distinctions here, and they are distinctions which must necessarily be passed over in economic theory. (It was 'obvious' to Keynes that 'consumption is the sole end and object of all economic activity',[44] obvious only because Keynes's economic theory could not distinguish the various kinds of property, and the various modes of holding it.) Similar considerations explain why the sense of property tends to transform itself into the pursuit of aesthetic value, and why beautiful objects are consecrated to God. A paradigm of the personal gift is the ornamented, decorated object, which retains its worth beyond the life of any owner. Among such things the important examples are the house, its furniture, and all those assorted oddments that used to come in a decorated *cassone* from bride to groom.

Property and Household

It is important to say a little more about this connection between the sense of property and the sense of home (or household). Home is the place where private property accumulates, and so overreaches itself, becoming transformed into something shared. There is no contract of distribution: sharing is simply the essence of family life. Here everything important is 'ours'. Private property is added to, and reinforces, the primary social bond. It is for some such reason that conservatives have seen the family and private property as institutions which stand or fall together. The family has its life in the home, and the home demands property for its establishment. Whatever abstract arguments might be offered against that connection, it has a savour of irrebuttable common sense. And so far as I can see, the abstract argument is very feeble, representing the connection between 'family' and 'property' as an accident, peculiar to something called the 'bourgeois' family, the imminent demise of which it seeks to foretell. I shall say more about this concept of the 'bourgeois family' in the next chapter. But it must be pointed out at once that this particular form of attack is rooted in the shallowest of observations. For where do we find the 'non-bourgeois' family, in which the connections between kinship, household and property are supposedly loosened or undone? Here the radical critic usually chooses to refer to some hypothetical future, of which neither he nor anyone else has a concrete understanding. If he attends to history it is usually in order to misdescribe it.[45] For consider some typical 'non-bourgeois' families. The Homeric *oikos* (from which word our own 'economy' is derived) referred not merely to a social unit but also to a household, endowed with property, and standing under rights of ownership and obligations of hospitality. (Nestor, exhorting the Achaeans beside their ships, cries: Friends, be courageous, and consider the shame of other men, and remember, each of you, children, and wife, possessions and parents . . .' (Il. xv, ll. 661–3). And lest it should be thought that Homer spoke only for the ruling class, perhaps it is well to refer also to Hesiod, *Works and Days* (l. 405f.), and to the comments in the pseudo-Aristotelean *Oeconomica* (Book 1).) The modern proletarian family is similarly constituted, as was the extended aristocratic family of the Renaissance. In studying such social units one will see how deeply intertwined is the private aspect of social life with the institution of property, and how much of a distortion it must be to prise the two apart. Those who imagine that the proletarian family somehow escapes from the bond of property, simply because it cannot afford, or does not require, the purchase of a house, are confused indeed. Property does not consist in the accumulation of proximate objects: it is a particular form of *right*. A right of way is property; so is a right to use a common lawn-mower, a right to shut a door against another man. Even the occupancy of a council flat is a property right, defeasible at law, but in practice no more defeasible than a private lease, and carrying with it as fierce a sense of territory as pertains to any country house. The difference that exists is of course important: it enables the proletarian family to accumulate moveable goods and gadgetry (cars, televisions, washing-machines) in a manner which changes the aspect of the home. And it may be that these goods, and the specific appetites towards them, point to political considerations that condemn the whole arrangement. But to discuss that complication will only obscure the present issue; the essential connection between household and family is undeniable. It follows that a conservative must be concerned with the distribution of property, and not only with its accumulation. Given his belief in the political importance of the family, and his reliance on family allegiance in forming respect towards an established state, he must desire the distribution of property through all classes of society, in accordance with whatever conception of household might be generic to each of them. How, and in what measure, is this distribution to be effected? And to what extent is it the concern of state to further it?

Distribution and the Market

It is, I think, an inescapable consequence of the existence of property, and of the active nature of man, that there should be exchange and accumulation. There are philosophies that envisage the institutions of private property as existing without these consequences. We are asked to imagine a society of men endowed with such plenty that they have only to reach out a hand to satisfy their needs, and possessed of natures so lassitudinous that the desire to overcome and dominate is unknown to them. The literature is full of such visions, and nothing that Aristotle, Hobbes or Nietzsche have said will prevent them from being produced and pondered. But let us be realistic: men seek domestic peace and security; they seek fame and applause; they seek power and influence; they seek friendship and love. Of all those, only love cannot be acquired through property, and love without security is tragic. Moreover, the other aims are not only furthered by property: they require property, since they require the ability to assert a massive right against intrusion. The desire for property will therefore be mingled with the desires for security, status and power. All these ends are furthered by exchange (since no one can produce everything that he requires), and equally by accumulation (which brings security and power). Since talent, ability, energy – indeed the sheer attachment to life – are unequally distributed, so too therefore will be property, a fact which can be called 'unfair' only by invoking that concept of 'social justice' which we have already seen reason to reject. Thus the very process whereby man first humanizes the world and renders it intelligible as an object of his social will, also creates the divisions which, on one view, set men against one another. The socialist, who seeks for the redistribution of wealth (believing that only in a condition of equality will social conflict be brought to an end) has devised methods for achieving his aim, and I shall later consider three – taxation, nationalization, and expropriation – since their place in the activities of state is so fundamental that no political dogma can ignore them.

'Distribution' can be considered both from the political and from the economic viewpoint. One may consider the justice of a particular form of taxation, or the political wisdom of expropriation, or the relation between the distribution of property and the quality of social life. These are political questions; they depend upon the conceptions – justice, friendship, and community – through which the social organism is understood by those who compose it. One might also consider the economic benefits of progressive taxation, or the effect of taxation on investment income, or the fiscal benefit consequent on a general ownership of moveable goods. These are economic questions, which must be answered through an adequate theory. The answers to them will contain no recommendation that is not itself subordinate to questions of general policy. It is no part of social life to engage in these economic speculations, although a politician must needs have some grasp of them. But whatever grasp he may seek or acquire, it will be useful to him only if he is possessed of a political dogma – a set of beliefs capable of generating coherent policy. And therefore, before the questions of economic management can be properly discussed, it is necessary to review the political factors that will be at stake in their solution. We must therefore examine the way in which questions of distribution will enter the basic principles of conservative thought.

Distribution is, in England, the great socialist cause. But we must notice that the desire to arrive at an 'equitable distribution' is not the desire to abolish private property, but the desire for an adjustment in what liberal (or 'classical') economists have thought of as the natural order. English socialists have in general upheld the institution of private property, partly in response to the intuition that I have elaborated, the intuition of a deep connection between property and family life. With the 'radical' critique – the view that private property is simply an evil, to be abolished as soon as possible from the world – I shall be concerned only later.

Perhaps it may be wondered why we should now consider socialism even in its parochial form, the form which aims at redistribution. For, having defended private property, can we not leave it to take its course, establishing itself in society according to the natural laws of the market? The answer is, of course, that we cannot. Not only would it be absurd to dismiss out of hand the demand for redistribution (as though the many who have argued for it were men of no understanding). It would also be wrong, having given essentially conservative reasons for the maintenance of private property, to adopt a merely liberal stance towards its distribution.[46] We can see from the account given that the right to property must be deeply entwined with national and social history, and cannot at any moment be reduced to a mere résumé of human agreements. Property is an institution, requiring realization and protection in the forms of state, and a man's right to it is not some over-riding law of natural justice, but a right conditional on his own allegiance to the society which made his ownership possible. Hence there is no injustice involved in a law of forfeiture; and if we can show that the order and equilibrium of society requires the appropriation of individual property, then reasons of state will require that the right to private property be defeasible in the public cause. No one doubts that reasons of state may be abused, either in Neronian fashion, or in the more subtle way of bureaucratic power. And even here, in that twilight where the equilibrium between individual right and public necessity is established, there are principles of justice which no government should ignore. But it is no longer possible to imagine, amid the vast contingencies of modern society, that the need for private property should be allowed to dictate a 'natural' right of man, and that the law of the market (whatever it is, indeed) should therefore be enacted by every ruling power. Whatever natural justice dictates, it will be but a part of the law of property, and insufficient to determine the nexus of legal rights in which the individual lies constrained. Nothing better illustrates this than the richly historical law of land in England, a law which, codified many times, and finally in the great land laws of 1925, represents a thousand years of careful dealing between state and citizen, and expresses a subtle sense of the ways in which a title to land may be lost, gained or granted. It has been recognized throughout history that the law of the market is inadequate to represent the smallest part of what is here at stake, and that any estate may be encumbered with adverse rights that have arisen neither out of contract nor out of any other form of human choice.[47]

Moreover, one must bear in mind that, even when property is 'private' and changes hands by private treaty, it may be held subject to interests which prevent it from being exchanged at its 'market' price. The legal owner of trust property, for example, is encumbered by the rights of the beneficiaries, who become the equitable owners of the content of the trust. This introduces immeasurable complexities into property rights; property can now remain owned but immovable, bound by terms which prohibit active dealing. The case of a trust for purposes (as in the endowment of a college or hospital), where no list of beneficiaries can be made, shows private property at the extreme point of attenuation, on the verge of becoming wholly public. For here, while what is held is 'private property', the right to dispose of it lies with no group of individuals (unless it be the trustees, who have no true rights, but only obligations). Such arrangements, while they do not provide our paradigms of private ownership, at least show how 'private property' already contains within itself the possibility of its own restriction. Property rights are precisely the kinds of thing that can be indefinitely qualified in the interests of some 'higher' institution, and why not in the interest of the highest of institutions, which is the state?

But it is only a minority of men who would now see the market economy as the true end of private property, and 'state control' as an unmitigated evil directed against the citizen's natural right. It has never been true, and it is now indeed evidently false, that the choice in these matters lies between 'individualism and socialism', as one liberal[48] declared in the House of Commons in 1923 (the subject for debate being the surprisingly abstract issue of 'The Failure of the Capitalist System'). But we must still face the question of the legitimacy of state activity in the realm of private property, and the precise 'mode of production' (if there be one) that a conservative might find himself committed to uphold.

Taxation

Let us begin by considering taxation, since, in one form or another, its necessity cannot be denied without at the same time denying the need for government. In England taxation has always loomed large among political issues and, being one of the matters which divided the Stuarts from Parliament, contributed much to our greatest constitutional crisis. When full security in the fiscal relations between state and citizen was established in the last century, it was with the introduction of a permanent income tax by the Peel administration in 1842.[49] As we shall see, it is no accident that a Tory government should have been responsible for this measure, and no accident that arguments of justice should have been used in support of it. Given the necessity of taxation, its legitimacy as an institution need not be doubted. Justice intrudes, however, because we must ask the questions 'How?', 'How much?', and 'When?'

Gibbon, describing the grandiose injustices of the Roman emperors, wrote frequently of 'oppressive' taxes; and I doubt that many of his readers have been unconvinced by the epithet. Solzhenitsyn and others have described in similar terms the Bolshevik and Stalinist systems of taxation, ruthlessly applied in the attempt to destroy every vestige of private profit. And again, turning from the abstractions of political theory, to the concrete examples which such writers have so vividly presented to us, few can fail to be moved to indignation by what they read. It seems then that the sense of justice provides us even here with a criterion of legitimacy. But it is not a criterion that is readily understood. One important liberal thinker has concluded – by an argument strikingly reminiscent of Marx's thesis that an employer who makes a profit must do so by the extortion of unpaid work – that taxation is nothing but forced labour, and therefore inherently unjust.[50] If we are to concede such an argument, then we abolish the conservative enterprise, and cease to acknowledge the web of obligations by which citizens are bound to each other and to the state. Politics collapses once again into that specious 'social contract', through which no lasting institution, no developed government, and no bond of allegiance, can be formed.

The first problem is to know what the state is doing in extorting taxes. The answer seems to be simple: it is providing itself with funds to meet the needs of state, and therefore the political needs of the citizen. Natural justice therefore suggests that each should be taxed according to his means. However, in almost every country we find significant departures from that ideal, departures which indicate that taxation is used, not only to finance the offices of state, but also to redistribute wealth, even when that wealth has been legitimately acquired. The wealthy are required to part with a greater proportion (and not just a greater amount) of their income. This is not because the poor are granted *relief* (for that is usually an independent feature [51]) but because the wealthy are being prevented from keeping what they earn.

There are two arguments for progressive taxation that might carry weight, but neither is likely to recommend itself to a conservative. The first is purely political and goes back at least to Tom Paine (*The Rights of Man*, pt II, ch. 5). Progressive taxation has a long-term tendency to equalize the possession of property, not by giving to the poor, but (what has always proved easier) by taking from the rich. Such an argument must appeal to a socialist, especially to one who believes with Shaw that socialism is merely 'the economic side of the democratic idea',[52] but it has no persuasive power beyond the reach of that particular ideology.

Progressive taxation is an act which jeopardizes the ties between the state and its more successful citizens, and can be regarded as a social necessity only if the nation so swells with the resentment of the underprivileged that the rich must be punished to appease them. No conservative is likely to accept that view, since he will instinctively incline to the belief that resentment is appeased, not by equality, but by the 'validating' of inequality, in the forms and allegiances which pertain to the maintenance of civic life. To adapt a thought of Aristotle's, it is not the large inequalities which men resent, but the small ones. A man does not suffer from the prosperity of another against whom he is not practised to measure himself. But the change in his position relative to his immediate fellows is deeply and keenly felt. Thus we should not be surprised if the 'erosion of differentials', or the 'loss of parity' give rise to a resentment far greater than the 'inequitable' distribution which preceded and survives them.

The other argument is economic, and as such subservient to policy. It might seem that the fiscal benefits of progressive taxation must be small, since it disinclines the more talented from work, and so lowers the total product available for taxation. However, this need not be so. It is an evident fact that, beyond a certain point, a man will not be disposed to spend what he earns – unless he is of the wasteful disposition that usually accompanies, not the earning, but the inheriting of wealth. In other words, if the surplus is not confiscated by the state, it will accumulate, and not be returned to the market. It will translate itself into a castle, a pile of gold, a collection of pictures, a library, or some other idle, deleterious thing. Sometimes the individual may indirectly return the surplus to the market, in the form of a capital investment which creates employment. But there is no guarantee that he will do so. Suppose we accept the Keynesian hypothesis,53 that the growth of the economy requires the active stimulation of demand. We might then believe that the appropriation of this idle surplus could be used to feed the economy, either through public spending, or through redistribution, so that the poorer classes may transform it into consumable goods. We might also think that economic growth (or the lack of economic decline) is a political necessity. In which case, progressive taxation becomes a guarantee of national livelihood.

Even if one were to accept that argument (and in the next chapter I shall give reasons for rejecting one of the principles upon which it rests), the most it could justify is a very limited form of progressive taxation. To put it roughly, the economic solution to the problem of falling demand will be given by the point of intersection between the curve that measures the growth of demand through redistribution and the curve that measures the fall in the taxable surplus caused by the disincentive to earn. The optimal point of taxation would be that where the marginal disincentive to earn balances the marginal benefit of confiscation. Wherever that point may be (and it would be a matter of great complexity to calculate it), it will certainly be lower than the actual maximum that all governments, including Conservative governments, have imposed. Even if we are to allow ourselves to be influenced by these economic arguments (and that means imposing upon ourselves the duty to discover the truth about a matter governed by no agreed scientific theory) then we should be hesitant to accept the present structure of income taxation. It may be that only small adjustments can be made towards the ideal which proposes itself. But the direction of those adjustments is clear.

Income tax is not only a budgetary necessity; it is also the form of tax most readily comprehensible to the citizen. Having the nature of a repeated blow to a part that is already numb, it is the form of confiscation that is most lightly felt. Moreover, it is felt by the whole nation; and not by any subordinate or ruling class: it therefore imposes severe restraints on government expenditure, and leads to a natural balancing of social forces. If the working class suffers the fiscal effects of some policy at the same time, and to the same degree, as the upper and middle class, then all will be united in their attitude towards it. In no sense need taxation become the cause of social unrest, as it was in the France of Louis XVI, when the nobility were exempt from it, or as it is now in England, where the middle class is subject to punitive measures which in the nature of things it can neither accept nor understand.

These punitive measures are explained by the survival in political consciousness of Victorian class resentment. Somewhere in the heart of every socialist, the image of Mayhew's London lies indelibly engraved, and despite everything that has happened to dispel such things from the hearts of more ignorant men, no present reality has power in comparison with the ghosts of that vanished age. It would be well if the life of England could be resumed without interruption from this self-dramatizing company. No society can survive if its rulers contemplate with fixed attention evils that can no longer be remedied, and conjure in themselves resentments that can never be appeased. But this feeling still dominates. It has resulted, for example, in the use of taxation to attack hereditary wealth, both through the imposition of heavy death duties, and through the (now inescapable) capital transfer tax. This tax, since it undermines not only the transfer of wealth between generations, but also the exercise of private gift, constitutes the first direct attack in English law against the institution of private property. In being such an attack it wars not only with property, but also with family and friendship. Private gifts are penalized, as is the natural desire to establish and endow a household. In this one may feel the premonition of evil to come, when men take from their parents nothing but the fact of birth, and nothing tangible passes from generation to generation except by stealth. Suddenly the continuity of things is broken, and the past and the future begin to conceal themselves behind the present pursuit of immediately expendable gain.

Perhaps there is social policy at work here: but it is a policy that shows little understanding of the basis of social life. Moreover, one may doubt the wisdom of government that seeks to impose social policy in such a way, a way which immediately removes from its citizens the sense of a 'natural' obligation to comply with it. The state must persuade its subjects that the obligation to pay tax stems directly from the fact of citizenship. Such an obligation is thwarted when taxation is used as a weapon against the very institution of private property. It is impossible, therefore, to regard with equanimity the introduction of a wealth tax. For again, small fiscal benefits accrue, at the cost of alienating those families which have made the greatest contribution to our national pride and history. Yet another cornerstone is pulled from the edifice of national culture, and it is hard to understand the self-destructive impulse which may lead the powers of state towards such a policy.

It seems, then, that the conservative attitude in fiscal matters will be directly opposed to the attempt to bend taxation permanently and directly to some external aim of redistribution. This does not mean that the conservative statesman will subscribe to the view that the *only* legitimate use of tax is to secure the revenues of state: he too will be prepared, when necessary, to use it as an instrument of social control. But he will do so only rarely, and the instinct which guides him will seek, not disruption, but continuity.

Public Ownership

Space forbids that we dwell longer on this complex matter, since the yet more important question of 'public ownership' must now be faced. A sinister picture was painted by the early socialists of the effects of competition, of the greedy struggle of man against man for an ever-larger share of the market. Now, in so far as the competitive spirit is a constitutive part of rational nature, connected with the very sentiments of pride and self-esteem through which we imbue our world with value, it is pointless to bewail its more tawdry manifestations. The conservative is unlikely to feel confident that an economic arrangement could be devised which would both preserve the motives and the self-esteem of labour, and also dispense with the competition which results from them. In dealing with deep and obdurate facts of human nature, one can only refrain from judging harshly. Nevertheless, one does not have to be a Saint-Simonist to see that matters are far from simple. The unbridled

law of the market breeds monopoly – or if not monopoly, business olig-
archy [54] – which not only stifles competition, but which may also set up
an independent corporation or cartel in rivalry to the state. It has been
argued that the cure for this is public ownership, or 'state control'. However, state 'control' only protects the state if it vests the power of monopoly *in* the state. In Russia, where these questions are well understood,
that effect is achieved, since the workers in a state monopoly are carefully marshalled by trade-union officials who are themselves the servants
of government. In the West, however, the state has usually made itself
not less, but more vulnerable, through public ownership. It has allowed
trade unions both to support the principle of monopoly (by excluding
workers who do not belong to them) and at the same time to retain the
'right to strike' whereby to bring any enterprise to a standstill. Thus the
power that the state wrests from the monopolistic owner (who can be
expected to be interested in maintaining the growth and activity of his
industry) is vested not in the state, but in 'organized labour'. This body
is both hard to appease and easy to antagonize, and being often in a
position of power without authority, will naturally see itself in self-
protective terms, pitted against the state as against a master from whom
to win favours. In the case of essential services the result may be dis-
astrous. When those services are (as they must be) brought under the
administration of state, there ought also to be legal sanctions, curtailing
the activity of the workers who are employed in them. No state can
readily tolerate the persistence of a 'right to strike' among its immediate
servants (policemen, firemen, the army, the civil services, members of
parliament, postmen, the judiciary – the list is extended with every
nationalization that is not a mere *acte gratuit*). Indeed there have been
statutes in force which restrict or abolish that right in the areas where
it is possible to agree that a worker is employed, not privately, but
publicly.

Many issues surround this one of public ownership, and a conservative view is difficult to state. But the foregoing considerations suggest a
distinction which is of some importance, that between a nationalized
industry and a public service, between a competitive enterprise taken
into public control, and an activity essential to the maintenance of
public life. An advocate of private enterprise could certainly make use
of this distinction in clarifying his approach to the complexities of a
modern state. Consider the Post Office. The postal service is indispensable to the life of the community; without it, neither private relations
nor ordinary business could be conducted in the customary manner.
(The example of Italy shows how difficult it is, in a modern state, to run
a private business without the benefit of regular postal delivery.) Automatically, therefore, the maintenance of a postal service becomes one of

the responsibilities of government. The railways are similarly placed, for clearly, once the activities of railway companies had so transformed the nature of public life as to become an irremovable part of it, they were, from that moment, a matter of public, and hence of state concern. This shows how an enterprise which begins as a private industry may, in time, become a public service. It is in the case of a public service that the powers of state may, without violence to the normal rights of property, be invoked to support, protect and (where possible) provide a statutory constitution to a business enterprise. Even in America this is recognized. It is through the incorporation of independent enterprises that the 'frontiers' of the state extend, often to the point of strain. There is no alternative here, and the conservative, if he wishes to participate in the government of a modern state, must recognize and participate in the inevitable.

In the case of mere industry, however, he may still be reluctant to countenance state intervention, not, as some think, out of any overweening sympathy for the successful, but out of fear of being troubled by the weak. It is no part of friendship to cultivate dependence. Likewise it is no part of state activity to bring about the financial dependence of its citizens. But the state does this whenever, in nationalizing an industry, it removes the natural guidance of self-interest, creating instead a pocket of redundancy in which thousands may be kept from the knowledge of their uselessness by the reluctant dispensations of a central power. Here, it may be, the conservative would prefer what has been called the 'hard discipline of the market',[55] if only because it effects more quickly what will happen in any case.

It would be lengthy and difficult to rehearse the relevant arguments. But a matter of principle needs to be affirmed. It is the absolute duty of the state to have power over its subjects. The state's relation to the citizen is not, and cannot be, contractual. It is therefore not the relation of employer to employee. The state has the authority, the responsibility, and the despotism of parenthood. If it loses those ties, then it must perish, and society along with it. The state must therefore withdraw from every economic arrangement which puts it at the absolute mercy of individual citizens. This counsel has been many times ignored, and never more blatantly than in modern times. Through the vast and rampant civil service, through local government, through nationalized industry, through all the advisory bodies and meddlesome councils that surround it, the government disperses its power among ignorant multitudes. If it cannot coerce them, then it is at the mercy of any force (a union, for example) which can.

The true civil servant is a servant. He may see himself, if the state allows, as a private employee, with private and contractual rights. He may exert against the state his 'right' to strike. He (along with a million others) may engage in activities which, while legally sanctioned, are tantamount to rebellion. But when that is so the state is weak to the point of non-existence. What policy can restore its power? One answer suggests itself. Reward extravagantly those servants who are essential; but make them servants. As for the others, let them strike, and permanently.

Capitalism

But if the state is to withdraw in this way from *direct* participation in economic arrangements (offering its support to the indigent out of charity and not from some contractual right), then it must tacitly uphold that mode of production which has been called capitalist. For the third method of interference in the flow of private property – the method of expropriation – has about it too much of the air of penalty to be used except with the full majesty of state, as in times of war, or against the overbearing insolence of criminals. It cannot be held forth as a simple remedy against the over-accumulation of private wealth. And if wealth can accumulate – even to a modest degree – and if redistribution is only partial, then nothing will prevent it from accumulating in the hands of those who most actively pursue and desire it. From them, therefore, it must be borrowed by those who wish to begin any enterprise of their own, and at once the economic structure of capitalism is forced on us, as a consequence of that lending power. For there is the beginning of wage labour, when one man has nothing to bargain with except the gifts of natural power. The only way to avoid this would be to impose a system approximating to feudalism (or at least to feudalism as described by Marx), where wealth is largely inherited and barred from exchange, where men are born into a web of obligations that circumscribe its use and their own activities, and where the free sale of labour is thwarted. But while the imposition of this kind of feudalism was practised with some success in Maoist China (so that people were regarded as born into their station and free to move from it neither in place nor in attainment, all production being handed over to an immediate overlord who took full responsibility for the labourers within his charge), the arrangement seems to have proved impermanent. Besides, such measures lie outside the purview of contemporary British politics.

The reference to feudalism enables us, however, to clarify the problem – and it is undeniably a problem – of conservative economics. From its beginnings the Conservative Party has been characterized by a relatively firm and enterprising fiscal policy, being responsible, not only for constant restrictions on free trade, but also for the introduction of regular income tax, and for legislation which governed the sale and conditions of labour. In the light of history, its recent conversion to Keynesian economic theory might be seen as a natural intellectual development, a further move away from the view (variously propounded or assumed by Smith, Ricardo and the Mills) that economic affairs are self-regulating (so that little good and much harm may result from the attempt to interfere with them), towards the more plausible view that the posture of state is all-important, and that, without the state's surveillance, destitution and unemployment could result at any time. The triumph of Conservatism over Liberalism, and its continuing ability to confront and assimilate the labour movement, are due in part to its economic sense, to its recognition that, after all, the free movement of labour, and the concentration of capital, are matters for discipline, and that the 'crises' to which they are subject are by no means accidental, but a chronic liability of industrial power. (Which is not to argue for the *truth* of the Keynesian theory, but only for its political utility.)

But although there may be truth in the idea that the Conservative Party has been brought steadily under the influence of economic theory, we must again remind ourselves that no economic theory makes proper sense until conjoined to some adequate political dogma (a dogma which defines the nature and rights of the social arrangement to be served). The appeal to economics is like the appeal to the doctor, based not in self-confidence, but in hope or fear. It is as much to political dogma, as to any economic theory, that the Conservative's restrictions on capitalist enterprise have been due. And such restrictions are by no means peculiar to our times. On the contrary, free trade has always been a cause to fight for, not a norm to be assumed. The fact that its restriction is now embellished with theory suggests not so much an intellectual conversion as a loss of political self-esteem.

The Marxist Challenge

Nevertheless, in invoking the comparison with feudalism, I have already made an important concession to theory, specifically to the theory of Marx. It is a distinctive contribution of Marxism, and one to which all historians and politicians are indebted, to suggest that social and historical facts can be illuminated in terms of the economic structure from which they derive. Marx persuasively contrasted two structures, capitalism and feudalism. The former requires freedom of exchange, wage labour, accumulated capital, and leads by inexorable steps to the creation of a property-owning and a propertyless class. The latter requires serfdom, *corvée*, and an attachment to place and person that hampers free exchange.

113

Now it is difficult to imagine the presence of real wealth without the tendency to exchange and movement. In those societies that have been *called* feudal (on account of the specific obligations which they encapsulated) the prevalence of money suggests a real reference to exchange as the basis even of the power of a monarch. (In 'feudal' England, for example, villeins could buy, sell, pledge and hire everything from livestock to land; their feudal bond often amounted to little more than an attachment to place and manor, coerced as much by custom as by force.[56]) Now some Marxists believe that there is a genuine and absolute distinction in *reality* between feudal and capitalist modes of production, and that the transition from one to the other is the single great economic fact, explaining matters as disparate as the Peasants' Revolt, the rise of Protestantism, and the formation of towns. There is an element of fantasy in these explanations, and a consequent emptiness in the attendant description of the real alternative to capitalism. Nevertheless, we can extract from them an important underlying idea. 'Feudalism' and 'capitalism' are the names, not of historical realities, but of theoretical ideas. Societies may approximate to either form, but in reality will always contain some idiosyncratic mixture of both. There may have been (in some sad community, lost in the Dark Ages of our civilization) a genuine feudal arrangement; there may have been (perhaps in late nineteenth-century Chicago or in Victorian Manchester) a genuine capitalist town. But just as history points to an absence of the first, so must it confirm a similar absence of the second. A glance at modern Europe shows how deviant are its economic arrangements from those of the free capitalist enterprise described by Marx. And a glance at America, with its great anonymous monopolies and cartels, further demonstrates that even in the absence of state intervention, the *homo economicus* of classical theory has little capacity to survive.[57] No longer do we encounter the small enterprising 'bourgeois', pursuing his private gain in the open forum of the market, accumulating profit with which to strike a bargain for labour between man and man. Naturally, by their inner life and logic, the corporations pursue their profit, in a market which they can only partly 'fix'. But they contract with *all* their members: with managers, shop-stewards, salesmen, machinists, advisers and clerks, all of whom become wage-labourers, in an organization the profits of which accumulate anonymously, and the purpose of which may be no more stable from day to day than is the purpose of the whale. Moreover, the contract is made under mutual duress: a manager soon becomes indispensable, and can 'fix' his terms. Even the lowest employee – whose wage would else have been determined by his meniality – becomes possessed of similar power, operating, not as an individual, but as part of the union which secures for the manual workers as a class that indispensability which they could never acquire alone.

114

The concepts of Marxism correspond, then, only to theoretical and idealized arrangements, and while this may render them useful in the study of history, it gives us little ground for accepting the political economics with which they are commonly combined. For one thing, it becomes absurd to divide reality into the exploiters who employ and the exploited who are employed by them (and who therefore sacrifice their hours of 'unpaid' labour). Just about *everyone* is employed. It follows that the class normally identified as the bourgeoisie is as much given to contract away its labour power as the class which is supposedly oppressed by it. Both produce a surplus (for that is merely another way of saying that their common enterprise is profitable), and they both suffer what Marxists consider to be the injustice of its 'confiscation'.[58] All the distinctions here are obliterated by a philosophy which in any case consigns the idea of 'justice' to the realm of 'ideology', so as to represent (and misrepresent) contractual relations in terms of the exercise of power.

Suppose John contracts with me, so that I make a profit and he earns a wage. This contract will share with every contract the merely *relative* freedom which the law has long observed. (I may be the only employer and John may be starving. Alternatively there may be fifty employers, all competing for John's unique dexterity, and John may have independent means.) It follows that we can distinguish those contracts which exemplify just dealing from those which do not. Moreover, apart from brief periods of free-market activism, this distinction has always been made and often enforced – for example, by the Church (through the canonist doctrines of 'usury' and the 'just price'), by the justices of the peace, by the state – and not always in the interests of one particular party. There is no 'natural right' to the surplus which a man has contracted not to enjoy: the only injustice must therefore lie in the extent to which his necessity is manipulated by the man who employs him.

The Feudal Principle

I have dwelt on the Marxist theory for a specific reason, which is this: that since it presents idealized models of economic arrangements, it enables us to describe in clearer terms the conservative attitude to the restriction of property. It is not feudalism that a conservative will advocate, but merely its 'main principle – that the tenure of property should be the fulfilment of duty'.[59] That remark of Disraeli's, expressive of the idealistic vision of *Sybil* and *Coningsby*, is of course as false to the reality of 'feudal' Europe as is the Marxist analysis of its economy. But just as there can be idealized models in economic theory, so too can there be such models in politics, which extract from the imperfect arrangements of history some ideal of political obligation. The Marxist analysis cannot mention the ties of obligation which bound villein to lord and lord to villein, except as elements in the ideology which served to 'conceal' the realities of power. But the politician's preoccupation is precisely with this ideology. Hence he must attend to the concept of obligation, and ignore the economic theories which fail to make sense of it. Conservatism seeks to build ties of obligation into a relation which, left to itself, may prove unable to produce them. Since the conservative remains unpersuaded by the vision of a communistic future in which the human desire to possess, dominate and prosper will be extinguished, he must aim to discipline property in accordance with the obligations that make it tolerable. But it will be through law, and not through force that he will seek to achieve his purpose. His strictures on the free flow of property and the free sale of labour will flow from the 'feudal principle'. But they will flow through the channel of law, and will have as their aim, not the destruction of private property, nor its equal distribution, but only the relief of the hardship with which industrial production has been linked.

And now let us face, for a moment, the broad historical perspective. No society has successfully assimilated industrial production, or the discontents which stem from it. Nevertheless, industrialization, mobility, the divide between labour and management, the reckless pursuit of growth – all these have spread with such rapidity across the globe that it would be foolish to suppose their existence to be accidental. The conservative task has been, not to oppose whatever force has wrought these things, but to maintain through all its onslaughts the reality of social order, and the continuity of political life. Even a Marxist may have to admit that 'until the end of the eighteenth century the common people of France and England adhered to a deeply felt "moral economy" in which the very notion of . . . a dissociation between economic values on the one hand and social and moral obligations on the other was an outrage to their culture'.[60] He too may have to admit that it was in the last century, and under the impact of forces which had no necessary connection with capitalism or indeed with any other system of control that there arose an 'anti-political economy whose harsh profit-and-loss purgatives voided the body politic of old notions of duty, mutuality and paternal care'.[61] By then, capitalism had been active in Europe for four centuries – as long a span as any historical explanation could assimilate It seems, therefore, that the loss of this 'moral economy' is a more complex thing than the typical historical perspective can venture to explain

Now I have represented property as a corollary to conservative dogma rather than its principal preoccupation. It is quite reasonable to assert that for conservatism social and political unity take precedence over the free accumulation of property. English socialists claim credit for the 'heroic struggle' against the evils of industrial production. They prefer to forget that the Factory Acts, the legalization of trade unions, even the welfare state, were either Conservative inventions, or made possible by conservative forces that had long been struggling to bring such things into being. (In like manner, men once execrated the Court of Star Chamber as the symbol of royal power, while preferring to forget that it was also the only court in which the 'feudal principle' could be affirmed, so protecting the peasantry against enclosures.) Naturally these processes of adaptation served also to consolidate the interest of a ruling class. For social continuity was the motive. But if that way of looking at things conveys any truth it is only this, that those responsible profited as much from the security which they generated as did the restless classes which depended on them. No doubt a ruling class is well placed to undertake such things (whether or not it also represents itself as the 'vanguard' of something whose interests it 'really' serves). But that is neither here nor there.

The broad historical perspective, we shall increasingly find, is not broad enough. It remains fixated on the century which made it possible, and stares so intently at the industrial process as to conjure vast and hallucinatory images of its significance and power. The explanations that it generates seem inexorable only because they derive from the period when 'inexorability' was godlike and immune. But it overlooks the enduring political activity that has steered us through these 'inexorable' changes and seen the old 'moral economy' restored. Of course, there have been changes, and vast ones. Moreover, they have been attended with a strange unhappiness. If the historical perspective has anything to tell us, it is that we cannot let the matter rest. Something deeper needs to be said, about the emergence from the debris of industrialism of the peculiarly 'modern' man. It is the function of the next chapter to explore his condition, and to examine how far he can or ought to be a conservative.

Conclusion

What might be the conservative dogma concerning property? I have argued that the very state of civil society requires an institution of rights in things. It follows that any political view which regards the state as the protector of society must also demand the continuance of property. Moreover, a view which recognizes a title in custom and usage will find nothing wrong with the inheritance and accumulation of wealth. Furthermore, it will seek to protect both inheritance and accumulation, in so far as they stem from the bond of family, and in so far as they lie endorsed in the condition of society. This means that it is income, and not wealth, that the conservative will wish to tax. But he will be forced by the very concern for the civil bond which generates his belief in property to consider the question of its distribution. He will wish to instil into the accumulation of property those obligations without which part of society benefits, while another suffers, from its single-minded pursuit. As I have suggested, a qualified endorsement of modern capitalism seems to be the consequence of these opinions, even when that endorsement accompanies no aversion to general poverty, and no commitment to 'growth'.

But if, as some say, the capitalist mode of production (even in its modern, highly attenuated form) is the sole or principal cause of the evils which beset us, is conservatism still possible as an item of belief? In answer to that question we must show that the condition of modern man, whatever anxiety may attend it, is not the result of private property but of something else. Here we enter a dark area of politics, where both conservative and radical aim blows which miss their targets. But as for the liberal, his contribution is now at an end, for even if he has tottered on his fence so far, he is bound to fall off in the ensuing darkness.

CHAPTER 6

Alienated Labour

There is a natural instinct in the unthinking man – who, tolerant of the burdens that life lays on him, and unwilling to lodge blame where he sees no remedy, seeks fulfilment in the world that is – to accept and endorse through his actions the institutions and practices into which he is born. This instinct, which I have attempted to translate into the self-conscious language of political dogma, is rooted in human nature, and in elaborating its foundations I have also been adumbrating a tentative philosophy of man. This philosophy distinguishes from the activities of animals the peculiar behaviour that we recognize as human; the behaviour of a creature who has not only instincts, drives and needs, but also values; who exists, not only in the present, but in the past and the future; who does not merely suffer reality, but who also makes himself part of it, and impresses on the world the imprint of will.

The Modern Consciousness

But the task has now met an obstacle. To defend the unthinking prejudice of the normal active man was easy in an age when prejudices followed at once from the dogmas of received religion, or when social continuity ensured that those who rose to self-consciousness nevertheless departed only in the smallest items of belief from the happier mortals who were fated never to question what they knew. Suddenly, however, we find ourselves confronted with that monstrous entity, the modern man, the man for whom all connection with an order greater than himself has to be won through an effort of his own, and who looks for that order, not necessarily in what is or has been, but more often in what will be or in what might be. His restless longing to be rid of the here and now is stilled by no religious faith, and by no patient belief in the necessary imperfection of mortal things. His transcendental urge translates itself into an all-consuming nostalgia, nostalgia not for the past, but for a future which – like heaven – can be only negatively described.

119

Nor is his restlessness peculiar to the self-portrait that he has been painting over the past two hundred years. It belongs – at least, he believes it belongs – to the entire human world which served to create him, and in his attempt to understand himself he has been forced to understand the condition of all those beings who lie stranded about him on the shore of history, beings who may not follow his newfangled idiom but whose state nevertheless demands a description which has not been heard before. To the German Romantics we owe the concepts with which 'modern' humanity can be represented, and those concepts reflect a philosophy which I have tried intuitively to follow. But it is now time to make the central problem explicit. And it is here that we must part company once and for all with liberalism and engage only with those opponents who recognize the depth of human things. For what, after all, has been the prevailing weakness of the liberal ideal? Surely, this: that it reposes all politics and all morality in an idea of freedom while providing no philosophy of human nature which will tell us what freedom really is. It isolates man from history, from culture, from all those unchosen aspects of himself which are in fact the preconditions of his subsequent autonomy. When the liberal tries to make concrete the ideal of freedom which he proposes, he finds himself always constrained to endorse (whether wittingly or no) the habits and predilections of a particular way of life – the way of life of the emancipated urban intellectual. As for the rest of human nature, the human essence, what Marx and Feuerbach called the 'species life' of man, it seems to survive in his philosophy only in atomistic form, a confused bundle of individual desires and needs. Human fulfilment lies in the satisfaction of as many choices as short time allows. Such a philosophy presents no idea of the self, over and above the desires which constitute it: it therefore has no idea of self-fulfilment other than the free satisfaction of desire. It tries to stretch the notion of choice to include every institution on which men have conferred legitimacy, without conceding that their sense of legitimacy stems precisely from their respect for themselves as beings formed, nurtured and amplified by these things. It is not that men have desired and chosen them, for without them there would have been no choice to make. Nor is it that they know how to draw back from every inherited arrangement and pronounce it legitimate by some sudden sovereign act of will – any more than they can stand back from themselves and ask 'shall I, or shall I not, be this thing that I am?'.[62] The conservative, like the radical, recognizes that civil order reflects not the desires of man, but the self of man. Neither will hesitate to propose or defend a system which frustrates or diverts even the most innocent of human choices, if he sees those choices in conflict with the order that breeds fulfilment. But the conservative is also sceptical. He may have a nostalgia for the past, but he will not parade it as a declared ideal, and he will regard his opponent's far more compelling nostalgia for a non-existent future as a kind of intemperate folly, a last inverted survival of the belief in a Golden Age.

Nevertheless, faced with a world which, whether sick or not, believes itself in its self-conscious part to be so, the conservative must seek to define afresh his position, and his sceptical history has left him only an impoverished language in which this might be done. It is for this reason that he would do well to respect the radical's attempt to redescribe the state of man so that the modern consciousness may be seen as a proper part of it. Much as the English conservative, through love of constituted liberties, may feel drawn to the liberal cause, its philosophy is neither his nor anyone's. It describes not man but man's brief caricature, and most of all is that caricature ridiculous when set beside the realities of modern life. In what follows I shall have to borrow (largely from the Hegelian side of Marxism) the concepts with which to refine our political vision, so that this modern man can at least be discerned by it. The discussion will perforce be brief, touching on matters that require great analysis. But I hope that it will suffice to indicate a direction which the conservative might follow without detriment to his strength or to his refined lack of purpose.

Alienation

The concept of alienation was borrowed by Marx from Hegelian philosophy in order to describe the condition of man under capitalism – not just the condition of the labourer (as was Marx's first thought), but the condition of everyone. Only with the abolition of private property, he argued, could this alienation be overcome, and man restored to himself, to his essence, which is his 'species life'.[63] This abolition would come about as a necessary result of historical processes which Marx saw already at work in society, processes which involved the transfer of power from class to class, ending in the final emancipation of the proletariat and the deliverance of all men from the bondage of exploitation in which both exploiter and exploited had been held. At that point the truth of history would be revealed and private property would disappear, having no longer any part to play in the dealings between men.

In support of that idealistic vision, a kind of political theology has arisen, and one which requires a certain degree of faith from those who would attach themselves to it. Nevertheless, it is no accident that the descriptions which Marxism offers command such widespread assent. Naturally, many social troubles have attended the demise of the 'classical' period of our culture. Industrialization, over-population, the loss

121

of religious conviction, the mobility and subsequent prosperity of the lower class, the rise of the media, the debasement of language, the almost universal detachment from place and station – whatever the cause of these things, their existence must be recognized, together with the political problems which derive from them. But alongside all of them, representing itself simultaneously as cause and effect, stands the same unsettled ghost – the spirit of alienation, the collective sense that there may be no social order to which we severally belong. I shall study this ghost, not because it is the greatest of modern horrors, but because it is the most frequently encountered. It will serve to remind us that not every society is governable, and that there are political problems which lie beyond the purview of economics.

Recognizing, therefore, that there may be truth in the description of man's 'alienated' condition, and recognizing too the possibility of a deep and elusive connection between that condition and the 'fetishism of commodities' which Marx saw as a necessary result of capitalistic modes of production, the conservative will wish to present his own description of alienation, and to try to rebut the charge that private property is its cause. It may be, indeed, that he will find himself able to propose no complete or developed remedy. Not all human ills have a remedy, and, in this case, there is surely none that has been proposed which has any permanent power to find enactment. Marx, far from proposing a remedy, relied on a prediction, to which he gave little substance besides a rhetorical eulogy of the abstract 'emancipated' state of man, and a vigorous dismissal of all those concrete ideals which others might confuse with it.[64] In the third volume of *Capital* he (or his editor, Engels) goes so far as to declare that the premise of this emancipation is a shortening of the working day, a premise that has been fulfilled in the increasing idleness, and (some would say) the increasing alienation, of western society. And if, as I believe, private property is actually a necessary part of any positive conception of human freedom, the pursuit of Marx's 'emancipated' state will involve embracing a contradiction. Nevertheless, the conservative must try to find his remedy – since it is in the solution of this kind of problem that the possibility of a modern politics resides.

Ends, Means and Labour

The alienation of man is manifest first in his attitude to his work (or 'labour'). Work must not be thought of as just any kind of activity which terminates in production: machines do not work, nor do horses (not, that is, in the sense that I intend). Work is a form of rational conduct, which has, or can have, both end and means, and which is engaged in as a matter of intention – even when the labourer has no 'choice'. It was Marx's contention that work is the *primary* activity of man, since it is only through production that the edifice of society, and the leisure which accompanies society, can be erected. A man is alienated in his work, and from his work, however, when he is able to see it only as a means, and not as an end. The distinction between end and means is hardly clear enough to allow this description to stand unqualified. Let us ignore for the present the Marxian diagnosis, and try to give a direct characterization.

In writing this book, I am working. Moreover my work is a means to an end – in fact to several ends. (I might hope to earn money through its publication.) However, it is also an end in itself, in that I seek to write this book for the sake of it. The activity of writing is something which I not only desire but which I also value. It *means* something to me, as the idiom has it. I have already suggested that the idea of an end or value involves implicit reference to a realm of shared and public things. To value an activity is to have some sense of its objective worth, which in turn involves the presumption of a public world (actual or possible) in which that activity has an honourable place. In viewing my activity as an end I therefore enact my sense of myself as a being in potential relation with his fellows. In doing what I value I find my identity as a social being confirmed. Hence I not only remain at one with my activity, I also remain at one with myself and, potentially at least, with my fellows.

Such a case may be contrasted with that of a slave, forced against his will to perform some repetitive task in which he can take no interest, and the profit of which lies always with another. Such a man does not desire to do what he does, still less does he value it, unless he is of that stoic frame of mind recommended by Epictetus, in which the mere consciousness of slavery is sufficient to constitute a refined mode of freedom – a frame of mind which we cannot assume to be the common property of the common man. The slave can see his labour as a means, but not as an end. As a result he is not *confirmed* in it: his own identity is not present in what he does. He sees what he does as *exacted* from him, and himself not as an end but as a means. In being alienated from his activity he becomes alienated from himself, and from the 'species life' which constitutes his essence.

The Industrial Process

Lying behind these very brief descriptions of two contrasting states of mind is an important idea of personhood, the idea that men as rational beings are persons because 'their nature already marks them out as ends in themselves – that is, as something which may not be used merely as a means' (Kant). It was the distinctive advance of the Hegelian phil-osophy to suggest that we can treat ourselves as ends only if we treat others as ends, and that in each case our activities must involve some concrete notion of the value of what we do.[65] We can therefore be possessed of the autonomy which Kant valued above all other things, only if we live in unalienated union with our fellows. Our very being as individuals presupposes immersion in society. In so far as modern man stands in danger of losing his freedom, it is not only on account of the despotisms which threaten to engulf him, but also (and this is more im-portant) on account of his state of alienation from the social context which would once again imbue his activities with a public meaning. (For it is the state of alienation which, in inviting despotism, makes despotism possible.)

If we present the concept of alienation in some such way, we can see, both that it is indeed a condition of modern consciousness, and also that it does not necessarily have its roots in private property, as Marx sup-posed. Nevertheless, the belief persists that it is precisely private prop-erty, and the capitalistic modes of production which stem from it, that have reduced the labourer and the clerk to the position of slaves. Yet the loss of identity between man and his world seems distinctive, not of capitalist modes of ownership, nor of the institution of private property, but rather of the industrial process, the artificial division of labour,[66] and the large-scale absorption of the public life of man into the ethos of work, so that fulfilment and value seem not public but private affairs, to be pursued only at home. Man no longer fully enacts his identity with his fellows, but works *alongside* them without feeling the value of what he does. Certainly the institution of private property was not always associ-ated with this feeling; nor for example were the capitalistic modes of production introduced by the great banking families in medieval and Renaissance Florence. (Or if Dante lived the life of alienated man, then let us not complain that we must do so too.)

It is true that, for Marx, 'industrial capital is the realized objective form of private property' [67] – in other words, that without private prop-erty the industrial process as we know it would disappear. Such an asser-tion stands in need of proof. And the proof must not be trivial. It would be trivial, for example, to assert that, since private property is a pre-condition of the industrial process, it is therefore a source of the evils which attend it. (For what remains of that assertion when it is shown that private property is also a precondition of society?) No such criti-cism can be serious until accompanied by a full description of the alternative.

124

The Slander of Private Property

Some (Marx included) have tried to turn on its head the argument that I gave for private property, in order to establish a *direct* connection between private property and alienation, bypassing considerations about the nature of production. They have argued that, in seeing the end of his work as *property*, man terminates all his activity in an object, and therefore comes to see value only in objects and not in the human activity which they represent. In order to find his own value, therefore, he begins to represent himself to himself as an object, as something that may be bought and sold, a means among means. Man becomes his property, and is dehumanized, both in the pursuit of property and in its possession. The point has been expressed by Fromm [68] in the idea that property has become an 'idol', and in being enslaved to an idol man is himself reduced to an object, frozen into thinghood. (The origin of this is a peculiar theory of Feuerbach's concerning the nature of religion.)

The argument is both more popular and more suspect than the one which I in part endorsed. There is certainly a peculiar conception of idolatry lying behind it. Those great idolators who once inhabited the Aegean would certainly not have recognized themselves in Fromm's unseemly portrait, any more than the author of the *Divine Comedy* could be recognized in Feuerbach's description of religious man. For the Greeks, the worship of gods in rivers, trees and artifacts was part of a process whereby nature became human, and man something more dignified than any merely 'natural' thing. Why is there in the *Iliad* resolution, purpose, activity and character beyond almost anything else in the literature of the world? Surely, it is because the Greek hero had wholly imbued his world with rational will, and made of it a perfect image of himself. And private property played an essential part in the image that he thereby fashioned.

Possession and Consumption

The slander of private property becomes more clear if we return to our original description, and draw a distinction between possession and consumption and, correspondingly, between durable property and exchangeable goods (or commodities). There is a difference between a man who pursues something out of appetite, in order to satisfy the appetite in the consumption of the thing, and a man who pursues a thing from some conception of its intrinsic value, not in order to exchange or consume it, but in order to possess it. The object of an appetite does not have the character of an 'end', in the special sense in which ends are the province of rational will. It is, rather, a means to the satisfaction of desire, and is consumed and abolished in the act of gratification.

In order to clarify the distinction that I have in mind, I shall consider first, not the institution of property, but the realm of ordinary human relations. Specifically, I shall consider the distinction between lust and love. Here there is usually no question of legal ownership. But there is a clear contrast of attitudes which may find its equivalent in property relations. Lust may be satisfied by many things, and takes its nature from the fact that its objects are equivalent means to the satisfaction of a single desire. Love is satisfied by the individual object, and exists only in so far as that object is seen as end in itself and therefore irreplaceable. Love aims at a form of 'possession'. (Consequently, lust has a market value, whereas love does not, and the elevation of the market as the sole principle of value must involve the forswearing of love – cf. the opening scene of *Das Rheingold*.)

I mention the example, because it shows the absolute difference between animal appetite and the human attempt to 'possess' something, in the sense of making it part of, and an extension of, oneself. In the case of a person this attempt may seek fulfilment in the institution of marriage; in the case of an object, in the institution of property. Hence the highest form of ownership is that of an object desired for the sake of its beauty. This desire excludes the consumption of its object, and does not regard the object as one among equivalents. Working back from such examples towards the kind of self-conception that is involved in them, one will recognize that there are many aspects of the relation of ownership which cannot be seen in terms of consumption, and which are characterized by the thought of an object as in *some* way intrinsically desirable (though it will also be to *some* extent exchangeable, even if only under the pressure of necessity). In particular, one should mention again all those aspects which come under the notion of 'household', the aspects through which the domestic image of man is constructed. These are pursued, not through the urgency of animal appetite, but through the desire to construct a thing of value, in which human relations, property values and aesthetic meanings are usually all inextricably mingled. Things of the household may not be considered to be fully durable, but they are ends and not means, to be possessed and not consumed. To the extent that they possess this essence they will be regarded as in part irreplaceable, as a house is irreplaceable by the insurance moneys that 'represent' it. (The degree of permanence is less important than the nature of the relation to oneself. A car, a herd of cattle, anything which a man has cherished at least in part for what it is, and in which he seeks to reflect his identity as a social being, comes to validate for him the relation of ownership. Although it is the fate of cattle to be slaughtered and consumed, one would have to be very stupid not to understand the grief of a farmer whose prize herd, stricken by disease, is condemned to destruction by authorities, who nevertheless restore its market value.) Some part of what I am getting at can be understood through the art of interior painting. The Dutch and Venetians, for whom portraiture became an obsession, developed this art along with that of 'isolating' objects in their human significance. In the Dutch interior we see, simultaneously, an exploration of the self in its freedom, and a representation of the ultimate value of *things*. The portrait will contain some arrangement of reflecting things, which, conceived under the aspect of ownership, are seen as representing to the world the inner life of a room and its inhabitant. In still life, we see further the attempt to overcome through art the attitude of consumption, to represent as end what is normally seen *only* as means. The dead rabbit is the rabbit 'reduced into possession', to use the legal phrase. The apples and the silver dish stand in a real but temporary relation to each other, and that relation is a reflection of the soul of man as the spirit of domestic freedom conceives it.

The Fetishism of Commodities

The reader may doubt the need for such a fanciful digression; however, we are discussing not elementary facts of economics, but subtle features of the self-image of man, features which art makes directly accessible to us in the way that volumes of political theory may not. As I said in the last chapter, the attitude of consumption is different from that of possession, and the ascendancy of consumption belongs, not to the essence of property, but to its pathology. We can now see why that is so. For if a man's efforts are entirely directed towards the accumulation of objects which have no other relation towards him than that he may consume them, then none of his productive activity presents him with a coherent picture of the ends of conduct, independently of his mere subsistence as an animal being. Property – now reduced to the status of 'commodity', i.e. to its fluid, expendable form – no longer has a distinctly human character. It is in a world of mere consumption that people become prey to that 'fetishism of commodities', persuasively described in *Capital*,[69] in which the constant pursuit of the expendable and the replaceable negates the fulfilment of rational life. People come to live in a world of means without meaning, for the commodity is only a means to its own consumption, and consumption is not an end in itself, since nothing pertaining to the self is changed by it. (The ascendancy of the technocrat is already a sign of this species of 'fetishism'; and seeing one's life under the aspect of means, with all one's desires transformed into appetites for this or that consumable, then one can 'live' the political organism too only as means, and not as end. It would seem that not capitalism, but rather a form of technocratic socialism, would be the natural accompaniment of commodity rule.)

It is true that the distinction between possession and consumption is a matter of degree. And it is true that consumption is not an evil but a necessity. Nevertheless we must draw distinctions between the various activities which have property as their aim. And then we see that the *mere* pursuit of consumption, without the development of a nexus of property rights, constitutes part of the pathology of personhood. Some thinkers have denied the distinction that implies this. Followers of Veblen would say that the only difference here is one of 'conspicuousness'. A man accumulates property only in order to make its consumption more spectacular. But why then should there have been private patrons of art, or the development of that material and visual intricacy known as civilized living? The English gentleman is known and respected precisely for his ability to make consumption as quiet and inconspicuous as breeding allows.

In those reflections we might see why a conservative should be dissatisfied with economic theories which advocate – as the sole remedy against recession – the active stimulation of demand. For what is this active stimulation, if not the transformation of property into its most fluid, most expendable, and most meaningless form? It must inevitably involve the generation or extortion of superfluous appetites, at the expense of social and personal fulfilment. The question poses itself : why should a man labour, if all he acquires is *that*? Would it not be better to wind down the economy so that needs alone are satisfied, and all the rest is leisure? The suggestion is not yet coherent, since leisure itself must be tolerable, and the problem of alienation may arise all over again. The issue of leisure is, indeed, an important one, and we shall not have a clear conservative dogma in these matters until we have discussed it.

It is important to see, in fact, that the distinctions which I have tried to make cannot be reflected in economic theory, construed as an exploration of the basic laws of accumulation and exchange. The animal nature of man imposes an exchange value on everything, simply by forcing that exchange under the impact of necessity. When a man is starving or in danger of his life, then (unless he has the heroic nature which *homo economicus* is forbidden by science to have) the artifact òf self collapses. In such circumstances the exchangeability of everything becomes suddenly apparent. There is a degree in all this, and those two facts between them settle a market value even on objects which cannot normally be seen under the aspect of exchange. The later Marx, who sought to derive his description of the unhappy condition of labour from an all-embracing theory of economic value, therefore passed over the distinctions to which I have referred. In doing so, he was forced to drop the concept of alienation as the description of the unhappy consciousness, and replace it with that of exploitation. It follows tautologously from the labour theory of value that any man who is able to sell nothing but his labour must work without payment for another (his master) who robs him of his surplus labour-hours. But there is no movement of logic or reflection that would force us to the conclusion that this is how the wage labourer must *see* himself in his activity. (Consider a Mississippi boatman of the kind described by Mark Twain.) Any suggestion that the state of man under capitalism *must* be an unhappy one is eliminated. Or rather, everything depends, not on the theory of exploitation, but on the psychological implications which are still contained in the idea that the commodity is a 'fetish'. The question of the 'state of man under capitalism' is a question, not of economics, but of social psychology.

Ownership and Control

It seems, then, that there may be features of modern society which tend to the negation of rational satisfaction, and that they may go together. The first is the mechanization of production, and the associated artificial division of labour; the second is the fetishism of commodities. They each have the same tendency, which is to present the world as one of means only, and not of ends, a place where rational life is replaced by consumer calculation. It has been thought that in such a world men, forced to see themselves as objects driven by appetites that they do not understand, live detached from their social life, rarely achieving direct and natural union with their kind. Politics then stands in danger of being overwhelmed by economics, the philosophy of utilitarianism governs the workings of the administrative intelligence, and people are given over, as Arnold once put it, to modes of thought which are 'mechanized and external'.[70]

But no change in the control of the means of production will suffice to alter this: if a factory labourer is compelled to view his activity as means, then this is so whether or not the final product lies in the hands of the individual, the collective, or the state. For it is the nature of his activity, and not the form of control, which imposes this picture upon him. Likewise, it is not private production which turns objects into ephemeral commodities. One thing that can have this result is mechanized production, which makes not true objects but only replicas; and replicas, because the measure of their value lies only in their quantity, and because they are of necessity replaceable by some other exemplar of their kind, stimulate the market in commodities, since they can be used and thrown away. The direction of human activity towards these things itself creates the appetite for them, so that men may be alienated not

129

only in their activities but also in their desires. Their desires are extorted from them, or imposed upon them, by their participation in a world which devotes itself to the manufacture of objects which have no relation to genuine human need.

If man is alienated it is indeed because he does not fully belong to his world. The world of commodities is a world of ephemera, whereas man's *rational* need is to see himself as part of something lasting, and in all his true urges towards property, that instinct is his guide. However, the description that I have given has been necessarily stark. I have described an extreme, not because I believe that it locates the present reality, but because it presents us with the contrasts in terms of which to envisage the actual complexity of the modern world. Only a minority of workers participate directly in mechanized forms of labour; the rule of the commodity is only partly established; in general – and nowhere more than under modern capitalism – the relation of men to their work is varied, complex and imbued with intimations of, even if not the reality of, genuine satisfaction. Nevertheless, although the reality lies somewhere between the extremes of alienated labour and the natural, social, man, who finds his duties in his station, his station in his duties, and his work and leisure as equally harmonious offshoots of himself, the reality is one that must be faced by any political outlook. As I have argued, there is no cure in the transfer of ownership. On the contrary, if, as Marx says, the real grief of labour is that 'its product . . . stands opposed to it as an alien being, as a power independent of the producer', how much more will this be so if the nature of labour remains mechanical, while its end product becomes a mere abstraction, seen to belong to no particular man, being the concrete embodiment of no intelligible interest? Nothing is more frightening than the prospect of the rule of the commodity in a wholly socialist state. In such a state, the degradation of property becomes absolute and irremediable, and, as in Huxley's *Brave New World*, the world of objects benignly consumes the world of men.

In the attempt to make sense of the condition of man under modern economic arrangements I have strayed from the path of politics into difficult regions of human psychology, and what I have said is inevitably contentious and one-sided. But before proceeding it is necessary to return to the political realm and to reassert the one important fact that the philosophy of 'fetishism' overlooks. This philosophy envisages property not as an institution, but as a form of mindless attachment to things. The institutional reality of property lies, however, in the nexus of property rights. This nexus is a human artifact; but it is an indispensable artifact, one which arises inevitably out of man's desire to belong to his world and to find fulfilment in it. It is part of private property to possess a right of way across another's garden, a right to seclude yourself in a private place, a right to wear a suit of clothes, to eat at a certain table, to dispose of the clippings of your hair and toenails as need or fancy should dictate. There could be no society without such rights, since it is part of social nature to claim them. (To suppose otherwise is to suppose men to have social relations with their kind, while remaining in a mere state of nature towards *objects*.)

Now the condition of alienation from one's kind exists only to a certain degree, and always in *some* degree. Suppose that the final culmination of labour in a 'right of use' is forbidden, or that a 'right of use' cannot translate itself into domestic life (where rights exist as the embodiment of personal values). Then labour must remain in a state of alienation, a means without a social end. It is not private property which generates this state. What, then, is its cause? The hypothesis considered was this: alienation is the product of the *forms* of production. These forms do not require private property. They exist wherever there is mechanization, an artificial division of labour, and an artificial stimulation of demand (whether or not demand can embody itself in property rights). If we accept that hypothesis, then we might think it necessary to destroy these habits of production, and these patterns of demand. To do so would, of course, require tyrannical and oppressive measures, measures which could be carried out only at the risk of social disorder. But suppose we do accept the hypothesis, then we will have to admit that 'profit sharing' and 'worker control' contain no remedy. The former offers an added inducement to the labourer, but it cannot change the conditions in which he works. On the contrary, it is more likely to keep him attached to them.

However, the hypothesis is an uncertain one. We cannot claim to know what generates the 'fetishism' that I have described. Sometimes, in cases of collective danger, men will throw themselves willingly into arduous detail labour. For the end of action is now immanent in all the processes that lead up to it; the spirit of social unity imperative and absolute. End and means are one and the same, and no fragmentation of the labour process can sunder them. The labourers who rose at five each morning to work on the construction of Spitfires were certainly far from the condition that I have described. Admittedly, their state is not our state, and to perpetuate the war-time feeling of camaraderie, to which many still look back with nostalgia, is secretly to long for the resumption of war. Nevertheless, they present a vivid example, demonstrating the precariousness of any theory through which we might seek to explain these elusive phenomena. One thing, however, is certain. The condition of war is not the normal one. If labour is to have a meaningful end, this must not be just because it has a vivid common purpose.

The State of Leisure

What, then, in all this confusion, is the most cogent political dogma? I have tried to describe one of the sicknesses of modern humanity, and to separate the description from the diagnosis. It would be unprofitable to proceed without facing the question of policy. Is this state of things irremediable? And if it is not, is there anything that a *conservative* might do, by way of advancing towards its resolution? Some might regard alienation as merely one of the inevitable but tolerable imperfections that characterize every social arrangement. But that is hardly plausible. Alienation is not a condition of society, but the absence of society. It may lie beyond the purview of liberal politics, but, for the true conservative, its existence poses a direct political problem.

The condition of alienation involves the perception of self as object, propelled towards a satisfaction that is merely animal and individual, partaking of no community with one's kind. But, while certain conditions of labour may generate this outlook, leisure, properly conducted, does not. Whatever image a man may derive from his leisure will have a tendency to imprint itself upon his work, not necessarily by 'making drudgery divine', but by reminding him of the end towards which his activity is directed. The reality of civil life is therefore intimately bound up with the quality of leisure, and it is in the nature of leisure that the conservative will see his principal support and motive. A builder, for example, confirmed in some ideal of dignity and serenity, will attempt to imprint that character on his work. He will 'do the job properly', for that is the kind of man he is. Another workman, lacking the consolation of a dignified private life, may see his activity only as the prelude to some act of personal consumption. He will work without pleasure and without pride. The difference between the two has nothing to do with ownership. The material reward is the same – a set of counters in the game of exchange. But there is a difference in the two men's image of what they are doing, and of themselves as agents in the doing of it. That difference reflects two separate experiences of social life, and this social life exists not merely in work, but more particularly in leisure.

In the next chapter I shall demonstrate how the ends of life may develop in leisure. If these ends exist, then they must become part of the motive of labour. It is evident that there is, and can be, no easy way of making them so. It is difficult now to believe in a world of craftsmen, formed according to the gospel of William Morris, each imprinting his image on the object of his labour and so seeing the end of labour in the means. But it may be possible to extract from that ideal a sufficient picture of the possibilities, a picture from which to work for the restoration, both to the labourer and to the bureaucrat, of the dignity which the industrial process and the ethos of individualism combined to take away. But these are delicate matters of policy, by no means to be solved by panaceas. The situation is as much worsened by the fraud of 'public ownership', as by the undiluted process of the 'market'. If we study the history of the labour movement, from the agitations of Francis Place, through the struggles of both Tories and radicals on behalf of factory legislation, to the final tottering of the Labour Party in our day, we find that the objectives of that movement have been either accomplished or removed. The dissatisfaction which lingers points therefore to no evident remedy. The longing persists for humane relations between those who work together, and for a satisfaction in labour that will make it something more than a means to its own prolongation. Factory institutions – clubs, teams, festive days – confer social unity on those who work there. But they do so because they import into work the attributes of leisure. It is to the state of leisure that we shall therefore turn, in order to understand the manner in which social unity might remain a political enterprise.

The Narrow Historical Perspective

But at this point I must take account for the last time of a persistent worry. Throughout this chapter I have employed conceptions which a true Marxist would regard as unimportant. I have been discussing the social appearance of things, believing that politics must engage with this appearance. And how things appear is how they appear to *me*, *here*, *now*. Thus, if tradition is integral to conservative politics, it is because it represents, not history as such, but history made present and perceivable. (See the argument of Chapter 2.) The historical perspective to which I have several times alluded may be unconcerned with such things. It rises above the world of activity and searches for a comprehensive pattern, a pattern divorced from present politics. Consider the Marxist view of history, according to which social appearance moves in obedience to laws which are hidden from the creatures who obey them. Such a theory is unsympathetic to policy, and unlikely to generate it. (It is not surprising, therefore, if Russian foreign policy has changed so little since the time when Marx warned against 'the immense and unresisted encroachments of that barbarous power, whose head is at St. Petersburg, and whose hands are in every cabinet in Europe'.[71]) The sentiments that I have expressed belong to 'bourgeois humanism' and inevitably reflect the station to which history and upbringing have consigned me. They are destined to disappear, together with every dogma, policy and project that I could presently imagine. No one can fail to be impressed by such a prediction. It is hardly surprising if this narrowing perspective dominates

133

the thought of our times, constantly recalling us from the business of politics to the spectacle of history.

I have already given reasons for rejecting the great prediction in which the Marxist theory culminates – the prediction of man in his 'emancipated' state, without private property, without greed or exploitation, without ideology or religion, in a state of complete and lasting brotherhood based on nothing but the supposed desire for it. But if we abandon the great prediction, what of Marxism remains? Only this striking, convincing, and yet futile hypothesis: that the nature and movement of society may be partly explained (in so far as anything so complex can be explained) in terms of the productive forces which constitute its active principle, and the economic structures (the forms of control) through which those forces find expression. Such an hypothesis has no evident bearing on political activity. Its lesson for the conservative is no more obvious than its lesson for any other political being. If it refers to inexorable processes which political activity cannot change then it is of no greater significance in politics than is the theory of anatomy in friendship. If it refers to processes that we can govern and control, then it is useless until we know the direction in which we wish to bend them.

The narrow historical perspective shows that, knowing too much, a man may be uncertain of everything. Faced by the complexity of history, he sees his activity as absorbed in the impersonal forces which propel him. Nothing is more tempting, in such circumstances, than the 'reductive' view, the view of man reduced to his own self-interest. And if not the self-interest of an individual, then the self-interest of a 'class'. It is a necessary but trivial truth, that the class which benefits from some historical process is the class whose interest is served by it. It is a necessary but trivial truth, that the exercise of power lies always with the powerful. It only remains to describe the process of change in terms of the self-interest of the powerful, and everything falls into place. The theory is almost vacuous; but for that very reason there is no fact which it cannot appear to explain. But for the man who takes this reductive view, the present is clouded in mystery. To justify his activity is to show that it presages or permits the ascendancy of some other, future, state. To take his will from his surroundings is simply to surrender to the powers that be. If he sees himself as agent, it is because he has projected himself forward into another world. He does not belong to *this* world; he is at odds with everything that has nourished him. To sustain his self-image therefore, he begins to glamorize his posture of detachment, to arrive (by negation) at the imaginary 'purity' of the social outcast.

134

Self-conscious Alienation

The channels of intellectual expression are flooded with the products of this self-conscious alienation. And it is partly due to its morbid insistence that men have been persuaded that all things have changed beyond redemption. Perhaps the best way to illustrate the phenomenon is through an example. I shall consider the attempt by R. D. Laing and his followers to subvert the values of family life. This example has the singular merit of being not only self-glamorizing but also evangelical, so that its political meaning will be immediately apparent.[72]

The Laingian attack on the family has an idealistic, Rousseau-esque and romantic beginning, and shows in diminutive form the philosophy of *Émile*, in a world which Émile could never have inhabited. But its development makes use of a familiar instrument of subversive rhetoric, a juggling with the distinction between appearance and reality, in order to show that the way the normal man envisages things is somehow upside down, that his vision, being conditioned by 'myths', is mere 'false consciousness' or 'ideology'. Now it is a useful first step in subversive thinking to represent itself as 'demythologizing', and to set up, as its enemy, something called the 'bourgeois man' for whom myths are supposed to be uniquely necessary. (The fact that the real intention is to replace old myths by new goes unnoticed in the reader's conviction that he, at least, is not an example of that 'bourgeois man', whose myths nevertheless seem to include every aspect of the self-image of every normal person.) Laingianism begins, not from the family, but from the idea of mental illness. A natural attitude to mental illness is to suppose that the mentally ill are set apart from others and, if necessary, submitted to clinical treatment, as a *result* of their illness. This process of isolation is not thought of as an attempt to deprive the patient of his freedom; for, in his illness, freedom is already lost. The master thought of Laingian psychiatry consists in the reversal of that doctrine. It is the patient who becomes ill (and so sees himself not as person but as animal or object) because the clinical scientist treats him so. The patient has not lost his freedom: it has been stolen from him by the clinical refusal to treat him as a person. And from that arises his 'ontological insecurity', his sense of himself as 'object'. In short what others would regard as illness is nothing but 'alienation' in its purest and most innocent form.

This pattern of argument has a special appeal. For it presents a vivid picture of alienation as something that is *brought about*, and suffered in its full form by an innocent victim. And the true causality of the phenomenon is in the established order, of which the clinic is only a kind of administrative 'voice'. It is only necessary to add that the real culprit – the institution which begins the process of alienation – is the family, in particular that mythical 'bourgeois family' upon which every form of blame can be safely pinned, for the subversive charm of the argument to be complete. The argument now enters the area of 'relativity' where, since nothing is certain, anything can be proved. To put the ensuing doctrine in a nutshell it is this: the concept of mental illness is really a fabrication; the sick person is the innocent who dares to express his alienation as it really is. 'Mental illness' is invented as a label for him: it denotes a kind of crime, a reprehensible rejection of the values inherent in the established social order. Through this invented concept 'bourgeois' society attempts to suppress the complaint of the alienated, in the interests of the family as its master institution. (This is all well set out in Laing's *The Politics of the Family*.) Thus the 'schizophrenic', who on one view (that of Aaron Esterson) is none other than the scapegoat who has enacted in himself the full alienation implicit in the structure of family life, *has* to be cast in the role of a thing. The procedure of the clinic is to make him accept that role, and come to recognize that he can reacquire a self only by accepting the values that he had tried to reject. This covert plot of bourgeois society, being 'ideological', is necessarily self-confirming. There is no way in which this fully alienated being can establish the validity of his posture in the face of an overmastering 'normality' which he is unable to oppose.

Of course there is a great body of myth behind these doctrines, and it is no part of my concern to unearth it in its entirety. Its guiding features (implicit in Sartre's *Saint Genet*, Foucault's *Histoire de la Folie* and many other works in the theology of modern satanism) are the belief in a covert identity between 'bourgeois', 'family' (which as we have seen between them constitute the essence of 'property'), 'paternalism' 'authority' and the rest; the belief that the complex state of 'alienation' can be transferred to a chosen victim by a kind of unconscious conspiracy; and the much odder belief that, in exposing the culprit, we prepare the way for a radical freedom of the self, beyond anything envisaged in that tradition of substitute 'freedoms' proposed by the rulers and ideologists of bourgeois society. This myth, like any other, is bound to be vulnerable to historical fact. (For example, it seems to be true that the aristocratic family is more paternalistic, the peasant family more authoritarian, than the family known as 'bourgeois'; that the middle class has shown an ability to dispense with the family which has never been shown by those classes which are normally thought of as economically 'beneath' it, that the family has in consequence only ever seemed dispensable in those societies which are dominated by the ideology – manifest indeed in the Laingian outlook – of bourgeois individualism.) But that in itself is no objection, at least, not if the theory can show that it has a coherent application that will enable us to make sense of, and perhaps even avoid, the condition of alienation which besets us.

Its confusion is revealed as soon as we ask how the man who has suffered the extreme of alienation is to obtain that psychological freedom which the family denies. The first thing that he must do (or that his parents must do in recognition of their guilt) is to transfer a considerable amount of money to an existential analyst, who is characterized by the fact that he does not see it as his task to 'teach the other to conform to society or to any particular morality', but rather to help the other to 'actualize his own existential possibilities'.[73] Not only the process of recovery, but also its end result, are described in terms that are internal to the individual. He must simply 'actualize' his 'possibilities'. The clinical process should be one of self-determination and self-discovery, in which the individual is answerable to no one but himself, and need accept no morality that is not of his own devising (since values are in any case only 'relative'). But of course there is a paradox involved in recognizing (as the myth recognizes) that the self is a social product, while at the same time attempting to give it a 'freedom' that is merely individual. What does this 'freedom' consist in? It is doing what you want to do, or rather 'actualizing your possibilities', and therefore doing what you *really* want to do, that is, so long as you do not murder, or steal, or perhaps you can steal – at any rate, sexual intercourse of all kinds is permitted, or perhaps not when there is danger of 'harm' to another, or when children are involved or something, but at least. . . . What emerges is either incoherence, or precisely that 'particular code of morality' which the psychologist was supposed to avoid. And it is likely to be very similar to (if not even identical with) the code from which the patient began.

The Laingian myth is interesting because it is both subversive and also inherently paranoid. It sees the world in terms of a struggle between 'us' and 'them', and the cure of alienation as a kind of internal victory over 'them'. It has no place for the idea of reconciliation, since it recognizes the validity of nothing outside himself with which the individual can be reconciled. Indeed, to recognize an 'objective', 'public', 'established' or 'external' validity would be to abandon the entire picture upon which the myth depends – the picture of the essential innocence of the *truly* alienated man, the man who is seen as 'mentally ill'.

Such doctrines trade in the concept of 'alienation'. But a proper understanding of that concept must lead us away from the individualistic notion of a paradisaical innocence, and return us to the idea of the self as social product, a product of that structure of 'primary' relations for which the word 'family' is the normal label. For the mass of men the ego can discard the social morality which created it only by an act of

137

suicide. If that is what innocence consists in, then innocence cannot be desired. As soon as the psychotherapist recognizes that his patient might have a need to be reconciled – with father or mother, his conscience, the moral order, with God – and might be suffering precisely because of that need, then he must reject the idea of an 'essential' innocence, and with it the whole subversive rhetoric with which Laingian psychiatry has sought to conceal its nihilism.

One might say that, if anything has enabled bourgeois individualism to display a brave and appealing face, it is precisely the pattern of conflict, guilt, and reconciliation. This is the Lutheran ideal of conscience. To remove that ideal in obedience to the Laingian imperative is to destroy what is valuable in the bourgeois outlook, while retaining what is not. Without it, there is only individualistic rhetoric, a fragmentation of all serious values, and the sickly sentimentality about the sufferings of others which serves to mask a fundamental lack of sympathy for whomsoever might be successful, healthy, or strong. The Laingian vision is, of course, as far from being truly 'anti-bourgeois' as any other theory which depends upon radical fashions for its appeal. Its unscrupulous sentimentalization of individual experience adapts it perfectly for the market in cut-price ideas; while its flimsy ideal of an 'inner' purity fosters that sublime illusion of the middle classes, the illusion of an individual united with no social order, who has nothing to lose but his mental chains.

We see, then, in such examples, an extraordinary attempt on the part of alienated man to glamorize his condition, precisely by detaching himself yet further from the institutions and allegiances that would restore him, and which are still enjoyed by those who have yet to recognize their 'bondage'. This phenomenon – the self-consciousness of alienation – has many features, apart from the relativistic outlook that I have described. It belongs with the yearning for a purely individualistic religion, and for an instant return to paradisaical blamelessness. The psychiatrist (who does not reprehend but only listens) fulfils the role of confessor, and, because he demands no contrition, seems to endow the self and its past with the redeeming attributes of God and Eternity. It suffices to 'know oneself' in order to discover that one is, after all, a noble figure, cheated of happiness by some primeval tragedy, but free from personal blame. Thought, detached from objective reference, becomes self-directed and fetishistic. So too does activity. The alienated man regards his body not as one among human bodies but as *his* body; it must be improved and refined through exertions that have no connection with the activities of daily life. Whether he be banker, teacher or wine merchant, he will not allow his body to take on the shape which those occupations generate. He holds his body aloof from them, subjecting it to rigorous discipline in park or gymnasium, flattening every protuberance that would detract from its charm, and polishing every part which might indicate its vitality. Meanwhile his soul lies spread on the analyst's couch, morbidly discoursing on the ways in which body and soul have failed each other.

Idleness and Leisure

The narcissism to which I have alluded points to a new difficulty. For many people the world has been narrowed, confined within the limits of the individual. (Hence the latest American magazine extolling the cult of physical fitness bears the title *Self*.) We have witnessed something singular and strange, which is the pursuit of alienation, and the almost deliberate subjection of leisure to its rule. Leisure becomes idleness, the cog which turns but moves no part in the machine.

Such fads and fashions are important. For we live in a world of mass communication, and the self-image of alienation can be preached *ad nauseam* to all mankind. Members of the media often believe, with every appearance of sincerity, that it is part of their duty to present to the common man the image of 'alternatives' – alternatives to everything by which he might otherwise be content to live in a state of security. Most people are sufficiently *bornés* to view this kind of thing with incomprehension. But, in so far as they are affected by it, the result is not a broadening but a narrowing of the mind, a detaching of the individual from all that confirms him and makes him real, a jettisoning of him from the world that he recognizes, into an inner seclusion, where he is lost, valueless and alone.

The problem is one of ideology – of how society is *perceived*. The self-conscious spirit of alienation, wishing to represent its own detachment as a form of purity, actively seeks to describe the world in abject terms. It asks us to see alienation everywhere, even where social bonds are most immediate. Glamour for self comes through scorn of others. But in becoming articulate the spirit of alienation opens itself to opposition. It can be understood and thwarted. It is no longer a mysterious thing, but a commonplace babble of the urban mind, the mind of the impassive and idle observer, for whom the world is nothing but a heap of facts.

There is no salvation in that nihilistic outlook. We are compelled by our nature to believe that the web of human destiny is spun by human hands, and that there is no point at which the pattern need disintegrate. Of course, no conservative will be happy to see the spread of relativism, since people need values and have them only to the extent that they believe in their authority. It is a philosophical question whether relativism is *true*. Politically speaking, however, it is better that few men believe it. Like Plato, a conservative may have to advocate the 'Noble Lie'. He might in all conscience seek to propagate the ideology which sustains the social order, whether or not there is a reality that corresponds to it. For even if there is no reality, the politician can in any case do no better than provide new myths for old. As we shall see, there is a difference in quality between the myths of leisure, and the myths of idleness, and we shall always have reason to prefer the first to the second.

Concluding Remarks

We have seen the final incompetence of liberalism to confront or examine the major problem of modern politics: the problem of the actual cohesion of society. Alienation, I have argued, does not stem from private property, nor even from capitalist production, but, in all probability, from complex and inescapable features of industrial prosperity. There is no clear socialist attitude towards it which does not base itself in a discredited prediction. But the conservative will feel able to confront alienation, once he has seen that it is a matter of degree. There will always be issues of policy, both small and large, in which the advance of alienation can be arrested or reversed.

However, there is a vociferous opposition to the attempt. The historical perspective, for all its protestations to the contrary, wills the destruction of society. It rises to self-consciousness only by glamorizing its detachment, attempting to destroy the capacity either to respect or even to perceive the social order that surrounds it. 'Demystification' makes a mystery of human things; it must therefore be part of conservative dogma to describe the world, not in neutral, but in ideological terms.

Uneasy though the state of modern man may be, it is not hopeless. Everywhere one may see, sometimes sick, but for the most part living, the forms and institutions through which ideology is formed. We must now examine these institutions, and the special kind of autonomy without which they cannot flourish.

140

CHAPTER 7

The Autonomous Institution

I have suggested that it is part of conservatism to resist the loss of ideology. The 'value-free' world is not a human world: it contains no intimation of society. But how should ideology be generated, and what form should it take? This is not, to repeat, a question of policy, but a question of dogma, a question of the fundamental suppositions at work in determining the particular political choice.

It is of the first importance to develop the conservative viewpoint in the proper order, working always towards the full conception of citizenship, and never tacitly assuming it as a premise. (As it is assumed, for example, in the liberal aim of freedom, or in the idea of a 'Natural Right'.) Thus while it is true that conservatism involves the maintenance of a hierarchy, and the attempt to represent the unpleasant fact of inequality as a form of natural order and legitimate bond, it is impossible (and not just impolitic) to begin from this. There is an order of argument and conception, which leads the conservative onward to the hierarchical state. And that order begins in what is smallest, in the activities where man first relinquishes his savagery for the comforts of civilized life.

The Need for Roots

Our task is to locate the practices and institutions in which we are at rest, and in which we view ourselves not as means but as ends. Such practices must themselves *contain* the ends of conduct, and hence must generate the ideology through which those ends can be valued and pursued.

It is perhaps not a happy description of this task as a search for 'roots', for although that word captures the ideas of tradition and allegiance which the conservative requires, it also suggests a kind of nostalgia which he cannot afford. Naturally, nostalgia for the past is more reasonable than nostalgia for the future; nevertheless it is, like every form of sentimentality, a way of 'standing back', a refusal to engage in the practice

141

of rational life. It consigns its subject to inaction, and its condition is that of Dante's Limbo: without hope, living in desire. While the love of country and tradition is to some extent confirmed in the nostalgia with which the Englishman views his eccentricities, his countryside, his architecture, and the ghostly presences of England, this nostalgia depends upon the possibility of something more concrete – of a deliberate activity of citizenship of which it provides only a sepia-toned reflection.[74] Here we see the distinction between true conservatism and mere 'conservation'. There is no sound politics of antiquarianism. It does not matter whether the 'antique drum' sounds from the pastures of rural England, or from the warm backyards of the slums You can follow it, but you cannot lead it.

Our search, then, is for the immediate forms of social participation, those forms which intelligibly present to the citizen the fact of his public life, and so generate his values. As I suggested, it is to leisure that we must look to find the essence of these forms. They contain the intimation of value, and hence must be 'autonomous'. Yet their autonomy may require protection and sanction through law. In order to explain those thoughts I shall consider examples, beginning with the simplest, which is that of sport.

Competitive Sport

Competitive sport represents an activity in and through which millions of people constantly express their allegiance to town, region and country, and their sense of the 'proximity' of these things. The aim of a team is of course to win. But winning is defined by the rules of the game, and cannot be achieved except within the institution that defines it. Thus the aim of football is both internal and highly complex, not only defining but also entirely permeating the activity which leads up to it. No footballer can possibly see his activity 'as a means only' or himself as 'alienated' in that activity from his self-identity or from his 'species-life'. Here is a tangible and rational end, which permeates and redeems the means to its realization. Moreover because it has that character, the player can be an object of immediate imaginative involvement. Social feelings of an elaborate kind can be projected on to his activity. His strength, courage, loyalty and perseverance warm the hearts of his following as though they were their own. The spectators are confirmed as social beings in the act of watching, as the team in the act of playing.

The example is an ancient one, and of some importance. It shows that, for men, the truly satisfying activities are often those which have no purpose. The full elaboration of the attitudes which are congealed in spectator sport would take us far from the realm of common politics.

(Consider the psychological complexities of Pindar's Olympian Odes.) However, because the example is so clear, it deserves analysis. I have referred to 'autonomous institutions', and autonomy can mean many things. It can mean financial independence; or it can mean self-government. In the sense that I intend, however, an institution is autonomous if its purposes are peculiar to it. Whatever aims the institution has are aims which can be achieved through that institution alone. (One cannot win at football by playing cricket.) Of course there might be an external purpose too. A football team may earn money. But it is autonomous so long as its real meaning lies within itself. Members of a team sometimes earn money; but the interest of football for those who are immersed in it lies in the game and its outcome. Later I shall raise the question of how far this 'ideological autonomy' requires financial and administrative independence. For the moment, such questions must be held to one side.

An autonomous institution is not just *any* arrangement with an internal purpose. It is also an *institution*. It is an arrangement which can outlive its individual members, and which offers to them a transcendent bond of membership. It is in such arrangements that activity most readily generates and confirms an ideology. The case of spectator sport demonstrates this. The player who actively pursues the goal, and the spectator who pursues it only vicariously, both rehearse therein a sense of shared identity. The pursuit symbolizes the social values which are inspired by it – loyalty, courage, competition, endurance. Here, then, is a simple and spontaneous institution, which, in pursuing its internal purposes, generates a consciousness of social ends.

The Politics of Institutions

A Marxist thinker once argued that the 'hegemony of a social class' is exercised largely through organizations that are (or seem to be) 'private'.[75] By private he meant (in part) what I have meant by 'autonomous'. Being an Italian, he identified the principal autonomous institutions as the Church, the municipalities, and the schools (all since penetrated by the middle-class ideology whose best-known expression is the Red Brigade). There is an important insight in Gramsci's assertion. Autonomous institutions and class distinctions go naturally together. But this is not because a ruling class requires such institutions in order to exercise its 'hegemony'. On the contrary, it is the institutions themselves which, in diversifying human pursuits and occupations, make stratification inevitable. Later I shall explain why this is so.

The example from which I have begun is of immediate polemical significance. For it is fairly obvious that the interest in competitive sport is both spontaneous and, if not exactly classless, more characteristic of the lower than of the upper class. (It is not 'winning' that defines the ethos of the field or the grouse moor.) How, then, could a Marxist claim that *this* kind of private association is the instrument of class dictatorship? King James I struggled (against puritan opposition) to legalize Sunday sport. This was not merely because it eased the minds of those who might otherwise turn to less pacific interests. It was also because many of the people wanted it. Who, in this petty struggle, was active in the pursuit of class hegemony? The Stuart Court? (They did not, as Parliament sought to demonstrate, really possess it.) The puritans? (They hardly constituted a class, even though Parliament for various reasons supported them.) The populace? (Not, for the Marxist, a coherent possibility.) It is the institution that comes first; 'hegemony' (if it exists) is at best a consequence.

The Family

The point becomes more obvious if we turn to the second example, which is that of the family. It hardly needs saying, in the light of all that has gone before, that the support and protection of this institution must be central to the conservative outlook, and that changes in the laws which are calculated to loosen or abolish the obligations of family life, or which in other ways facilitate the channelling of libidinal impulse away from that particuar form of union, will be accepted by the conservative only under the pressure of necessity.

The family is the prime focus of leisure, and the origin of self-respect, being the first institution through which the social world is perceived. It is also autonomous; it is a form of life which has no aim besides itself. What is achieved through family union could not be achieved in some other way. The family is therefore instinct with concrete values, providing each of its participants with an unending source of rational objectives, which cannot be specified in advance but which arise from the realities of family life. The child who saves his pocket money in order to make a gift to his mother acts under the first impulse of rational conduct, acting towards an end the reality of which is more vivid to him than anything he might abstractly understand. Thus he makes his mark in the family, learns the 'ways of freedom', discovering himself and another through the act of love. To say that such a child is learning the habit of alienation (because it is *money* that mediates and fulfils his aim) would be to utter some kind of morbid joke.

I have previously taken the family as the clearest example of an institution based in a transcendent bond. It is a clear example because it is an extreme one. Almost nothing about the family union rests in contract

144

or consent, and none of the values which spring from it can be understood except in terms of the peculiar lastingness with which it is endowed. While a football team has an identity which can outlast the contributions of particular members, it is not for its lastingness that it is valued. (Although it would be of less worth were it to be constantly formed and re-formed without some trappings of continuity.) In the case of the family, however, the experience of continuity is immediate and dominant. Parents play with their children and so re-enact childhood. They also educate them, preoccupied by the future character and happiness of their offspring. This motive reaches forward beyond death, and also backward, to a sense of former dependency and a remembrance of the parents who protected it. In the commerce between parent and child, past and future are made present, and therein lies the immediate and perceivable reality of the transcendent bond which unites them.

It matters enormously to parents that their children should be something, and not just anything. It is natural to seek preferment and security for them, and to be pleased when they acquire it. It is also natural to wish to pass on to them every attribute that might survive one's own departure. The principle of legacy – whereby a household outlasts its members – is therefore a consequence of family love. So too is the principle of hereditary privilege. This is not confined to a particular class. It is as much a desire of the labourer to work for the advantage of *his* child (rather than anyone else's), as it is a desire of the landed aristocrat. Massive legal interference in legacy and hereditary right constitutes a direct affront to the securest of social feelings. It is therefore impossible for those affected by it to be persuaded of its legitimacy. In this matter conservative politics directly supports and stems from a fundamental social bond. It seeks to conserve social continuity, so that people may envisage generations which stretch before and after them. Without that vision much of the motive for procreation is lost, and the child himself becomes an accident, an anxiety, and a reminder of one's isolation. The parent at rest with his child has a dominant desire, which is this: what I am and what I value, I here pass on. The complexity and consolation of this thought has never been better captured than in the passage of *Ulysses*, sometimes known as 'Ithaca', in which Bloom projects towards Stephen the image of himself as father. Reflect on these things, and you will see that, however vociferously men may declare their attachment to other ideologies, in their most solemn and silent innervations they are naturally conservative.

Autonomy and Law

The two institutions that I have so far mentioned are basic examples of the institutions of leisure. They are inevitable manifestations of civil life, and no one can doubt either their essential autonomy, or the value that is bound to it. Moreover, they each generate ideology, and so ratify the impulses which find expression in them. In the first case the ideological content is precise: it is the assertion of team spirit, competition, courage, endurance, all connected with particular loyalties to place and people. In the second case the ideological content is more general, embracing everything of value, everything that might be 'passed on'.

But now, what attitude can the law take towards these institutions, and towards their claim for autonomy? The question is an interesting one, and provides a clear demonstration of principles for which I argued in Chapter 4.

The institutions of sport require little protection, since their spontaneity makes them immune from internal decay. Nevertheless, they have a special kind of existence in law. This existence is extremely difficult to define, precisely because of the need both to grant legal status and to conserve autonomy. The natural form of such spontaneous institutions is that of the 'unincorporated association' – an entity which, since it is not a legal 'person', poses complicated problems for the law. Where there is an external purpose, then it is usual to 'incorporate', in order to safeguard assets and liabilities should the purpose fail. But because associations arise spontaneously, simply to do the peculiar and often indefinable things that they do, it is impossible to lay down by fiat that they should incorporate as soon as formed. The law is forced nevertheless to *recognize* them. It therefore grants protection and assigns liability to institutions which possess no legal personality. The great jurisprudential problem of the unincorporated association stems precisely from the fact that the only *legal* relation that can exist among its members is a contractual one, whereas the *reality* of the institution transcends that of any contractual arrangement.[76] A vivid example, then, of the law accommodating itself to civil society. It is also an ancient one, responsible for some of the finest intellectual constructs of Roman law, such as that of the *universitas*, adapted in medieval times to its present use.

The family illustrates the point more poignantly. Every legal system includes a branch known as 'family law', which is specifically concerned with the obligations generated by this peculiar transcendent bond. The bond of marriage is not contractual. Marriage is chosen, but its obligations are largely indeterminate, being generated by the institution itself, and discovered by the participants as they become involved in it. (It would be absurd for a man, faced by his wife's mortal illness, to say 'I did not bargain for this', and so think himself justified in leaving her.) Family law has changed in response not to individual claims, but to variations in the social arrangement. The law offers its protection to that arrangement conceived as a whole, not to this or that individual grievance that may arise from it. (Consider why it is, for example, that the law seeks to make divorce, not easy, but difficult.) Once again one notices the collusion between social values and legal norms. And since there is no external purpose to marriage, there is no definite point at which the law will say that the obligations of marriage have ceased. The obligations endure until the parties can persuade the law to absolve them.

Education

The two examples that I have taken illustrate certain fundamental conceptions to which the conservative must refer in his quest for ideology. But naturally enough, these two simple and natural institutions do not exist alone in any developed society. There are as many autonomous institutions as there are forms of social flourishing, and not all of them will have political significance. I shall consider, as my principal example, the institutions of education, through which politicians have rightly perceived that a major battle for the soul of society must be fought, some moved by a sense that education has certain inherent 'standards', without which it imparts nothing to the value of human life, others moved by the knowledge that it also confers 'privileges' which they demand to be more widely distributed. Through the smoke of this quarrel we discern the vital distinction, between education as means, and education as end. Whether or not there are 'privileges' involved in education is not a matter that is likely to concern the conservative. It is in the nature of all institutions to create privileges and determine their distribution. Forced redistribution of a privilege that arises internally will usually abolish the institution. Imagine for example the attempt to spread the privileges of kingship to more than one: to succeed is to abolish both the institution and the privileges which attend it. Egalitarians have been divided in the matter of education (in their practice, if not in their rhetoric). Some aim at an 'adjustment', others at the direct subversion of the whole arrangement. I suspect that only the second are thinking reasonably.

Education is a peculiar process, and one that presupposes that its subject is a rational (or potentially rational) being. Whatever the degrees and nature of the discipline administered, a child receives education only if his rational nature is engaged in the process. He is learning, reasoning, reflecting, and whatever constraints hold his nose to his book, his mind will be held there only by the exercise of his own understanding. This process is so very different from the kind of 'training' that is administered to a horse, where there is no question of understanding but only of exact performance, that it seems absurd that anyone should have confused the two. But it is a fact that they have, and that the word

147

'conditioning' has been used to refer to all forms of disciplined education, as though the process and the product differed in no material particular from the training of a horse. The purpose here is the usual one: to 'demystify' or 'demythologize'. It is the purpose of refusing all validity to the lived surface of human things and to the concepts (such as that of the 'authority' of an institution) which are contained in it, allowing only an alien picture of the 'depths' of established power. And it is of course not authority but power which trains the horse, and which treats the present horse only as a means to his future and more useful incarnation. Education too involves the exercise of power – power vested in a school or teacher. But school is conceived as an arena of legitimate and not merely of established power. Of course, there is a problem as to the true origins of a teacher's authority in the modern state. One of the undesirable consequences of making education (or rather the attendance at school) compulsory at law is that it becomes impossible to construe the teacher's authority as acquired by parental delegation, so that the two institutions of home and school do not so readily call upon the same fund of natural deference. The teacher's authority is seen as arising independently, and if it can rely on no agreed 'fiction' for its validity other than the inherent right of the state to command obedience, then the institution of school is in danger of losing its autonomy, and becoming prone (as in France and Italy) to whatever disaffection may attend the authority of the state.

Nevertheless the absorption of school into the machinery of state is not complete, and the idea of educational autonomy is still vivid in public life. This is because the aims of education are again internal. In education a child learns to pursue things which must be pursued for their own sakes. The values of these things are not (as a rule) to be seen in any end to which they lead, but rather in their capacity to embody social meaning. (Consider the study of history, of language and literature, even of natural science and mathematics as these first capture a child's attention.) In a bureaucratic society it is natural that men should attempt to see education as a means (for example, a means to social advancement, or to a 'higher standard of living' or, more cynically, to reducing unemployment). To take that view is to abolish educational values in favour of other, usually more material interests. But the value of education lies precisely in the *immediacy* of the aims involved in it. The reasons for learning a subject that is truly educational lie in the subject itself. Education, and the accretions of tradition which surround it provide their own direct picture of a human aim. In education, therefore, we again see the reality of leisure, and the restoration of human things. Naturally, not all men would wish to spend their leisure in education; nor would they gain from doing so. Apart from the family, we

148

find a division among autonomous institutions, some adapted to the fulfilment of one person, some to the fulfilment of another. And the very
idea of 'autonomy' suggests that this must be so. Values can be diverse
and yet not conflicting, and, so long as there is a suitable establishment,
to relate the activities of men in every autonomous field, these can exist
in relative independence without risk to the social order. I shall return
to that point in the next chapter, but will first concentrate upon a complex issue in the theory of education, in order to reveal just what is meant
by educational autonomy, and just why it is politically desirable.

Relevance

The issue is that of 'relevance', and the confusion which it has introduced into the study of the humanities in higher education. It is one of
the merits of university education in England that it has been built
around certain recognized academic disciplines, with 'combined degrees'
taking a subordinate place, governed by the intellectual standards of
their constituent subjects. (And this has been made possible largely by
the standards of education achieved at school, which sometimes enables
a university teacher to assume a knowledge of English grammar, of
Latin, of literature, of history, and of calculus.) But the humanities
stand opposed to certain 'factitious' degrees, usually put together out of
pieces that have no obvious connection, in order to continue the illusion
of an educational process that may in fact have ceased by the age of
ten. The invention of these degrees is connected with the rise of humanities departments in polytechnics. Their guiding principle is the principle
of 'relevance', according to which education is not an end but a means,
even in those non-technical disciplines where such a construction might
have previously seemed impossible.

The first gesture towards 'relevance' is the creation of the 'second-
order' subject, or 'meta-discipline'. Consider again the art of football.
This requires great skill and physical endurance, but little education.
'Football' might appear as an American 'course unit', but it is not a possible subject for an academic degree. Which is not to make any deleterious comparison between the amateur footballer and the graduate in
sociology, but rather to repeat the point just mentioned, that autonomous institutions are of their nature many and varied, so that the ends
of one cannot be transported into the practice of another without detriment to the values achieved through both.

Now someone with a consuming passion for football, and with no
ability to play it, might wish to communicate his enthusiasm, preferably
in comfortable and leisured circumstances. And others, equally deficient
in aptitude and skill, might welcome the opportunity to live for three

149

years at public expense, thinking about nothing but football. A subject is therefore invented, called 'Football Studies'. It contains a variety of papers (or 'modules', as they would be called at the polytechnic). For example, there is the sociology of football (involving the study of the structure of crowds and the 'charisma' of players); the philosophy of football (beginning from Aristotle on *catharsis* and centring on the role of alienated labour in spectator sports); the psychology of football (containing dry reflections on how the motion of the ball is perceived by the human eye, together with much wetter reflections on 'football and the unconscious'); the ethics of football (including studies of 'social responsibility' and the true origins of hooliganism in capitalist society); the history of football and its relation to class structures; and so on. This subject is welcomed by many sociologists – for it is 'relevant' to the working-class student, and directly applicable to social and political problems facing the world of today. It is more useful, the sociologists suggest, for a student 'faced with the problems of living in industrial society', to study for this degree than for a degree in classics or theology. The degree is adopted at once by the University of Stirling (where for sociological reasons, classics and theology are already banned). Famous football teams, anxious for publicity, endow chairs and studentships at their local polytechnics. Soon the academic world is saturated with teachers of football studies, and the dole queues are swelling with their graduates.

The Artificial Degree

The example is hypothetical, but it parallels the history of 'Black Studies', 'Women's Studies', and now 'Gay Studies' in the American colleges. The method – that of throwing together rival disciplines and of creating artificial links with areas of 'relevance' and 'social concern' – is also widespread in England, and an important part of the misunderstanding of education that ensues, when education is conceived as means and not as end. Its first product, and one that has proved most damaging to our educational system, was the formation of 'Schools of Education', and the invention of the entirely fraudulent Graduate Certificate in Education, which conveys neither the understanding of a subject nor the ability to teach it, and which is now required of all who would work in a state school and who lack the advantage of a non-university training. It has produced schools of 'American Studies', of 'Communications Studies', even of 'Industrial Relations'. It has the support of sociology (or 'Social Studies'), and is entrenched wherever sociology has been victorious in its aim to represent itself as Queen (or perhaps Lord Protector) of the Humanities. For sociology, containing no agreed theoretical structure, and having all but eliminated from its content the reflections of those perceptive men who founded it (men like Durkheim and Weber, whose style was the historical style, of elevated critical insight), may exist largely as a vehicle for mindless statistics and political prejudice. There is nothing to which it cannot be applied, and its application is always and inevitably 'relevant'.

It is, of course, hard to identify the quality which makes a discipline genuinely educational. Some might think that the factitious nature of the second-order degrees derives from the factitious unity in its first-order subject. To say that there is one subject of 'Communications Studies' for example – which focuses on speech, gesture, painting, music, television, politics, and photography – is, they might argue, like saying that there is one theory of holes, which covers the holes in shirts, in shoes and in the earth; black holes, key-holes and holes in an argument. (Perhaps such a subject might venture to ascertain the truth of Laurence Sterne's assertion that 'there is more sin and wickedness have entered the world through key-holes than through all other holes put together'.) But the absurdity in the imaginary subject of 'Hole Studies' is of a different order from the absurdity of 'Communications Studies', being more like the absurdity of the latter's continental rival – 'semiology' – which dominates what remains of the humanities in Italy and France. It stems from adopting a first-order classification which indicates no theoretical basis, where no other basis is possible. But even when the first-order subject has no theoretical unity, it may still have a practical unity. And in the case of the major humanities – English, classics, history – there need be neither theory nor practice involved in their study, but something more elusive, and, from the educational point of view, more valuable than both.

The true failing of the factitious degree lies in its second-order nature, and its consequent attempt at an unearned 'relevance'. It is precisely this which keeps the discipline at one remove from a serious understanding of its subject. For consider the hypothetical subject of 'Mathematics Studies', a degree option for those who dislike the barren rigours of old-fashioned mathematics, and who wish to see mathematics in its 'wider context', as a discipline potentially relevant to the problems facing industrial man. This degree offers courses in the sociology of mathematics (which studies the effect of 'disprivileged background' on mathematical eminence, and of mathematical competence on social standing); the psychology of mathematics (which is again very dry except for the 'module' devoted to the unconscious); the philosophy of mathematics (which, being unable to presuppose any competence in logic, stays with the jargon of 'dialectical' thought); and the history of mathematics; with options in 'Mathematical art', 'Pythagorean cosmology', 'Number symbolism', and 'The universal history of the number 2'. Nobody will suppose that such a subject produces understanding, either of mathematics, or of anything else. It is impossible to gauge what qualities of mind would be adapted to it, or what value or discipline would result from its pursuit. The subject is a pure fantasy, and even sociologists might consider it unfair to inflict it on students – at least, not before 'further research'.

What is wrong with such a subject is not that it leads to no career (for that is true of almost every academic subject), nor that it is unscientific (for that is true of English and philosophy, both of which have been represented by thinkers of the highest seriousness as representing the best in academic discipline). What is wrong with the subject is simply that it involves no critical reflection on an identifiable field of study, and, for that reason, embodies no educational value. The true critical appraisal of mathematics is reserved for those with a mathematical understanding. It is not possible to emerge from this degree in 'Mathematics Studies' with the ability to assess or dispute a mathematical proof, or with any other intellectual ability that would show itself in reasoned critical reflection, applicable beyond the range of examples which have nourished it. The second-order subject has neither the scientific method required for an established body of results, nor the more elusive discipline of the humanities, the discipline which leads to genuine critical intelligence.

Critical Intelligence

It is difficult to define critical intelligence, because it is difficult to make clear, in terms external to the specific forms of education, just what the value of education is. But let us consider another example, that of history. History is not a true science : it has few theoretical concepts and no experimental methods. The facts which it studies are studies not under the aspect of scientific law, but under that of everyday memory and perception. Nevertheless, the study of history involves the direct application of intelligence to those facts, rather than the self-conscious reflection upon its own 'methodology'. We speak of a historical understanding, which is something distinct from both factual knowledge and philosophical reflection, involving an ability to reason about history, to understand historical processes, and to bring an intellectual training to the assessment of familiar and unfamiliar facts. Sometimes a historian explains, sometimes he merely describes; in every case he is bringing into relation matters which illuminate one another, and showing some perception of their human essence. Voltaire, Hume and Mommsen were great historians, simply on account of their articulate understanding of human things; and while accuracy is a precondition of historical analysis, it is of no independent significance. No one can regard the licence of Thucydides as a flaw in his historical understanding. On the contrary, his brilliant procedure of 'dramatization' succeeded in representing an entire human episode as intelligible, in a way that no 'science' of historical facts is likely to rival. It is through such examples that the idea of 'critical intelligence' is understood.

What I have implied about history is true also of classics, philosophy and English, at least as these are usually conceived. But nothing similar is true of the second-order discipline. It should be obvious, therefore, that the 'relevant' degree is either associated with a serious first-order discipline (which will then naturally take precedence over it, as mathematics takes precedence over 'mathematics studies'); or else wholly independent. And in the latter case it can involve no discipline at all. For it will then be without any coherent body of facts to study, and without any critical method to apply to them.

I say that all this should be obvious, but apparently it is not so. Not only do our children have to suffer daily from the fraud of 'Education Theory' (the ascendancy of which ensures that those who most love and understand a given subject are those least likely to teach it in a state school). There is also a sign that governments will listen to those for whom education is a means to an end, and at best a branch of technology. They might therefore come to consider that second-order subjects are a source of genuine understanding and useful expertise. For example, a prominent member of Lord Bullock's Committee on Industrial Democracy was Professor of Industrial Relations (a course not unlike the 'Football Studies' envisaged earlier) at the University of Warwick.[77] This perhaps bears on the single most ominous feature of the report, which is its uncritical adoption of uneducated fantasies, such as the fantasy (now impossible to believe outside the closed world of sociology and educational theory) that 'self-expression' is essentially 'creative', and that 'education' has made unprecedented advances since children were encouraged not to 'accept authority' but to 'make up their minds' on the subjects presented to them. Indeed, at every point in the report where it is possible to insert an idea (and these are few enough, both premises and conclusion having been preordained by the then ruling party) we find similar fragments of sociological liturgy.

What is wrong with this liturgy is not that it embodies palpable falsehoods or unwelcome prejudices. What is wrong is that it is the expression of a mind working at one remove from its subject. Sociological liturgy is simply the easy rigmarole of the 'second-order mind', which substitutes ready-made concepts for critical understanding. Such a mind has no ability to test its ideas against reality, or to understand reality through its stock of ideas. The ideas are essentially factitious, often deriving from subjects which have neither method nor theory; and the facts, being of that complex kind which must be understood in terms not of scientific theory but of critical intelligence, are essentially elusive, being masked by nothing so much as the blind statistics which are the common recourse of a mind devoid of concepts. To the second-order mind social realities are not merely incomprehensible, but also imperceivable. Here indeed we have the true 'mind' of alienated man, of man for whom the pursuit of means has swallowed and obliterated the understanding of ends.

The Autonomy of Education

I have dwelt on the example at some length, not merely because of the neglect of such issues in recent politics (which has had time to consider less the fate of higher education than that of school), but also because it illustrates the most important points of principle that I wish to generalize.

First, it shows the manner in which education, as traditionally conceived, contains its end internally, so that the aims of education are inseparable from the means by which we arrive at them. It is in this sense, and no other, that the institutions of education are autonomous. Their autonomy is not necessarily (although it may be in fact) affected by the financial dependence of educational institutions upon the funds of state. Everything here depends upon the attitude of the state, just as it once depended upon the attitude of the Church. Naturally, if government lies in the hands of men who are active in the pursuit of 'social goals', and who do not recognize the validity of any independent reason, then *every* autonomous institution stands in danger. But this is an accident of policy. And the accident is not peculiar to the goal of 'social justice': it follows equally from the single-minded pursuit of economic growth, or international power, or racial purity (although not of tradition, since that is a goal which is internal to the institution).

Second, the example shows that, precisely because its aims are internal, the institution of education may be a point where the values of men are formed, elicited and sustained. Education is essentially a 'common pursuit', formed by traditions, and directed towards recognized ends. To engage in it is to envisage a form of community, and to desire it is to desire that community. It is in this kind of pursuit that the grip of alienation is loosened, and fellowship is born. Naturally it is very difficult to describe that fellowship: but it is shown in the ability of such an institution to survive, just as it is shown in the institutions of entertainment and sport. There is something about the ends of education which prepare them for this social interaction – something about their close-

154

ness to human life which is perceived in the pursuit of them, but lost in the description.

Values and Institutions

A third point should be noted, which is that the values implicit in the pursuit of education (or in the participation in any such autonomous arrangement) cannot necessarily be reduced to a code of conduct, a system of rules, or an ideal of the 'good for man'. They consist, rather, in an intimation of a human world, and of access to that world through understanding. Hence the idea of education coexists with that of culture. In the language provided by a culture all ideals and morality may be more finely and more accurately expressed. Nor is this peculiar to education. Every arrangement which allows men to value an activity for its own sake will also provide them with a paradigm through which to understand the ends of life. The working-man's club, the business-man's marina, the institutes and societies of urban and rural life – however remote these may seem from some snobbish ideal of fellowship – are in fact the stuff of human society. Through them men and women are able to define themselves, and to discover the language in which to express their common essence. Such institutions contain a 'presentiment', and in terms of that presentiment other aims may be located, and sometimes described. An autonomous institution provides language, custom, tradition, fellowship: a member may transport that mental framework to the rest of life, and so make sense of himself as a political being. Indeed one may say that the autonomous institution is the alternative to the ceremony of initiation which anthropologists have presented as the essence of primitive life.

Such reflections enable us to see that an institution which has an internal aim may also have an external value. Consider friendship. The internal aim of friendship is the well-being of someone loved, but its benefit is greater than that. What the friend desires is only a part of what he achieves. He achieves, for example, a reciprocal affection, and his own security. But he does not aim at what he achieves, for that would be to treat the other as a means, and so to deny the spirit of friendship. Likewise a man will achieve education only if he desires it for its own sake. But what he achieves will be far more than that. He will acquire the ability to communicate, to persuade, to attract and dominate. In any social arrangement, such abilities must constitute advantage; but education can never be pursued as a means to them; even if they are its natural consequence.

Standards

Because the nature of education is determined by its internal aim, these advantages can be removed from it only by the destruction of that aim. And it is precisely against this aim that the ethos of 'relevance' is directed. Similarly, when conservatives uphold the ideal of 'standards' in education they too are appealing to an aim which can be made sense of only by consulting, as I have, the institutions of learning, and not by reference to any advantages that those institutions may incidentally confer. And in fact the autonomy of the institution *must* require that emphasis on standards; an institution does not have a defining purpose unless it purposes to do the thing *well*. And that means that it may have to be selective, not just in respect of those it engages to administrate it, but also in respect of those it chooses to admit. No more than a football team can a university admit just anyone; and if we see this demand of education extended backwards along the line from maturity to birth, we shall have to concede that there always will be a point – the point where the pursuit of educational values becomes earnest – at which *some* form of selection takes place.

Moreover, while of course this does nothing to defend one manner of selection against another, it does immediately grant privileges to those who come to the institutions of education better prepared – for example to those whose parents encourage them to read and write, to those better endowed with natural intelligence, to those with the resources to employ private tuition. Even if we abstract from every *actual* educational arrangement, including those which have sacrificed the aim of education to that of social equality, we are forced to recognize an inevitability here: a collusion between the institution of the family and the later institutions which prepare a child for the adult world. Unless we are to snatch our babies from their mothers and rear them in battery farms, this 'inequality of opportunity' could not be eradicated. And even then its full eradication might depend upon depriving the gifted child of some part of his natural understanding, say by subjecting his skull to repeated hammer blows, or by removing parts of his brain.

Autonomy and Advantage

Now the social advantages conferred by autonomous institutions are not all of the same kind. Some institutions provide only the fellowship of their members; others (such as education) provide indefinite possibilities of relating to people who do not necessarily belong to them. And this is natural: some people do not want their universe to be indefinitely expandable – expandable, say, beyond the yachting club or the publi house. Others do. Thus while every institution may return privileges that are not involved in its aim, these privileges cannot be of equal value. Some enable men to form ties of a new kind, others only ties of the same kind. In the former case – which is the case of education – the achievement of the aim accords also the gift of social mobility. (Even if this is not obvious *a priori*, it will, I think, prove to be a historical truth.)

The persistence of autonomous institutions already points in the direction of a stratified society. The advantages conferred by education are to some extent transmissible across generations and, even if not so transmissible, are inevitably bound to divide those who can obtain them from those who cannot. The example shows, incidentally, the absurdity of the aim of 'equality of opportunity'. Such a thing seems to be neither possible nor desirable. For what opportunity does an unintelligent child have to partake of the advantages conferred by an institution which demands intelligence? His case is no different from that of a plain girl competing with a pretty girl for a position as model. The attempt to provide equality of opportunity, unless it is to involve massive compulsory surgery of an unthinkable kind, is simply a confused stumble in the dark.

At once, however, we see an enormous political issue arising. It is not possible to provide universal education. Nor, indeed, is it desirable. For the appetite for learning points people only in a certain direction; it siphons them away from those places where they might have been contented. There are many occupations, from the operation of a signal-box to the management of a bank, which require great natural intelligence, and yet which may not appeal to someone who has been flattered by the gift of education. It is important for a society that it contain as many 'walks of life' as the satisfaction of its members may require, and that it accord to each of those stations its own dignity and recompense. And it must somehow safeguard itself from the loss of virtue in trade, profession and industry, by sustaining institutions which are not educational, and which do not merely siphon away gifted people to the point where they no longer wish to do what in fact they might otherwise have done willingly and well. It is difficult to express this point of dogma without sounding either patronizing or totalitarian. For it may seem that one is committed to the view that people should be 'confined' or 'allotted' to their station. But it is not necessary to believe that the authority of state need be invoked in creating the rival institutions of leisure, even if it may concern itself in sustaining them. Nor need it be invoked to forbid or encourage the adoption of any particular way of life by any particular citizen – provided, of course, that the way of life forms part of the civil order.

The Stratified Society

Nevertheless, we must face the question of how the institutions of leisure connect with those of work. It is difficult to imagine a contented society in which every signal-box was manned by a graduate in sociology, every shop-floor directed by a philosopher, and every field tilled by a barrister-at-law. It is necessary that the state should contain institutions which make contact with these occupations, where the leisure of men may be exercised and recompensed without the adoption of some specifically educational purpose. But what attitude can the state take to such a vast and complex problem?

Now in fact it *has* taken an attitude over recent years, and it is an attitude which has proved destructive of social values. The dictatorship of the Treasury has ensured, first that children with no aptitude for education should stay at school long after their lack of desire for it has become clear to them, and second, that large amounts of public money should be invested in the polytechnics, in the hope that these same children might be encouraged to stay off the streets for a few more years. The institutions of education, in other words, have been used largely as a means to reducing unemployment. There are two reasons for this. First, educational institutions have strong and definite internal purposes, which enable them to survive considerable abuse. Second, they have become dependent upon government support, and therefore answerable to government policy. And here we see that, when it matters, autonomy can be subverted at once if there is financial dependence on the state. It is for this reason that the best schools are now in private hands.

This attitude of state has made the problem of leisure acute. Not only have the institutions of education been subjected to pressure at variance with their internal purposes. More important, the rival institutions through which idleness might be transformed into leisure have been neglected. Without these rival institutions a child is forced, either to engage in the pursuit of education, or else to remain uselessly at school until suddenly ejected, on the brink of adulthood, into a world that expects that he should both work and provide his own amusement. It needs only the absence of work for the absence of amusement to become chronic and unbearable.

The problem here should not be underestimated. Autonomous institutions can be created, endowed, and protected through charter. They have legal status, and inherent authority. Nevertheless, they are not institutions of government. They are part of civil society, and depend on society for their strength. The state may commandeer them, and they may survive if it does not also force them towards an external purpose. But it always runs the risk of confining institutions within a predetermined frame. In lending its power to one institution, it withdraws authority from those that rival it. The rivals wither, while the favourite stands in danger of being absorbed into the policies of state.

What then happens to the people who do not desire, or cannot acquire, the benefit of education? It is surely a mark of deep disrespect to force them, despite that, to spend their early years in the vain pursuit of it. There *must* be rival institutions, and they must have comparable authority. And if social stratification results, then this must be accepted. For it will result in any case, as our discussion shows. Even when all men are forced through the mill of education, some emerge formed, and others emerge formless.

What rival institutions can we imagine? The custom of apprenticeship – which, while being a part of work, also demonstrates the continuity between work and leisure – has been eclipsed by the forces of industrial production. Much the same has happened to the exercise of craft, and to the clubs and organizations which surrounded and legitimatized the activities of popular recreation. But there is a degree in all this. Consider American rural society. It is neither barbarous, nor civilized, nor decadent. It is of no great interest to the outside world, but seems, despite that, to get on happily with itself. And we find in this society a proliferation of clubs and organizations, even old habits of craftsmanship that have disappeared from Europe. This is partly due to the lack of governmental presence. The American state is not given to regimenting its citizens into forms that are alien to them, and while the resulting chaos of childish eccentricities may have little appeal to an outsider, it is clear that it is not without considerable consoling power for those who engage in creating it. The result of this burgeoning of autonomous institutions is an extreme, though formless, social stratification. In England, history and continuity constrain all stratification into the mould of a great civilization, and ensure that absurdity does not easily survive. Nevertheless, England lacks the civil room, so to speak, in which the first gestures towards institutional activity can be made. In this at least, there is a lesson to be learned from America.

The loosening of the bond between state and education might therefore prove beneficial to the English. Other institutions might arise to console them, and so find their charter and enactment in the law. Consider the following example. A child is fascinated by electricity. (It might have been wood, or metal, or some other animal, vegetable or mineral thing.) He sets it up as a hobby, designing circuits and playing with lights. It becomes interesting for its own sake. We do not have to believe, with Schiller, that it is in play that the spirit of man first finds itself;[78] we can at least agree that play has a peculiar and immediate value.

Our child also learns through his diversion the rudiments of a trade. When in later life he becomes an electrician, his leisure will turn quite painlessly to work. Naturally, too complete an absorption in his hobby is unlikely to make him fascinating company. But he will find social consolation in associating with others of a like mind, learning through them and from them, moulding his character according to the common spirit which they come to share. The result of that process is a guild of electricians. This institution has peculiar value to its participants; it proceeds to embellish itself with the customs and ceremonies of social life, and becomes the focus of both work and leisure.

The example is not so far from contemporary reality. It shows two things. First, that, left to themselves, the institutions of leisure diversify as society requires. Secondly that some institutions, such as the one I have imagined, will be ideologically impoverished. They will not confer the social mobility or the social power that is conferred by education. This may matter if stratification is dangerous. But as we shall see, it does not matter, because it is not.

It is not easy to translate such reflections into policy, except by preventing the spread of fraudulent institutions which pretend to be educational while being no such thing, and by encouraging, wherever possible, the activities which compete with them. But this difficulty in stepping from dogma to policy is precisely the difficulty of overcoming the alienation of civil society. It is not surprising if it exists, since the problem is not amenable to a panacea. Alienation is overcome piecemeal, or not at all.

Concluding Remarks

In this chapter I have surveyed certain of the institutions which provide the ends of social life. I have argued that such institutions must be autonomous, focused on internal aims. I have also tried to show how the attempt to subject them to external aims is dangerous and impolitic. The role of the state here is that of guardian and foster-parent. It cannot invade the institutions of leisure without perverting them to its own uses, and losing sight, in the process, of what those uses are.

As we have seen, important conservative instincts are upheld in the aims of leisure. The desire for continuity, the bond of allegiance, the pursuit of excellence, even the stratification of society itself, all seem to be natural and even inevitable outcomes of institutional autonomy. But now we face a problem. If envy and resentment are not to be the result of this, then we shall want to know why and how. This leads us to the culmination of the conservative viewpoint: the ideal of a legitimate establishment.

160

Establishment

Some of the problems of the last chapter will begin to seem less intractable as we consider the idea of establishment, an idea which has caused some difficulty to conservatives, partly because their flirtation with liberalism has led them to conceive the matter from the wrong end, from the standpoint of the individual. We have now advanced beyond that standpoint, and must try to formulate our vision in more political terms.

Power and Authority

Establishment comprises both power and authority. It is a plausible assumption (defended in Chapter 2), that power and authority mutually require each other. Power without authority is 'unhappy' power. It is 'at large' in the world, distributing violence without earning respect. The transformation of power into authority confers recognition, and so removes the element of arbitrary force. Power and authority seek each other. Their search is the process of politics, while establishment is the condition which their meeting creates.

This process can be perceived, and its political importance ascertained, even in the life of the individual. Consider erotic love. Love stakes an enormous claim, and demands satisfaction. Its initial gestures point towards something which may be as much feared as wanted – for the power of love may be greater than the power of the individual who suffers it. What is surprising, however, is that, even in a society like ours, in which romantic love is taken more seriously than the legal forms which arise from it, those forms are nevertheless considered necessary. Wife and husband face each other with the authority of a legal tie. Thus an elemental social force becomes constituted in authoritative terms. The resulting law has to attend, not to the initial gesture of consent, but to the felt reality of the transcendent bond which results from it. There is and always will be love outside marriage. But it is love, and not some other power, which requires the forms of marriage. In these forms the violence of love is ended, while its strength remains. The authority of an established institution protects and makes intelligible the power which seeks for it. The daily demand for love becomes a painless ritual, but in no way relinquishes its essential power; while the confused sad feeling of one who loves and is betrayed becomes intelligible as a violated right.

The example points to a political meaning. Establishment requires three things: power, authority, and the process which unites them. Moreover the virtue of establishment consists partly in the mollification of power, and in the creation of the rights through which power becomes intelligible. But to understand the value of this process, and the particular institutions that the conservative will wish to see protected through it, we must turn our attention from individual feelings to the affairs of state.

Local Government

Some conservatives, wondering how the establishment of power can be justified, have sought not for the establishment but for the fragmentation of power, through some process of devolution which has not national but local government as its aim. It is important to understand the mistake in this – and along with it the fraudulent nature of 'local government' as it is practised in England – if we are to provide an accurate account of what establishment really means.

Local government was the reality from which America formed itself. However, less and less do the states retain their individual authority. As the apparatus of constitution grows, so can it form and reform the civil society not merely in New York and Washington, but also in Oregon and Alabama. Such autonomy as the states retain begins to be seen as delegated from central government, by whose decrees the states are ultimately bound. It is only comparatively recently, and under the pressure of international politics, that the image of *the* state of America has emerged from the confused idea of Union. And what has made that image possible is the progressive rendering up of locally constituted privilege to the centrally constituted power.

Now England has never been like that, and the advocate of 'devolution' cannot really consider that he is returning to the people something which they once surrendered. (Not even when there was a definite Act of Union caused by the accession of a Scottish King.) Local government cannot be conceived as a natural or prior right of the citizen, but only as a delegation of power. It is for this reason that, while in America much of the strength of the country derives from its separately constituted states, in England, the extent of local government indicates not a strength but a weakness in the political organism. It cannot be in this way that we should derive or justify our idea of what is established.

If there were to be genuine local government in England, then the national constitution might lead us to expect that it be an exercise of delegated power. This is in fact what we find. Yet it is true to say that there would be room for something else, and something healthier, within the framework of the English constitution. This healthier arrangement would construe local government simply as an administrative organism, financed by local people, in order to supply and maintain those services which agreement and tradition had placed in its hands. These services are to be maintained both for the benefit of the community which pays for them, and in accordance with certain established principles of order and charity. There might even be, as at present, a procedure of representation, so that those who surrender their money to local administration can see that it is neither squandered nor misapplied. Perhaps the fiction could be further embellished through the supposition of local events, contests and ceremonies for which the council takes responsibility, so conferring on the community all the trappings of civil life, in the manner of the little parliament of Mastersingers so brilliantly represented by Wagner. Members of the council would be chosen in whatever way (and not necessarily democratically) from those with an interest in the identity and continuity of the local community. Their framing of by-laws would be nothing more than a ratification of custom, defeasible in some higher court. The result is the town, autonomous not in law but only in usage, created from the leisure of its members, a representation of the values of civil life. Such an arrangement wields no power beyond the power of association, and defers to the state as its governing principle. Its authority is the authority of custom, an authority which should not be despised but which stands (as Hans Sachs admitted) in need of some other protection.

Such would be the ideal of local government pursued, not as a delegation of power, but as an institution of citizenship. Imagine now a community which establishes itself in that way, setting up a common fund from which to provide schools, police, and services, with a power to house and relieve those who are destitute. Those who administer the fund are able to levy rates according to need, and to exert limited powers of compulsion. Already we are moving away from the idea of administration towards that of constituted power. Imagine now, therefore, a local council which attempts to acquire by compulsory purchase street upon street of occupied houses, in order to replace them with new and expensive dwellings for people who are neither recognized members of the community nor seriously destitute. And suppose that it proposes this scheme as its main item of expenditure, seeking to increase the rate in

order to realize it. Given the status that I have imagined for local administration, such a body would be in breach of trust, and members of the
community would be absolved from their obligation to pay rates to it.

The situation I have just described is easily imaginable, and indeed
sometimes occurs, under the actual procedures of local government.
How is this possible? First, legal enactment has made it a criminal
offence to withhold rates, and with that act of state local government at
once became the recipient of enormous delegated power. It can no
longer be governed by any variant (however sophisticated) of the law of
trusts, but only by the more lenient and more cumbersome law of administration – a law empty of those equitable principles that control not
only the form but also the content of administrative decisions. Moreover, the administrative machine does not – as in my example – aim
simply to return its resources in symbolic or transmuted form to the
community that provided them; it has external aims, aims of 'social
justice', for example, or of government policy, which require it to call
on resources that are provided not only by local people but also by central government. There is no fund of local custom that could legitimate
such a machine, since it has become subject to the purposes of state, a
kind of vast and desultory civil service. Because of this massive delegation of central power, the local council has itself become a part of
national politics: it is formed according to the party structure of parliament, and is used as a practice ground for aspiring politicians. It is thus
that a business cartel can – as in Newcastle – draw upon the power and
authority of a national party in order to overcome all the local feelings
which might otherwise oppose it. The result naturally makes a nonsense
of planning law, just as it makes the idea of a 'local' school into a
constitutional fiction.

Clearly, to proceed further in the direction of delegated power is to
cause an increasing fragmentation of the state, and an increasing vulner-
ability to corruption. As the example shows, establishment in England
does not arise at the local level, but is transferred from the offices of
state. And often, what is transferred is power without responsibility.
The citizen's attention and interest is always diverted towards the source
of power – towards the national government and the parties which compete for its operation. Hence the 'local' representative need never regard
himself as answerable to those who elected him.

Delegation and Ratification

I have advocated the existence of autonomous institutions that are not
subordinate to government aims. The question to consider is not how
they can become instruments of delegated government, but rather how

they can be ratified by established power. This is a vital question, since it seems to me that it is only in some process of ratification that the tensions created by the multiplicity of subject institutions, and by the class divisions which they generate, will ultimately be resolved.

As the example shows, the delegation of power is not in itself the delegation of authority. The distribution of the powers of state to bodies which should be *directly* answerable to the citizen diminishes the authority of the state, without augmenting that of the subject institutions. Authority becomes naked power, but diminished power, with no serious allegiance except that which stems from coercion. Every delegation which separates power from the dignity of government therefore weakens both the power and the authority of the state. It is for this reason, and not out of economic conviction, that conservatives resist the nationalization of private industry, the proliferation of the civil service, the endless and fruitless activities of 'commissions of inquiry', and all the machinery of bureaucracy with which government has found itself encumbered.

Power and authority need each other. To delegate power alone is to weaken the centre of authority. Conversely, if power and authority reside together, new powers can be made subservient to the power of the state. Thus they acquire a nimbus of the authority which it is with the state alone to provide. I shall call this process ratification, meaning the gathering up of quasi-autonomous powers as subjects. Now it is clear that ratification must occur. If there is a power at large in the state, then it must not be allowed to generate its own authority, as the Mafia does. It must either be destroyed by the state, or else hold its authority from the state. In the latter case it will be constrained, as I shall argue, into a position of subjecthood.

In exploring the concept of ratification, I shall consider various examples. I shall begin from one of the institutions of state, in which power and authority are inevitably conjoined. Having drawn certain conclusions as to the necessary ingredients of ratification, I shall consider two further cases. The first of these – the Church – is a power losing authority; the second – the trade-union movement – a power attempting to gain it. Through studying these powers, both of which lie on the edge of establishment, we shall form a picture of what lies, and what ought to lie, at the centre.

Institutions of State

Much of what I said concerning autonomous institutions could be applied, in modified form, to institutions with primary aims that are not internal, in particular, to the subordinate institutions of state. I shall

165

briefly reflect on one such institution, in order to show that the external aim may be both remote from the actual motives of the participants, and yet intimately bound up with the institution's authority. The institution I shall choose is the military, specifically the army. This is an institution not of civil society but of the state. It also stands directly for, not only the authority of state, but also its power.

The primary aim of the army is to pursue by violent means all those requirements of state that can be pursued in no other way, such as defence against foes, suppression of rebellion, and the conquest of desirable realms. (Let us ignore the question whether all those aims are now feasible or politic: the issue of 'defence' is not one of fundamental dogma, but one of seeing who one's enemies are.) Now the primary aims of the army may often be in abeyance – there are times of peace and civil order in which the army has nothing to do. Nevertheless, it sustains its social life throughout those times, and this life cannot be understood in terms of the external aims which are allotted to it. The army has customs, modes of participation, social and private practices, which in sum compose the internal character of soldiery. Involved in those practices are many internal aims and values, aims of honour, comradeship and regimental duty. And these values, while they clearly serve the end of military discipline, have an effect in the life of a soldier which transcends the requirements of his occupation. A soldier takes back to the civil world the picture of himself that he required in the army, and this picture, while it reflects the external aim of the military, is also imbued with a particular self-justifying ethos. This ethos lends itself to the respect for established power.

Person, Office and Ceremony

Certain features of the arrangement are clearly of more than ordinary importance in bringing about this respect. The first and most significant is the separation of individual from office. This exists at its clearest in the army, but is an essential feature of establishment, and part of the appeal of establishment to all those who take no immediate part in it. This separation provides an immediate sense of who a man is, what his power and position entail, independently of any personal qualities that may serve to endorse them. It provides the guidance of a 'public world' to men who cannot grasp the endless sum of mere individuality. The soldier owes respect to his officer not because of that officer's personality but because of his office. In grasping the distinction he acquires the conception of a common order to which both he and his officer belong. Naturally, personality and office affect each other, so that an unworthy man may lower the dignity of office, as a worthy office may raise the

166

dignity of a man. But it is the recognition of the distinction between the two that accords to the office and its duties a kind of objective necessity in the eyes of those under its jurisdiction. Any genuine establishment must consist of such offices, successively filled by individuals whose personality is absorbed by them. Otherwise, it will wear the aspect only of arbitrary power.

The army displays another interesting feature. This is the pervasiveness of ritual and ceremony. While the respect for office is integral to discipline and hence to the external military aim, ritual and ceremony show the army not in pursuit of its ruling purpose but simply at ease. Yet, as everyone knows and observes, military parades and displays are of immense symbolic power, glorifying participants and spectators alike, and becoming a focus of common loyalties. All recently founded states – from the South American republics, through the Soviet empire, to the petty despotisms of Africa – have exploited to the full this natural charm of military ceremony, where power, through its transformation into symbol, acquires the aspect of authority. One of the weaknesses in western democracies is that a certain coyness about these things overcomes the urge to participate in them. On the one hand lingering memories of the Great War and its indescribable stupidities lead to a reluctance to express even the smallest respect for the pomp of military display, while on the other hand the desire for it becomes sublimated into a kind of helpless nostalgia, nurtured on Elgar and Lutyens rather than on any real political allegiance. To overcome these over-delicate sensibilities it has proved necessary to shift all ceremonies of state in the direction of a civil meaning.

It is interesting to note how, in civil matters, the loss of ceremony and the loss of the distinction between man and office attend one another, so that modern presidents and statesmen, in their efforts to claim for themselves, as *personal attributes*, what are in reality the dignities of office, try to dispense in so far as they can with the ceremonies of state, becoming 'informal' only in order to seem the more extraordinary. This trickery practised on the common people, who understand ceremony beyond any attachment to the personality of their leader, has been strikingly demonstrated in the comportment of recent Popes. Pope John Paul I, for example, attempted (during the few days that the Almighty permitted his office) to transform the ceremony of coronation into a public display of private virtue, and so subjected the necessary pomp of the Church to the private vanity of appearing to the multitude as a 'humble' man. Similarly, recent American Presidents have cultivated a kind of easy-going informality, which has not only vulgarized the gestures of government, but also made the Presidents themselves into objects of purely personal opinion. It is not the President but Mr Nixon, or Mr

167

Ford, or Mr Carter, who becomes the focus of attention. And so it is hardly surprising if Mr Nixon or Mr Carter are held personally liable for actions made necessary by their office, or if they are personally blamed, resented, voted for, and discarded, purely on account of some apprehension (however misguided, vulgar or parochial) of their quality as individual men. It is important to see how dangerous it is for a state to cultivate this identity between man and office. For how can a President order the bombing of a city, if the blame is individually his? The aggressive acts of state are, for the individual, morally impossible. Rather I should die than undertake to kill so many. But acting as President, the responsibility is mine only if I act illegitimately. And it is reasons of state which require that a city be bombed. Which is not to say that 'reasons of state' should always be listened to. There are just and unjust acts, even in war, whether or not the war itself is just.[79]

In reflecting on these matters, one may come to the conclusion that, among state institutions, that of constitutional monarchy is one of the wisest. In the figure of the monarch there is condensed all the ceremony of office, and all the majesty of state. The personality of the monarch, being detached from direct involvement in government, is freed from the oppression of responsibility. And yet, through the intellectual construct of the 'Crown', the monarch also represents the entire authority of state. If honours and authority stem from the Crown, then they are seen to flow objectively, not from personal whim, but from the life of the state. The process of ratification which arises from that will bear both ceremonial dignity, and the authority which the office of sovereign contains. Hence there is no better way of ratifying power than through titles of nobility. It is partly this which has enabled England to assimilate without rupture both the upward scramble of the 'middle classes', and the upward grind of the remainder.

Ideology and Myth

But now we can see how the institutions of state have their own way of generating ideology. Consider again the example of the army. The internal organization of army life generates a common code of conduct, the call of 'honour'. And while there is inevitably a certain rigidity about this code – for it must remain in harmony with the ruling military purpose – it is one which implicitly recognizes and endorses the distinctions between men.

Now this internal code of army life is paralleled in every purposeful institution. It corresponds to the professional 'ethic', to the 'solidarity' of the workers in a factory – indeed, to precedents, duties and answerabilities which proceed from any social organization, irrespective of whether they further or hinder its principal aim. Naturally these codes can be considered usually to be of service to the ruling purpose, but this is not necessarily the case. In business, for example, the professional ethic of fair dealing can put a company at an impossible disadvantage in international trade. This internal 'code' or 'ethic' is in its turn bound up with and reinforced by the features referred to: by the creation of offices and roles, and by the disposition to ceremonial enactment (nowhere more manifest than in the organized activities of the trade unions, which re-create, in some small measure, the glory of the guilds).

It is in considering again the true meaning of ceremonial enactment that we come across the most powerful and most intransigent feature of establishment, the feature of myth. All ceremony requires a symbolic depth – a sense that it reaches below the surface of things, and touches upon realities that cannot be translated into words. It therefore constitutes an enactment of something more than the chance union of these particular participants. It seems to point them to something 'transcendent', which they may only partly understand. The emotions which attach themselves to the ceremonies of state constantly outrun the objects which occasion them. Participant and spectator find themselves taken up into something greater, of which the reality of military or political power is no more than a pale reflection. Thus there emerges the myth of the 'glory' of the nation, the myth of its absolute unqualified *right* to allegiance. It is no part of my concern to translate this myth into other words, but clearly it belongs to every national culture, determining the form of its religion, art and literature, and being reinforced with every manifestation of civil or military power. It is out of such myths that war is made, and equally peace.

Now in referring to 'myth' I by no means wish to disparage these beliefs. On the contrary, they constitute the great artifact whereby institutions enter the life of the state and absorb the life of the citizen. In a sense the Marxists are right in saying that bourgeois man robs the world of history by creating myths which represent as natural and inevitable what is in fact historical and subject to change. But they are deeply wrong in supposing that it is only *bourgeois* man who does this, and that there is some other form of man for whom the necessity would not arise. For it is clear that my rudimentary sketch of military institutions (a sketch which points to their significance in the life of any state) ought to apply to all institutions of state, in whatever form of economic order. (Even when the state is founded on the eccentric myth of its own 'withering away'.)

Religion

But this brings us to the ruling idea of establishment as it has thrived, made itself tolerable, and incorporated the various forms of life of the peoples of Europe: the idea of a Christian society. In *The Case for Conservatism*, Lord Hailsham was straightforward enough to place the connection between English conservatism and Christian practice at the heart of his political creed, arguing that 'there can be no genuine conservatism which is not founded upon a religious view of the basis of civil obligation, and there can be no true religion where the basis of civil obligation is treated as purely secular'.[80] In support of this, Hailsham quoted remarks by Burke and Disraeli, neither of whom ingenuously believed in the religion to which they subscribed. They believed, if at all, in the self-conscious manner of the romantic, out of longing for an innocence which is lost in the process of reflecting on it. Naturally there are serious and complex attitudes involved in such belief. T. S. Eliot's Anglicanism, for example, was highly self-conscious but not hypocritical. But it is implausible to suggest that Burke, Disraeli or Eliot were types of the normal religious man.

Moreover, while there is a connection between conservative and religious feeling, it is now difficult to argue for their identity. Not only does that serve to exclude from the conservative viewpoint precisely those people who most seek the means to regain it – those for whom the passing of God from the world is felt as a reality – it has also left the creed of conservatism helpless in the face of the Church's growing disposition (in its vocal parts at least) to reject it.

Nevertheless, before discussing the issue of Church and state, we must look a little more closely at the motive of religion, if only because some might think that religion is one thing and politics another, and therefore that policy can be pursued without regard to the beliefs of the ordinary citizen. Of course, political activity may be independent of the existence of God, and independent of the Will of God, but it is not independent of the belief in God. It is the possession of that belief which enables men to direct their most powerful dissatisfactions away from the ruinous hope of changing things, to a more peaceable hope of being one day redeemed from the need to do so. It follows that the state of religious belief will be reflected in the state of civil society, and will seek its constituted expression in law. To think that a politician can proceed while ignoring the actual religious beliefs of those he proposes to govern, is to view politics as a detached machinery of administration. Such a view is either unworkable (cf. Iran), or tyrannical (cf. Russia), and in any case hardly conservative.

The reflections of the last paragraph might lead one to suppose that religion is an essentially conservative force. It is certainly true that both Burke and Disraeli believed it to be so, and while their professions of faith were not necessarily a consequence of that belief (any more than are Lord Hailsham's), it is surely right to suggest the presence of a deep and complex intellectual connection which underlay their commitment. The nature of this connection can be perceived at once, as soon as we consider again the character of the social bond. This bond, I have argued, is transcendent: it contains obligations and allegiances which cannot be seen as the result of contractual choice. It is a small step from belief in a transcendent bond to belief in the transcendent Being who upholds it. The vision of another and vaster world, from the laws of which all actual obligations spring, can lend support to bonds that were never contracted. Seeing such bonds as the expression of Providence, a man will be the more disposed to accept them. He will accept as a divine command what he might reject as a personal undertaking. It is some such message, the cynic might say, that is contained in the quoted remark of Hailsham's.

Nevertheless, the acceptance of transcendent bonds does not *require* belief in transcendent beings. The Japanese, who are famous (indeed, notorious) for their willingness to accept the former, are equally re-markable for their reluctance to believe in the latter. And the Romans, to whom we are indebted for the concept of piety, were casual and even non-committal in matters of religion. (A feature which they shared with the more dexterous representatives of the Papacy.) It would seem then that the conservative vision of society can survive in the absence of clear religious belief, despite the fact that it will always benefit from its presence. However, there is nothing more dangerous to the state than the transfer of frustrated religious feeling to petty secular causes. It is such a feeling that would people the world with invalids, in order to lavish upon it the luxury of 'social justice'. In so far as religious feeling exists, it is therefore better that it be channelled towards its proper object. And if its existence sustains the social bond, then that is another reason to propagate and also to influence it.

Church and State

But we cannot discuss these issues until we have considered the nature of religious institutions. Whatever part religious feelings play in provid-ing the background sentiments of establishment, it is with the *offices* of religion that the politician must deal. So he will first have to concern himself with the Church. The power of the Church, while it ultimately depends upon the power of religious feeling, has the backing of historical precedent, hereditary privilege and popular trust. Whatever the legal position of the Church, it continues to provide the major institutions which reinforce the attachment of the citizen to the forms of civil life, and which turn his attention away from himself as individual, towards himself as social being. It provides ceremonial embellishment to every kind of leisure, apportions the days of work and the days of rest, seeks to dignify the occupations of the laity, and to support and fulfil every endeavour in which the application outstrips the aim. Be its fundamental doctrines true or false, it is nevertheless the most considerable of all political institutions whose authority is not identical with the authority of state. It is therefore fully established in European life, so much so that all the institutions to which I have referred have recourse to it as the one binding principle which joins them together. Consider the family, education, even the military.

But it is in the relations of Church and state that we find one of the most difficult problems for conservative dogma, and one of the most elusive features of establishment. It needs little knowledge of history to realize that much of European politics was until recently determined by the state of these relations. Every attempt to break away from Rome has led to the incorporation of a rival Christian church into the establishment of state. The influence of the Church of Rome shows, however, that there can be 'establishment' without military power, and that there can be the values associated with establishment even when the ratification of an institution is not 'enacted' by the powers of state.

We must recognize, therefore, that the fact of establishment, as I am attempting to describe it, outruns the limit of legal enactment. Establishment at the level of state may not be required, when establishment at the level of civil society is sufficiently entrenched. The Catholic Church, because of its amazing constitution, has bestowed on itself the quality of establishment throughout Italy, Spain, France, and even (what is now likely to be of great political significance) Poland. In comparison with the influence and power of Rome, the legally established Church of England seems more feeble even than that of Russia. Likewise the organized trade-union movement in England has some of the features of establishment, even though it is not (and as I shall argue cannot be) legally established under the existing constitution. Establishment, while it means something more than power, may require something less than direct incorporation into the apparatus of state. The authority which it requires may arise directly from its ability to generate consoling myths, provided these myths prepare men for the acceptance of a given civil order.

Now while, according to the ancient system of precedence, our Lords Temporal and Lords Spiritual stand in similar proximity to the Sovereign, the power of the second amounts to very little when it ceases to convey the authority vested in their calling. Whether it be a passing fashion, or whether it be the sign of a deeper uncertainty, it is undeniable that the leadership of the Church – and not only of the Anglican Church – has begun to set itself against the order of European society. Some see in this nothing more than the effort of the Church to remain established at all costs, however much the prevailing political forces may change. And certainly, from its beginning, the Church has had that attitude, as can be seen from Tertullian's assertion on its behalf, less than two centuries after the death of Christ: 'We are for ever making intercession for the emperors. We pray that they might enjoy long life, secure rule, a safe home, brave armies, a faithful senate, and honest people, a quiet world, and everything for which a man and a Caesar may pray. . . .'

However, it is most implausible that the Church should retain political power while losing its spiritual authority. The instinct to which it appeals is, in fact, a conservative instinct, manifest principally at the momentous occasion of death, when men feel their fragility, their need of protection and the proximity of transcendent things. The true meaning of the Church in civil life leads away from the political issues which have bemused its leaders, for whom 'third world politics' has replaced the spirit of mission. The consequent weakness in an institution which, while necessarily political, has lost the true principle of its politics, and therefore the allegiance of its people, is a source of almost universal discomfort, so that already the religious sense seeks fulfilment elsewhere than in any kind of orthodoxy. Mere legal establishment is no substitute for political centrality: the place of the Church is either at the heart of things, or nowhere. Whichever it is to be (and present turmoils make it difficult to say) it will have significance only if it attends to the consoling myths which have drawn people to it. Were the Church to become merely the helpless repository of secular causes – a kind of sanctimonious addendum to Gay Power – then the objective dimension of its authority would disappear.

Consider, for example, what becomes of death and burial under the rule of ecclesiastical fashion. The old rituals and dogmas of the Church served to create the sense of continuity in death; they spread around the dead person a kind of embrace as though receiving a soul into its natural home. When there is no custom, no common dogma, no solemn enactment, then death and burial become mysterious. Thrown back into the trauma of ultimate personal choice, people do not know how to proceed. Uncomprehended necromancy is summoned, alien religions are experimented with; even the world of art is called upon to make sense of this unknowable thing (as in the vast triumph of human confusion at Forest Lawn). The oneness between the living and the dead is destroyed, and the dead themselves, having lost individuality in a world where only individuals have meaning, are cast overboard, so to speak, to float in rubbishy waves back across the sea of history, encumbered by the flotsam of a thousand irrelevant creeds.

The fetishizing of death accompanies that of birth. For with the eclipse of religious feeling comes the loss of the consciousness of destiny. Men must distinguish the dictates of fortune, believing that matters which deeply concern them are nevertheless removed from remedy or blame. The belief in Providence relieves the harshness of this outlook. Distinctions of beauty, health, intelligence, and capacity are natural; they are also essential to our ideals of human perfection. Not to see them under the aspect of fortune is to lose one's grip of human things, to become fascinated by a fantasy of interference, to take steps towards that brave new world in which the pervasive meddling in what is 'given' destroys both nature and value together. Not seeing birth as a part of fortune, a man might sue his parents for their lack of genetic control, or lay blame for his deformity upon the doctor who refused to abort him. Do not think that these cases are fantastical. At this very moment they lie before American courts of law.

Such is the confusion that the idea of fortune served to control that, lacking it, men find it hard to accept, and hard even to entertain, one of the fundamental thoughts upon which civilization depends, the thought that there is a profound, mysterious and beneficial difference between women and men. The thought that I exist as an individual independently of my sex, is one with the thought that my sex might have been chosen. So that, being only accidentally male, I experience my sexuality as alien. It is not of my essence. It has become an attribute, which I might change as I change my clothes. Much passes from the world when sexuality takes on this aspect. In particular, the clarity in the relations between man and woman disappears – being an accident, sexuality ceases to determine their relationship. It becomes a confused performance, of no more emotional significance than a shaking of hands. We have experienced in full what Henry James described as the 'decline in the sentiment of sex'.

Thus we see that, in all probability, the 'demystification' of our religious outlook has brought with it the complete mystification of fundamental things; roughly speaking, of birth, copulation and death. At the same time the theory that there are not, cannot be, or ought not to be, important or irremovable differences between sexes, races, and even individuals, is upheld with a bigotry that has all the fervour of religion, yet with none of religion's consoling power. The absurdities of the secular ideology are such that one can hardly believe it to be the expression of an improved education or a growing enlightenment. Its claim to clarity of thought masks the fact that it engenders unclarity of feeling. People 'hesitate to feel': every chance to expend personality in emotion

174

is made meaningless, undignified, or momentary. It seems then that the withdrawal of religious doctrine does, after all, bring about a withering in transcendent social bonds. Religion – and in particular Christianity – was too much a part of the common way of seeing things. The destruction of its dogmas, its liturgy, its rituals, and its ceremonial presence, has left a vacuum. But this destruction has been largely deliberate, carried out by Churchmen and so-called believers. Therefore, if we accept that secularization hinders the recognition of social bonds, it becomes politically necessary to fight secularization.

The very unsatisfactoriness of the secular picture of man leads one to suspect that it will not in fact last. There will be religious revivals, and it is politically important to guide the direction that they take. Hence the need for an established religion, and, if possible, for an established Church. In times of 'disestablishment' religion fragments into fierce and muddled gestures – as among Levellers, Ranters, Muggletonians and Seekers during the Interregnum. It is with no surprise that one should observe the spread of Manichean idiocy in California. Moreover, one cannot regard as 'apolitical' beliefs which bring such unrest and slaughter in their train. A firm established Church, with a tradition of non-conformism that relies on the same sacred texts and practices, is able to gratify the search for religion both immediately and intelligently. There is evidence that popular feeling is already seeking for such a Church.[81] The loss of authority in ecclesiastical offices is therefore a feature not of the offices but of their present incumbents. The restoration of the Church may well become a serious political cause.

The Trade Unions

I shall return to the question of ecclesiastical politics – for clearly, those concluding remarks raise questions which are not merely questions of policy. I have assumed that the religious sentiments of our nation are not extinguished but merely eclipsed, and that this eclipse is largely the result of liberal-minded 'enlightenment'. And the vast social power of religion seeks enactment – if not explicitly, as in England, then implicitly, as in the dominions of Rome. How this is done becomes clear when we consider another institution that is, as it were, on the edge of establishment, the institution of the Trades Union Congress.

It would be a quibble to argue, because it is only *de facto* that the Lords Temporal are partly drawn from the trade-union ranks and because the privileges of the trade unions at law (for example, the privileges in contract and tort granted by the Liberal Trade Disputes Act of 1906, and re-enacted in the Conservative Trades Union and Labour Relations Act) are only *privileges*, and not part of the overt constitution of the state, that therefore the labour movement and all that it represents is not part of the establishment of British politics. The process whereby the trade unions have moved towards a position of establishment is a recent one, and as much the outcome of unintended accidents as of real political choice. But this move has served to anchor in the national spirit a new body of myth, and an indelible impression of the reality both of class distinctions and of the social mobility which has always mitigated the resentments which surround them.

But is the establishment of the labour movement complete, even at the civil level? Nobody seems to have a clear or coherent answer. Some conservatives seek to prevent the completion of the process, being frightened at the irresponsibility of trade-union power, and at the threat to democracy involved in the close and exclusive relation that exists between this powerful autonomous body and a parliamentary party to which it 'pledges' sole support. But that very 'pledge' has about it an air of myth, and the myth is one that derives directly from a value that informs the civil order – the value of 'solidarity', integral to the feeling of class. It would be hard to oppose it directly; much easier to incorporate the trade unions into the apparatus of state. Besides, if, as I have suggested, the constitution of England has in fact only a small part that is governed by democratic representation, and if the conservative's main interest is in the continuance of that larger part in which the institutions of civil life are enshrined, then it seems difficult to reject the undemocratic ethos of the Trades Union Congress, unless one believes it to be genuinely subversive.

Here lies a main source of confusion. If a power cannot be ratified (say, because its purposes are at variance with those of government) then it is subversive. Now extraordinary qualities of leadership would be required to fight the trade-union movement with the weapons of state; for it could be done only if the loyalty of the working class were first detached from that movement. If there are signs, therefore, that the trade-union movement really is subversive – that it seeks power without responsibility, and so resists ratification in the institutions of government – it would be necessary to create and encourage rival organizations which attract the loyalty of the present union membership. In particular it would be necessary to foster and encourage 'unofficial' strikes, since these are a usurpation of trade-union power, and a snub to its self-constituted authority. Moreover, one could envisage sound conservative principles that would wish for the proliferation of 'unofficial' stoppages. Labour disputes would again become contractual. That is to say, they would consist in a confrontation not between 'classes' but between a particular employer and his staff – a confrontation that may not spread beyond the factory, and would be resolved either in the

destitution of the parties, or in a revised contract of work. Such 'industrial action' (as it is so oddly called) would serve to remove labour relations from the centre of politics, and to confine them to the business of
civil life. Legislation against unfair dismissal (a Tory Party invention
that has in fact proved extremely damaging) could be suitably amended.
Dismissal on account of 'unofficial strike' could be made presumptively
illegitimate. The contractual nature of the labour relation would then
be fully upheld, as would its security. Within no time the trade-union
movement – as an independent power – would wither and die.

I make the suggestion not because it is feasible or politic, but in order
to show that the position of the trade unions is already such that radical
policies are difficult and perhaps unnecessary. For the trade unions have
not shown a reluctance to accept ratification. On the contrary, they now
seem to wish to hold their authority directly from the institutions of
government. This may seem surprising, but it is arguable that it is true.

New Corruption

It might seem that the trade-union movement would be loath to seek
constituted authority. For while there is some truth in the view that 'in
decisive questions people feel their class membership more profoundly
than their membership of society',[82] does that not make it impossible
for the trade unions to become affiliated to any kind of ruling class?
Does not their claim to authority rest on the view that the class they
represent is the class not of rulers but of ruled? If the aim is simply to
abolish the distinction, then it is an aim that will not succeed. Besides,
such an aim is incompatible with the myths that provide the trade unions
with their image of authority.

The trade unions are therefore faced with a choice. And the nature of
this choice is most clearly seen when it is recognized that it is in the
interests of the state to grant, if it can, legal establishment to all *de facto*
established powers. Power then becomes directly answerable to the
interests of state, and its autonomy is restricted in all those issues where
it may be blocked by policy. Compare the easy relations between Church
and state in England since the accession of William of Orange, with the
uneasy relations between Rome and the rulers and rebels of France,
resolved only in the magnificent gesture of Napoleon at his coronation.
And compare the disorder created by trade-union power in England
with its tranquil exercise in Russia. This answerability can have far-
reaching effects. It was the House of Commons that in 1929 fought the
proposals for the reform of the Book of Common Prayer. And when the
Worship and Doctrine Measure of 1974 was unsuccessfully opposed in
parliament it was to the great detriment of the power and authority of

the Church. (It was this measure that has allowed the creeping disestab-lishment of the Church, so that ludicrous 'alternative services' can be laid before the people as though it were freedom rather than certainty that they wished for.) It is still an office of government to ratify the choice of bishops. While the Church – resenting these intrusions – has tried to move further from the centre of power, it is also clear that there can still be a successful ecclesiastical politics that would force it either to lose itself in mediocrity and faction or to return to its social centrality. That is why the current popular feeling against the fragmentation of ecclesiastical authority can still find its political expression. In general it is through the process of ratification that the state makes institutions into subjects. And thereby it remains aloof from the interests that com-pose it.

It follows that there is a certain self-destructiveness in a trade-union movement that is fully established. Such a movement claims to possess the authority of a class; it cannot aim to destroy the feelings of class without destroying its own authority. If it is wise, it therefore hovers always on the fringes of direct establishment, since it loses more than it gains by pressing itself into the centre of power. Most of all, in losing its class identity, it loses its close relation to the working class. (Hence there is no need to foster unofficial strikes – they are already happening.) It is therefore in the interests of state that union leaders are able to accept and rejoice in peerages. It is in the interest of state that they are granted powers and privileges that completely outrun the power that arises autonomously. It is widely known that, under recent Labour govern-ments, trade-union officials have become recipients of extensive political patronage. (In 1977, according to one estimate,[83] thirty-nine members of the TUC General Council held no less than 180 state offices between them – most of them salaried.) Now the extent of this 'New Corruption' is vast – vaster by far than the patronage exerted by the Whigs or by the Stuart monarchy. But it would be misguided for a conservative to think that he is compelled by dogma to oppose it. On the contrary, this sudden emergence of a power into the offices of government spells the eventual diminution of that power, and its incorporation into the state. Initially it is costly. But in the long run it must be beneficial. The influence of the trade unions over their membership becomes less a matter of will than of office. And the oligarchical nature of trade-union power enables the state to deal directly with a small number of stubborn but often brib-able officials. It is true that what is thereby established is not the labour movement itself (which now will seek 'unofficial', and consequently less damaging expression), but a collection of interests that have used the labour movement as a means to power. And that is the greatest weakness in the arrangement. For either the labour movement has the will to be-come established, in which case it ceases to be the movement of 'labour'.

Or else it does not, in which case the government can only deal with it indirectly, through representatives who do not fully command its loyalty. The problem, in so far as there is one, is an irremovable problem of modern politics, soluble by no dogma, and amenable to no consistent policy. But at least we can conclude that this feature of establishment is no more an obstacle to conservative politics than it is an obstacle to politics of every kind.

Class

The examples that I have chosen show two things: first, that the process of ratification both depends on and generates ideology. Secondly, that ratification is basic to conservative government, in that it provides the process whereby the power of state links itself to and becomes one with the power of society. But as we have seen, there have been efforts to sunder the two, as well as attempts to win ratification by powers unsuited to it. In all this we have encountered the principal social reality of England: its clear, but flexible, social stratification.

To speculate further on the origin and structure of social classes is no part of my purpose: it suffices that they exist and that everything that I have described so far as integral to conservative dogma seems to point to their existence as a necessity. The conservative must believe that class distinctions can be represented either as a necessary evil or as a social good. And the question will turn upon the extent to which their power reflects, or can be made to reflect, a genuine acceptance on the part of those who do not partake of the 'privileges' – whatever they might be – which divide upper from lower in the social scale. The conservative is likely to think that this acceptance *can* be induced, and even that there might be no enduring sense of legitimacy without it.

In one of his deepest reflections on the relation between public and private life, Shakespeare wrote thus:

> Take but degree away, untune that string,
> And, hark, what discord follows! each thing meets
> In mere oppugnancy: the bounded waters
> Should lift their bosoms higher than the shores,
> And make a sop of all this solid globe:
> Strength should be lord of imbecility,
> And the rude son should strike his father dead:
> Force should be right; or, rather, right and wrong –
> Between whose endless jar justice resides –
> Should lose their names, and so should justice too.
> Then everything includes itself in power,
> Power into will, will into appetite.
>
> *Troilus and Cressida*, I, iii

179

We speak now not of 'degree' but of 'class': the social arrangements of the modern world do not contain the complexities of precedence which Shakespeare saw as morally indispensable. Nevertheless, what he wrote contains an insight. The disintegration of authority means the collapse of justice. Power is once again at large in the world, reducing itself from rational will to appetite: social fragmentation then begins. The purpose of establishment is to prevent fragmentation. Hence we must ascend from power back to authority. How can that be done, unless men are prepared to recognize – in this or that individual, in this or that office – a vested authority by which they are constrained? And is it not plausible to suggest that, if this habit of deference arises, however qualified and however disparately directed, it is better that it should find the world already adequately provided with objective signs of authority, in the form of office, position, and established right? And how, if that is so, can one either prevent or bewail the formation of social classes, in which the unequal distribution of power becomes ratified by an unequal distribution of authority? One must therefore accept the view of Shakespeare's Ulysses, that the artifact of authority is one with the artifact of class.

Does that give cause for complaint? Certainly the mere fact that one man has what another does not have is not itself the cause of envy, nor does it cast credit on the one who has or remove it from the one who has not, nor does it in any way directly undermine their sense of belonging to a common civil order. If it were true that class distinctions were merely economic – reflections of the relation to the means of production and of the extent to which that relation can translate itself into private wealth – then it would perhaps be true that in a wholly materialistic society (a society with no myths other than those engendered by money) class distinctions could at once translate themselves into open war. But England has enjoyed a kind of permanent (if at times uneasy) truce. The occasional outbreaks of war have tended to take a religious form. If we are to accept the economic definition of class, then we should have to say that the present war in Northern Ireland is internal to a single class: an idea that looks very odd when set beside socialist theories of 'class warfare'. And it is equally odd to use those theories in describing the English Civil War. For there is no single economic category to which the contending factions in that war can be assimilated. Historical explanation becomes immediately clear and plausible when we observe not economic control, but ideology – in particular, when we observe the religious and cultural rivalries that so suddenly burgeoned in that age. If we are to speak of 'class war', it is a war that is fought, if at all, on the level of myth, and achieves there a variable, but for the most part peaceable, compromise. Economic distinctions cease to be important in determining class feelings, and no change in the economic order is likely to eradicate them.

If that is true, then it is surely easier to understand social class in terms of an ideological picture than in terms of relative wealth or economic control. The middle class, for example, which devotes its resources to education, to the purchase of durable goods, to the general stance and improvement of the 'self' is, as a result of these costly interests, seldom conceived as an object of envy by a class that does not share them. Only a minority of the 'middle' class is in a position actually to *dispose* of wealth greater than that available to the average working man. And that minority in its turn is unlikely to be seen by the upper class – whose command of social intercourse in no way corresponds to any real command of material resources – as qualified for admission to its circle. Here all the complexities, and almost all the realities, have to be seen in other than economic terms.[84] Hence the myths which enable men to see a given social position as natural can develop independently of the transfer of wealth. It is this sense of the 'natural' quality of social divisions that is created by the autonomous institutions examined in the last chapter. Education, for example, 'naturalized' property, by making it the instrument of social intercourse. (In periods of the highest culture, therefore, wealth tends to take on a symbolic form, the form of luxury, splendour and *gloire*.) If there is a problem of class, it will be because the working class lacks the requisite institutions through which to 'naturalize' its predicament. If this is so (and many people have argued that it is so), then it is not because the working man must inevitably resent his station, but rather because he has acquired some 'classless' or 'relative' way of seeing it which removes its inwardness, and its consoling power. The solution to such a problem cannot lie in the abolition of class, but only in the sustenance of the institutions which validate a social picture. It is upon the strength and variety of establishment that this validation depends.

One might thus agree with the socialist historian who claimed that 'class is defined by men as they live their own history, and, in the end, this is its only definition'.[85] But then one moves away from the view that classes arise from men's varying relations to the means of production, and away from the view that classes must necessarily be at war. On the contrary, a class that can validate its experience in the existing social order will find ratification for its innate unconscious power. (It has therefore been suggested that the tradition of English non-conformism has helped to contain the power of the English working class.) There seems, then, to be no reason why we should think of class distinctions as evil or unjust. They stem from the basic principles of social order; hence it will be an important part of conservative politics to uphold the picture through which they acquire their validity. It can hardly be called patronizing to accept such a view; for the only question is the *truth* of the doctrines which determine it. Having been persuaded of their truth, the rest must follow, as a matter of *Realpolitik*.

The Welfare State

In the past the relations between classes which constituted this established balance were often mediated not by the state but by the Church. The Church was the principal agent of charity, and the purveyor of education and advantage to those restless in their situation. The idea of a universal education is not a modern invention; nor indeed can we be sure that the standard of education of the lowest classes of society has noticeably improved (except locally) since the decretals of Pope Gregory IX. (By the end of the fourteenth century all legal restrictions forbidding the education of villeins had been abolished, having been more or less ignored through two hundred preceding years. And by 1400 the Paris *scholasticus* was able to command each parish to establish a school, to provide for scholars both rich and poor the education of the *trivium* – an education requiring greater mental exertion than anything commanded by our modern governments.) This general supervision of the exercise of charity naturally sustained the institutions of private property and legitimatized inequalities of wealth. The recipient of charity was the recipient not of a personal gift but of an objective privilege associated with his actual impotence. The Church legitimated the self-seeking of the rich, as it consoled the misery of the poor, by constantly ministering to the spiritual needs of each only on condition that the one should alleviate, while the other should accept, the lot of poverty.

Wise men, seeing the gradual retreat of the Church from the offices of civil life, sought always to supplement or replace its ministrations through organized poor relief, and through public facilities of education and medical care. Over such issues conservatives and radicals have often fought together. But it was not until the last century that the full force was experienced of the political obligation to provide (either through compulsory insurance, or through some direct constitutional device) a complete system of provisions for those who could not naturally afford them. Thus Bismarck, in creating the Prussian state, incorporated into its constitution a standing principle of social welfare. It was thereby possible for the professional classes both to pursue the tasks which make them indispensable, and to gather adequate material reward for doing so (a reward adequate to maintain the self-image without which the professions would wither away). At the same time the poorer sections of the community were supported in the needs which they could not satisfy alone, and so sustained in the sale of their labour. The result was the welfare state.

This institution, which is the final feature of establishment that I wish to consider, has been recently experienced as a kind of universal restriction on the pursuit of professional life. It has provided a grievance to the professions, who have been deprived of the means to maintain the image of their class. Teachers in school and university, cast loose from any genuine 'professional' life, have often preferred to see themselves as the 'vanguard' of the working class. Having thus lost the respect of one class, without gaining that of the other, they peter out in aimless gestures of rebellion, victims of nothing so much as the mismanagement of the 'social welfare' which they idolize. Now the welfare state exists, and has become a social and political necessity. Nevertheless it requires the support of a highly qualified professional class, who will seek its rewards either at home or (since mobility is its most evident feature) wherever else it may be provided. It is therefore important to sustain all the trappings of 'private' advantage, despite the universal dispensation of medicine, education, shelter and bread. Every doctor, every lawyer, every teacher, in so far as his identity stems from his profession, pursues an ideal of professional conduct and of professional achievement. And that ideal will depend upon the flourishing of complex and partly autonomous institutions. The state may profit from those institutions, but it cannot wholly absorb them, without risking the hostility of the professional class. If it profits from these institutions it is because they have a life of their own, and it cannot be part of the pursuit of welfare to destroy that life. Politically the issue is as delicate as the issue of trade-union power. In every institution of establishment the interests and identity of the separate classes have to be consulted and reconciled. That is merely the business of government, and the unavoidable corollary of power. It is clear, then, what the conservative view of the welfare state must be. The English conservative will not – like his American counterpart [86] – regard it as an abomination, neither will he seek to extend it beyond the point which ordinary humanity requires. He will be reluctant to see the state make weaklings or dependants of its citizens, and yet at the same time he will not cancel what has become a hereditary right. The important thing has been to maintain, through all this compulsory charity, the professional self-respect which makes true charity possible.

The issue is again one of ratification. Poverty and indigence are powers at large in the state. Not to relieve them is to foster resentment. It is to encourage a permanent and universal sense of the moral instability of the social order. Yet to relieve want is one thing, to make all men equal in respect of it another. And to inflict on the professional classes a compulsory form of charity without regard to the moral specificity of the charitable motive, is to destroy the ability of that class, either to profit from its industry, or to make itself acceptable to those who do not belong to it. To bring all these forces together in an established system of right and duty is a matter of the utmost political delicacy. And the first step towards that end must involve the separation of the idea of public welfare from the egalitarian crusades with which it has become entangled.

Concluding Remarks

I have tried to show, through a series of examples, how the powers that flow through civil life can seek and achieve establishment in a constituted state. Establishment is the great internal aim of politics: the aim of government. It is through this that the forces of society become subject to the power of state, in finding authority through the authority of state. The conservative dogma is that the order of the state must be objective, comprehensive, and commanding of allegiance, so that the contrasting conditions of society can achieve their ideological gratification in the condition of subjecthood, without recourse to lawless self-determination. Without this completion in establishment civil society remains always on the brink of fragmentation.

But to maintain establishment it is necessary to uphold the offices of state as distinct and honorific. It is equally important to combat the attempt of power to constitute itself independently. Hence there is an important motive for trying to represent the authority of certain peripheral institutions as stemming from government. But when these institutions generate an internal sense of opposition (which is to say, when they represent themselves as being not governed, but oppressed), then the process of establishment, however desirable, becomes fraught with difficulties. It is these cases that require the greatest political acumen, and which generate the major political problems of our age.

It remains now to say something more general about the relation between individual and state, and about the distinction – briefly touched on in this chapter – between public and private life.

CHAPTER 9

The Public World

The last two chapters have surveyed those areas of domestic politics where social cohesion is lost and formed. It is in these areas, on behalf of 'freedom', 'equality', or whatever enthusiasm should command the time, that the fissure between state and society is opened. My description has been inward, concerned with the motives of cohesion and their ratification in the *status quo*. But society has both public and private life. It declares itself through gestures of authority, which embrace citizen and alien alike. The state is the completion, and also the champion, of society. It is only through the formation of a state that a society can come into direct, secure and explicit relation with its neighbours.

The Nation State

The state is no modern invention. Every society contains the seeds of constitution, in the form of custom, tradition, precedent and law. But it may have to fight to preserve these, and from every successful fight a degree of 'nationhood' emerges. For most of us the state means, not just government, but also territory, language, administration, established institutions, all growing from the interaction of unconscious custom and reflective choice. The nation state is the state at the extreme of self-consciousness. It has its territory, its people, its language, even its church. And it holds these things up to the world not as gifts of nature but as rights of possession, for which it is prepared to commit its citizens to die.

From the spirit of the nation state much good has sprung, and also much harm. Without this spirit the very idea of a 'balance of power' would be impossible, and peace correspondingly more precarious. But this balance of power depends upon a sinister invention – that of the conscript army. Nations fight wholly, absolutely and to the death. Every man, woman and child takes part in the struggle, and it is assumed that such is war. Renaissance Italy produced the highest culture, resplendent institutions, a constant surge of political life – all from a state of war. But war was semi-private, conducted by mercenaries who changed sides when plunder or payment tempted them. No mercenaries would have planned the battle of the Somme, the siege of Stalingrad, or the bombing of Dresden and Hiroshima. Now such things are war. But when a handful of British mercenaries was found in Africa, fighting against the conscript army of a state which has declared itself our enemy, howls of indignation echoed at once through Parliament. That was the voice of a nation state, dictating to its citizens that it is for it, and for it alone, to determine how they fight and die.

For good or ill, the nation state is the condition of Europe, and the most settled way of representing to the people the complex notion of allegiance. Given this fact, it is only an unfortunate society that cannot lay claim to nationhood. Nevertheless, such is the fierceness of a man's attachment to that which he regards as his own, that a society may endure through conquest, occupation and reform. Consider the fate of Poland, overcome again and again by rival powers, yet resolute in the defence of its identity, aided and abetted by the church of Rome. Consider too Alsace, and the many unfortunate states which, barely released from the benign authority of the Austro-Hungarian Empire, were almost at once incorporated into the great and barbarous empire of the Soviets.

If I have tried to argue against the reforming spirit in British politics, it is partly because it constitutes a threat, not only to the state, but also to society. The spirit of reform has been too much concerned with private 'rights', and not enough concerned with the public order that makes them possible. Since that public order is now the order of a nation state, foreign policy and national identity are its immovable precondition. It is perhaps true that nationhood has become necessary only in recent times. When a royal dowry could contain a whole domain, together with its laws and customs (so that Flanders could pass by a kind of domestic agreement from Spain to France), then it can hardly be thought that this fact of ownership had any great effect upon the continuance of society. But now we must struggle for that continuance, and lack the consoling ideas (such as the idea of 'Christendom') through which to view the sovereign as given to the society just as much as the society is surrendered to the sovereign power. The nation state has therefore become a necessity. At the same time, its citizens need to be protected from the state's encroachments, and it has even been said that the ruling conservative motive in this world of nations is to 'roll back the frontiers of the state'.

The phrase is a slogan, obscuring as much as it reveals. To some it suggests the diminution of the state; to others the exaltation of the individual. Neither suggestion belongs to conservative politics. If there is any meaning to this slogan it is this: that in order to maintain and assert its power, the state must concern itself first not with private but with public things. It is within the public world as the nation state determines it that the consolations of privacy may be sought.

The Statesman

The public world must be a reality, possessed of the power, dignity and centrality that will make it so. Politics creates the image of public life, and of the statesman as leader of the people. The conception of leadership is not an easy one. Far easier, indeed, for a statesman to present himself as an ordinary and unassuming man, with an arduous employment from which he would rather retire. Thus he earns sympathy, appeases enmity, lives in so far as he can without the burden of office. But he does not serve the people. There is a deep and ineradicable demand that decisions should both issue from the statesman, and at the same time represent the interests of subject powers. A statesman must be a 'figure of state' – someone whose identity bears the impress of the state, and who seems to act and speak for interests that are simultaneously the state's and his own. His decisions must be intelligible to the citizen as decisions which affect the general welfare, but which without the statesman's will and adroitness could have been neither conceived nor made. It goes without saying that much of the dignity of statesmanship is lost in the current deference towards the 'expert opinion', the 'advisory body', the 'commission of inquiry', the complex of established civil servants whose expert knowledge can never amount to wisdom, and who are in themselves in need of the guidance which no mere body of facts or statistics could provide.

There are various ways through which a statesman might represent himself as the public voice of the nation. Domestically he might achieve this through the ceremony of office. In a republic ceremony attaches directly to the president, providing an immediate sense of the reality of presidential power. In a monarchy, however, it attaches to the monarch: it represents, not the power and significance of office, but the dignity of state. It is difficult to doubt the wisdom of this. Since losing monarchy France and Italy have undergone constant upheaval, because in those countries opposition must necessarily be *disloyal*. The dignities of state are successively borrowed by temporary presidents, who represent, not the state, but some dominant faction within it. A rival faction, in setting itself against the president, must therefore first confront the state as his adopted mantle.

In England the dignities of state do not belong to the statesman but to the sovereign. Opposition is therefore contained within the institutions of government. It is no longer a joke to speak of 'Her Majesty's Opposition': that is the reality. The only special dignity which the Prime Minister enjoys is the dignity of office: all other dignities are bestowed, not equally or impartially, but at least widely, over all those factions which have power enough to want and strive for them. Nevertheless, the aspect of public ceremony still exists, and the true statesman must act in concert with it. He must be the public face of the nation, newly inserted into the gilded frame of monarchy.

Foreign Policy

More important, however, in creating the public world of politics, is the dealing between states. The statesman is seen as protecting his country's privileges, furthering its advantages, exercising the force, cunning or bargaining power which belong to the nation. An unfortunate effect of the reformist attitude is that it turns political activity away from international affairs towards domestic issues, which become exaggerated out of all proportion to their real significance. But it is in international affairs that the reality of government is most clear. Foreign policy, under the rule of reform, becomes cagey, non-committal and vague. Unable to measure up to the powers that surround us, we cease from the habit of bargaining with them and make public exhibition of our 'conscience' over past glory and colonial power.

The result has been a strange mixture of impetuosity and dither. In place of the 'concert of Europe', the League of Nations, and a hesitant treaty of defence, we enthusiastically subject ourselves to a law that is not our own. In place of colonial power we hand out vast sums to countries which are either hostile or indifferent to our interests, and whose people will never benefit from the gesture.[87] Either we are an international power or we are not. And if we are not we must secure our place by treaty. 'Foreign aid', 'the common market', 'Northern Ireland development' – all these are ways of concealing military issues behind an impenetrable veil of economics. We prefer to forget the ideas of war, defence and civil order, and instead offer money to enemies and bargains to friends. To distribute aid to countries (such as Vietnam) who are bound by no military treaty in our favour; to turn Western Europe from an alliance of nations to an anonymous bureaucracy; to allow civil war to continue undeclared within our frontiers – all these constitute a retreat from the public reality of nationhood. It is hardly surprising if the British people have come to doubt their national identity.

But for a democracy international politics is difficult and ungainly. A dictatorship moves with unchanging will and makes long strategic gestures. Bismarck had insight and genius. But without dictatorship he could not have created the German nation state. The present incumbents of the Kremlin are anonymous, inscrutable and perhaps not particularly intelligent. But they too, through maintaining a single stubborn policy over years, have made steady advances towards the empire which they desire. An elected government – unless ruled with grandeur and with a certain measure of disdain – makes gestures for the present moment alone. The price of butter in New York becomes more significant than the murder of an ambassador in Afghanistan. What then remains of the public world of politics?

To change all this would require long and careful tactics. But change it we must. Only then will the public life of our nation be restored to the order which domestic peace requires. To adopt some single-minded domestic purpose – the purpose of equality, say, or of free enterprise – is a familiar gesture in the face of international threat. But no purpose makes sense without the continuance of civil order. The true statesman must make decisions not out of some overriding policy or ideal, but out of the day-to-day necessities of politics, and from a desire to present in the public forum a symbol of national continuity. De Gaulle's greatness consists in the fact that, by two or three gestures of command in foreign affairs, he was suddenly able to transform the confusion of civil life in post-war France into a concerted harmony, to command renewed respect towards the institutions of state, and to establish stable government where there had previously been chaos. The conservative statesman, since he is not misled by dominant ideals or internationalist philosophies, is able to perceive the necessity for such gestures, and to make them when the moment requires.

The Private World

In this book I have argued for a view of legitimacy that places public before private, society before individual, privilege before right. Nevertheless, the satisfactions of social life, and the motive to engage in it, lie only with the individual. And this individual has become a sophisticated being, anxious for a sphere of privacy in which to seclude the eccentricities that fulfil him. His fulfilment, he thinks, is impossible without the 'right of privacy' which Englishmen regard as indefeasible.

But what does this right amount to when unprotected by the state? Nothing. What is fulfilment without the values of a social order? Nothing. And what is eccentricity without the norm against which to measure it? Nothing. This Anglo-Saxon privacy which we esteem is in fact nothing more than the public order, seen from within. It is not the vacuous freedom of liberalism, but a substantial and enduring thing, whose content becomes clear only with its limits. It is the principles determining those limits that I have attempted to lay down.

Silence and Practice

It may be wondered how this statement of position can be reconciled with the sceptical temper from which it was born. How can one willingly close one's mind, in so many ways at once? The direct answer is of course that one cannot. Nevertheless, there may be no persuasive alternative, it seems to me, to the attitude that I have sketched. At least, the usual alternatives are so radically under-described as to carry no conviction, and no authority that will outweigh that which is already incipient in the civil order. It is not by some act of faith that one closes one's eyes before the spectre of endless reform. The only necessity here is to live, and to respect the reality which makes life possible.

However, there is a problem. No one can retreat from the pursuit of truth once he has acquired the habit of self-conscious analysis. Yet the pursuit of truth leads one to doubt the myths that reinforce society. Some have set up as their ideal a society in which myths are no longer necessary. Like Marx, they have sought for a freedom from 'ideology', for a world in which there is no obfuscation of choice by the concepts peculiar to an established order. Marx's inability to provide the concrete description of this enlightened state may cause no surprise. For what remains of freedom when there is no self-conception, and how can there be self-conception in a world that is seen only in abstract terms? Without ideology the world is no more than the totality of facts, to be seen (if at all) only with the clinical vision of a dispassionate scientist. But fortunately we lack that vision, and lack the knowledge that would enable us to live it through. The dispassionate world does not contain the image of man; it leaves him empty-handed, staring at something that is neither human nor animal, a mere nameless thing.

Nature abhors a vacuum. Into the value-free world a host of airy ideologies has flown, and none less substantial than the secular myths which we examined in the last chapter. And in politics too these myths have appeared, bringing with them the idiotic language of 'progress'. Politicians can now speak as though the affairs of state move 'forward', or 'backwards'. The conservative is said to 'arrest progress', the liberal to 'advance' it. A conservative is a 'reactionary'. 'Revolution' means not the turning of the wheel, but the 'overthrow' of 'regressive' forces. In all this compulsive newspeak, we find the same frivolous myth. Things 'go forward', since that is their nature. The only truth here is that time moves forward, namely from past to future. But no politics can represent itself as announcing so trivial a truth. The movement of time is therefore mixed by free association with the movement of money. Things progress, in the way that money grows. Hence they get better each day, unless some conservative meddles with the process.

Even respectable historians can describe conservatives as 'staving off', for a period of years, an inevitable 'forward' movement, while others 'advance' the liberal or socialist cause,[88] Franco was not *successful* in Spain: he merely held up the liberal enlightenment. Metternich did not create or sustain an enduring order: he simply 'crushed', for a time, the spirit of history. And so on. A socialist state that lasts ten years is a prelude to eternity; a conservative state that lasts thirty years is only a gesture of survival. But once we see how foolish are the myths of 'progress', then we shall cease to see things in such a way. And then we might turn our attention to institutions of the present, and in particular to those institutions which sustain the ideology whereby men live and find fulfilment.

But the conservative who has risen above the fragments of his inheritance and reflected on the desolation that has been wrought in it, cannot return to an innocence which his own thinking has destroyed. He is not in the position of Sartre's existential anti-hero, forced to take responsibility for a choice which he lacks the concepts to describe. He knows what he wants, and knows the social order that would correspond to it. But in becoming self-conscious he has set himself apart from things. The reasons that he observes for sustaining the myths of society are reasons which he cannot propagate; to propagate his reasons is to instil the world with doubt. Having struggled for articulacy, he must recommend silence.

This problem is insoluble. It stands in the way of every political creed. The 'natural right' and 'freedom' of the liberal; the 'classless society' and 'emancipation' of the radical; the 'social justice' and 'equality' of the socialist – all these are myths. They have immediate appeal. But when we examine what they really mean, we see that they too can be defended to the élite which recognizes them, but only in terms which must be concealed from the common man. In discussing their basis we emerge from the sea of politics on to a strange desert shore of pure opinion, a place of doubt, bluff and subterfuge. The wisest course is to turn back and re-immerse oneself.

NOTES

1. The awareness that conservatism has no universal purpose, definable for all peoples and for all times, has led to a tradition among English conservatives, according to which their beliefs are essentially unsystematic, distrustful of theory, practical, empirical and day-to-day. (See, for example, Lord Hugh Cecil, *Conservatism*, London, 1912; Lord Hailsham, *The Case for Conservatism*, London, 1947, and, most recently, William Waldegrave, *The Binding of Leviathan*, London, 1978.) Such a tradition provides admirable support for conservative policy; but it cannot solve the intellectual problem – which is, why be a conservative in the first place?

2. The call for the political organization of conservative sentiment was vigorously made by Burke, who, although himself a Whig, spoke and wrote before the modern party allegiances had been formed. He is therefore usually considered to be a 'Founding Father' of the Conservative Party. Precisely when that party came into being is a disputed question among historians. In assuming that it was not properly formed before 1832 I rely on Norman Gash, *Politics in the Age of Peel*, London, 1952, and Lord Blake, *The Conservative Party from Peel to Churchill*. If I use the word 'Tory' in what follows it is to refer to the Conservative Party, unless the context indicates a reference to the loose association that preceded it. Likewise Conservative with a capital C refers to the party; with a small c to the system of beliefs which that party may or may not embody.

3. See, for example, Sir Karl Popper, *The Open Society and Its Enemies*, Princeton, 1950.

4. John Locke, *Two Treaties of Government*, ed. P. Laslett, Cambridge, 1960; and Robert Nozick, *Anarchy, State and Utopia*, New York, 1971.

5. See Kenneth Minogue, 'On Hyperactivism in Modern British Politics', in Maurice Cowling (ed.), *Conservative Essays*, London, 1978.

6. The distinction here corresponds in part to the distinction (much emphasized in nineteenth-century German sociology) between *Gesellschaft*, and *Gemeinschaft* (cf. F. Tönnies, *Gemeinschaft und Gesellschaft*, trans. *Community and Society*, New York, 1963). The argument of this section can be found more elaborately spelled out in Michael Oakeshott's 'Rationalism in Politics', *Cambridge Journal*, vol. 1, 1947/8, pp. 81–98, 145–57, and *On Human Conduct*, London, 1975.

7. Edmund Burke, *Reflections on the Revolution in France*, London, 1960.

8. Hobbes, *Leviathan*, London, 1651, II, p. 21. The thought lies behind Rousseau's *The Social Contract* (trans. G. D. H. Cole, London, 1913), and was criticized by Hume in 'Of the Original Contract' (in *Essays, Moral, Political and Literary*, London, 1791).

9. This recognition has, of course, been slow and painful, evident not only in the controversies over the 'New Deal', but also in almost every subsequent gesture of policy, whether foreign or domestic.

NOTES

10. I am indebted to John Casey for impressing upon me that such concepts are indispensable to conservative political thinking.

11. The great champion of this view in recent years has been Robert Nozick (op. cit.).

12. See the reflections in Jacob Burckhardt's *The Civilization of the Renaissance in Italy*, Leipzig, 1877–8, and in Émile Durkheim's *On Suicide*, 2nd ed., Paris, 1912.

13. See F. H. Bradley, 'My Station and Its Duties', in *Ethical Studies*, London, 1876.

14. Burke, *Reflections* . . . , op. cit.

15. The philosophy behind this is nowhere more succinctly or cogently expressed than in G. W. F. Hegel, *The Philosophy of Right*, trans. T. M. Knox, Oxford, 1967.

16. T. S. Eliot, 'Tradition and the Individual Talent', in *Collected Essays*, London, 1963.

17. John Casey, 'Tradition and Authority', in *Conservative Essays*, ed. Cowling, op. cit.

18. Burckhardt, op. cit., Introduction. The view should really be accredited to de Maistre, *Essai sur le principe générateur des constitutions politiques*, in *Oeuvres complètes*, Lyons, 1884, vol. I. De Maistre, having recognized the bond of constitution as 'transcendent', concluded that it must therefore be the work of God. This passage, from attachment to transcendent bonds to the belief in transcendent beings, is of great political significance. I return to it in Chapter 8.

19. It is interesting to note that the major textbook on the American constitution (by Edward Corwin) is called *The Constitution and What It Means Today*. It has been rewritten thirteen times since 1920. In other words, the study of the American constitution advances, not with the speed of science, but with that of law.

20. H. Marcuse, in *Reason and Revolution*, London and New York, 1941.

21. The philosophy has been expounded, in terms that stand in need of revision, in Hegel's *Philosophy of Right* and *Philosophy of History*. Vestiges of it survive in Bosanquet and Oakeshott. The idea is as old as Plato's *Republic*.

22. This logic is difficult to describe. An interesting discussion (conducted largely from the standpoint of the liberal view of constitution) may be found in R. Dworkin, *Taking Rights Seriously*, London, 1977.

23. See Ruth Benedict, *Patterns of Culture*, New York, 1934.

24. Aléxis de Tocqueville, *De la démocratie en Amérique*, bk II, pt II.

25. Walter Bagehot, *The English Constitution* (ed. R. H. S. Crossman, London, 1963), ch. III. Bagehot's defence of the ·House of Lords is a fine polemic, far above the level of recent discussions.

26. *De l'esprit des lois* (1748). The doctrine of the 'separation of powers' is given express enactment in the American constitution – a fact that has in no way served to make it more intelligible.

27. The peculiar structure of the British Cabinet, and its potentially tyrannical jurisdiction, are discussed in Bagehot, op. cit., ch. I, partly with a view to demolishing the myth of a 'separation of powers'.

28. See the Radcliffe Report, as discussed by Lord Cross, in *Dingle* v. *Turner*, [1972] 2 WLR 523.

29. [1903] SC 231.

30. The liberal view in these matters is given succinctly by Sidgwick, *Elements of Politics*, London, 1891, p. 295, where he defends the 'cosmopolitan ideal', according to which the 'business (of government) is to maintain order over the particular territory that historical causes have appropriated to it, but not in any way to determine who is to inhabit the territory, or to restrict the enjoyment of its natural advantages to any particular portion of the human race'. As though 'historical causes' could mark out a territory without at the same time marking out the people that inhabit it! It is

hard to imagine what conception of sovereignty, or of legitimacy, can be derived from an axiom so remote from the political feelings of ordinary men and women.

31. De Maistre, op. cit. See also the comments in Hume's *History*, ch. 47, relating to the constitutional crisis caused by James I's quarrel with the common law.

32. See *The Critique of Practical Reason*.

33. Pericles' funeral oration, in Thucydides, *History of the Peloponnesian War*, bk II, 33–46.

34. J. S. Mill, *On Liberty*, London, 1859, and Sir James Fitzjames Stephen's reply, *Liberty, Equality, Fraternity*, London, 1873. For the modern discussion, see H. L. A. Hart's succinct restatement of the liberal position in *Law, Liberty and Morality*, London, 1963.

35. See the excellent discussion in George Parkin Grant, *English-Speaking Justice*, Sackville, New Brunswick, 1974, pt IV.

36. See in particular the cases of *Eves* v. *Eves* ([1975] 3 ALL ER 768), and *Davis* v. *Johnson* ([1978] 1 ALL ER 1132).

37. See Oakeshott, *On Human Conduct*, op. cit.

38. Sir Isaiah Berlin, *Four Essays on Liberty*, Oxford, 1969, ch. 1.

39. *A Contribution to the Critique of Political Economy* (1859), London, 1961, preface. See also *The German Ideology* (1846), in which the view is stated more emphatically.

40. Someone might doubt this, remembering Marx's indebtedness to the theories of Adam Smith and Ricardo, in which 'labour' appears as a concept exclusive to economic theory. But there is another and greater debt: 'Labour is the universal interaction and *Bildung* (self-image) of man' (Hegel, *Schriften zur Politik*, 424).

41. See, for example, P. A. Baran and P. M. Sweezy, *Monopoly Capital*, New York and London, 1966, and J. K. Galbraith, *Economics and the Public Purpose*, London, 2nd ed., 1972.

42. In this paragraph I refer back to the considerations of Chapters 1 and 2; the reader of sociology will notice a connection with Weber's concept of '*Verstehen*'.

43. *The Phenomenology of Mind*, and the *Philosophy of Right*. Some aspects of the view are foreshadowed in Locke, and in Thomist accounts of the 'natural law'.

44. Lord Keynes, *The General Theory of Employment, Interest and Money*, London, 1936, p. 104.

45. See especially the work of Michel Foucault (in particular *Les Mots et les choses*, Paris, 1966, and *L'Archéologie du savoir*, Paris, 1970), in which the rewriting of history in mythographic form is taken to splendid and outrageous rhetorical conclusions.

46. The liberal view is succinctly summarized by John Stuart Mill, *The Principles of Political Economy*, London, 1848, 3rd ed., 1852, II, 2, i: 'The institution of property, when limited to its essential elements, consists in the recognition, in each person, of a right to the disposal of what he or she have produced by their own exertions, or received either by gift or by felt agreement, without force or fraud, from those who produced it.' (The grammar of this sentence is one rather unfortunate result of Mill's preaching of the feminist cause.)

47. The matter raised here cannot be readily summarized. See the doctrine of prescriptive right, defended honestly but inadequately by Mill (in op. cit., II, 2, ii); see also the discussion of 'competition and custom' in II, 4, ii, illuminating in its attempt to subsume history under liberal principle, and in its honest confession of failure.

48. The liberal in question was Sir Alfred Mond (later Lord Melchett).

49. *Temporary* income tax had been previously introduced by Pitt, again during Tory office (but before the formation of the modern Conservative Party).

50. Nozick, op. cit., p. 169.

51. See the excellent discussion in Adam Smith, *The Wealth of Nations*, bk V, ch. 2, as glossed by Mill, *Principles of Political Economy*, op. cit., bk V, ch. 2.

52. *Fabian Essays*, p. 33.

53. *General Theory*, op. cit.

54. The theory behind this assertion is in fact unproven and often disputed. While Baran, Sweezy, and Galbraith affirm that something like it must be so (deriving inspiration from the original cynical portrayal of the industrial process in the works of Veblen), there is some evidence that its truth is confined to business in America. Legislation governing monopoly is of such antiquity in Europe that business customs seem to have incorporated many of its tenets and aims. But see Thorstein Veblen, *The Theory of Business Enterprise*, Chicago, 1904, ch. 3.

55. F. A. von Hayek, *Individualism and the Economic Order*, Chicago, 1948, ch. 3.

56. See M. M. Postan, *The Mediaeval Economy and Society*, London, 1972, esp. ch. 9.

57. See Baran and Sweezy, op. cit.

58. This point follows either trivially from the labour theory of value, or more deviously from the view that all wage contracts are 'forced', and therefore consign one of the parties to a condition of slavery. The labour theory transforms Adam Smith's view that the true value of a commodity lies in the quantity of labour for which it may be exchanged (*The Wealth of Nations*, London, 1776, bk I, ch. 5), into the view that its value consists rather in the labour necessary to produce it. (See *Capital*, vol. I). It thus assigns values independently of demand, and while this may give the theory useful ideological force, it seems to deprive it of all predictive power. The view that wage contracts are forced depends upon the assertion that the proletarian, while not individually constrained to contract as he does, belongs to a class that is constrained as a whole. Even if that were true, unionization would suffice to remove the unilateral nature of the constraint.

59. Disraeli, preface to the 1870 editions of his novels.

60. E. P. Thompson, 'The Peculiarities of the English', in *The Poverty of Theory*, London, 1978, p. 82.

61. Ibid., p. 44.

62. Some modern philosophers have proposed methods of abstraction which they hope will enable us sensibly to ask such a question (or some strategic equivalent of this question). See for example the liberal theory of justice expounded by John Rawls, *A Theory of Justice*, Oxford, 1972.

63. See, for example, Marx's *Economic and Philosophical Manuscripts of 1844* (available, trans. T. B. Bottomore, in Erich Fromm, *Marx's Concept of Man*, New York, 1961).

64. See, for example, Marx's 'Critique of the Gotha Programme' (1875), in Marx and Engels, *Selected Works*, Moscow, 1958.

65. See the discussion of the Master and Slave, in *The Phenomenology of Mind*.

66. By the 'artificial' division of labour I do not mean that division which is implied (according to Adam Smith, *The Wealth of Nations*, bk I, chs. I–III) in every institution of exchange, but rather the peculiar process of specialization that is engendered by all mechanized modes of production. See É. Durkheim, *De la division du travail social* (2nd ed., Paris, 1902). The two kinds of division are independent: either could exist without the other.

67. In Fromm, op. cit., p. 123.

68. *Marx's Concept of Man*, op. cit.

69. *Capital*, London, 1970, vol. I, p. 76f.

70. See Matthew Arnold, *Culture and Anarchy*, London, 1876, and also Thorstein Veblen, 'Civilization and the Machine Process', in *The Theory of Business Enterprise*, op. cit.

71. 'Inaugural Address of the Working Men's International Association', in Marx and Engels, *Selected Works*, vol. 1.

72. The principal documents are Laing's *Politics of Experience* and *Politics of the Family*.

73. Aaron Esterson, *The Leaves of Spring*, London, 1972, pp. 248–9.

74. See again, John Casey, 'Tradition and Authority', op. cit.

75. A. Gramsci, *Il materialismo storico*, Turin, 1955.

76. See, for example, *Salmond on Jurisprudence*, 12th ed., by P. J. Fitzgerald, London, 1966, p. 325ff.

77. The invention of this subject may be attributed to the University of Cornell, whose school of industrial relations has set the pattern for those elsewhere. While going to press I notice that the Council for National Academic Awards has approved a degree in 'Sports Studies', at the behest of the Sunderland Polytechnic.

78. F. Schiller, *Letters on the Aesthetics Education of Man*, trans. and ed. M. Wilkinson and C. A. Willoughby, Oxford, 1967.

79. I here pass over the vast and intractable problem of the 'just war', over which medieval philosophers and jurists debated at such length. The point is simply that there are acts which would be criminal when perpetrated by an individual, but just when performed by a state.

80. *The Conservative Case*, London, 1959 (a revised version of *The Case for Conservatism*, London, 1947), p. 19.

81. As is shown in the popular response to the Reverend E. R. Norman's Reith Lectures, of 1978–9.

82. Trotsky, in Irving Howe (ed.), *Basic Writings*, London, 1964, vol. I, p. 378. Trotsky goes on to say, following a thought of Hume's, that 'the moral norm becomes the more categorical the less it is "obligatory" on all'. The history of religious and political persecution shows this to be false.

83. See Paul Johnson, *Britain's Own Road to Serfdom*, Conservative Political Centre pamphlet, London, 1978.

84. The attraction of the determinist view of history is perennial. An author devoted to providing some modified version of the Marxist hypothesis may notice the facts that cast doubt upon it and yet pass them over. Thus Perry Anderson, in *Lineages of the Absolute State*, pp. 270–98, is able to notice that the branch of the Polish nobility known as the *szlachta* had for many years an economic position scarcely distinguishable from that of the peasantry, without losing their sense of social distinction. And yet this fact receives no explanation from the theory in support of which it is cited. (Cf. also much of the history of the *samurai* in Japan.)

85. E. P. Thompson, *The Making of the English Working Class*, London, 1963, rev. ed., 1968, p. 11.

86. There have, of course, been American conservatives more wedded to the European than to the American idea of legitimacy. See, e.g., the humanistic conservatism of Irving Babbit and Paul Elmer More (especially More's *Aristocracy and Justice*, New York, 1915).

87. See the arguments given by P. T. Bauer, in *Dissent on Development*, London, 1971.

88. The tendency is natural for Marxists. But it is surprisingly frequent in 'fair-minded' historians too. See, for example, David Thomson, *Europe since Napoleon*, London, 1957. Nowhere in Voltaire's *Siècle de Louis XIV*, or in Thucydides, is there the slightest hint of the doctrine that history has a movement. The mark of a great historian is that it is not history which lives for him, but rather the men and societies which constitute it.

INDEX